A Charitable Orthopathy
Christian Perspectives on Emotions in Multifaith Engagement

EDITED BY
John W. Morehead
AND
Brandon C. Benziger

FOREWORD BY
Richard J. Mouw

AFTERWORD BY
Paul Louis Metzger

☙PICKWICK Publications • Eugene, Oregon

A CHARITABLE ORTHOPATHY
Christian Perspectives on Emotions in Multifaith Engagement

Copyright © 2020 Wipf and Stock Publishers. All rights reserved. Except for brief quotations in critical publications or reviews, no part of this book may be reproduced in any manner without prior written permission from the publisher. Write: Permissions, Wipf and Stock Publishers, 199 W. 8th Ave., Suite 3, Eugene, OR 97401.

Pickwick Publications
An Imprint of Wipf and Stock Publishers
199 W. 8th Ave., Suite 3
Eugene, OR 97401

www.wipfandstock.com

PAPERBACK ISBN: 978-1-5326-5413-8
HARDCOVER ISBN: 978-1-5326-5414-5
EBOOK ISBN: 978-1-5326-5415-2

Cataloguing-in-Publication data:

Names: Morehead, John W., 1964–, editor. | Benziger, Brandon C., editor. | Mouw, Richard J., foreword. | Metzger, Paul Louis, afterword.

Title: A charitable orthopathy : Christian perspectives on emotions in multifaith engagement / edited by John W. Morehead and Brandon C. Benziger ; foreword by Richard J. Mouw ; afterword by Paul Louis Metzger.

Description: Eugene, OR : Pickwick Publications, 2020 | Includes bibliographical references and index.

Identifiers: ISBN 978-1-5326-5413-8 (paperback) | ISBN 978-1-5326-5414-5 (hardcover) | ISBN 978-1-5326-5415-2 (ebook)

Subjects: LCSH: Emotions—Religious aspects—Christianity. | Religions—Relations.

Classification: BV4597.3 .C46 2020 (print) | BV4597.3 .C46 (ebook)

Scripture taken from the Common English Bible®, CEB® © 2010, 2011 by Common English Bible.™ Used by permission. All rights reserved worldwide. The "CEB" and "Common English Bible" trademarks are registered in the United States Patent and Trademark Office by Common English Bible. Use of either trademark requires the permission of Common English Bible.

Scripture quotations are from the ESV® Bible (The Holy Bible, English Standard Version®), © 2001 by Crossway, a publishing ministry of Good News Publishers. Used by permission. All rights reserved.

Scripture texts in this work are taken from the New American Bible, revised edition © 2010, 1991, 1986, 1970 Confraternity of Christian Doctrine, Washington, DC, and are used by permission of the copyright owner. All Rights Reserved. No part of the New American Bible may be reproduced in any form without permission in writing from the copyright owner.

Scripture quotations marked (NIV) are taken from the Holy Bible, New International Version®, NIV®. © 1973, 1978, 1984, 2011 by Biblica, Inc.™ Used by permission of Zondervan. All rights reserved worldwide. www.zondervan.com The "NIV" and "New International Version" are trademarks registered in the United States Patent and Trademark Office by Biblica, Inc.™

Scripture quotations are from New Revised Standard Version Bible, © 1989 National Council of the Churches of Christ in the United States of America. Used by permission. All rights reserved worldwide.

Manufactured in the U.S.A.   03/30/20

Dedicated to Terry C. Muck

The Samaritan in Jesus's story in Luke 10 does not simply love his beaten and near-dead neighbor with merciful thoughts. Nor does he perform stoic deeds of compassion. Rather, he takes pity on the Jewish man (Luke 10:33). As in the account of Jesus being moved to act compassionately in Matthew 9:35–38, compassion no doubt flows from the heart and shapes the thoughts and deeds of this Samaritan stranger. . . .

Building on the last point, we must be attentive to a holistic engagement involving orthodoxy (head), orthopraxy (hands), and orthopathy (heart) in our engagement of the religious other. Each dimension is very important.

—Paul Louis Metzger

Contents

List of Contributors | xi

Foreword | xv
—Richard J. Mouw

Acknowledgments | xvii

Introduction: Orthopathy, Evangelicals, and Multifaith Engagement | 1
—John W. Morehead and Brandon C. Benziger

Part I–Biblical, Theological, and Social-Psychological Foundations

1. "He Had Compassion for Them": A Key Biblical Foundation for Interreligious Relations | 13
   —Bob Robinson

2. Orthopathy in the Christian Tradition: Promises and Challenges | 31
   — Elizabeth Agnew Cochran

3. The Social Psychology of Emotions and Religious Intergroup Relations | 44
   —Rosemond T. Lorona, Thomas A. Fergus, and Wade C. Rowatt

Part II—From Heteropathy to Orthopathy in Multifaith Engagement

4. Evangelicals and Gross Religions: Disgust and Fear in Multifaith Engagement | 61
   —John W. Morehead

5. Courage to Engage: Fear, Hope, Despair, and Daring in Courageous Multifaith Engagement | 78
   —W. Scott Cleveland

6. Hope as an Affective/Cognitive Tool for Multireligious Understanding | 95
   —Terry C. Muck

7. Emotion, Valuation, Compassion, and Empathy: Engaging Cognitive Science and Theology on Willing Rightly on Account of the Other | 111
   —Michael L. Spezio

8. Loving Our Religious Neighbors: Reflections on Scripture and Twenty-Five Years of Mormon-Evangelical Dialogue | 134
   —Craig L. Blomberg

Part III—Avenues of Orthopathic Multifaith Engagement

9. The Love of Christ Compels Us: Orthopathy, Mission, and Evangelism in Multifaith Environments | 153
   —Karen L. H. Shaw

10. Emotional Evangelism, Affective Apologetics | 169
    —Adam C. Pelser

11. Hospitality and Religious Others: An Orthopathic Perspective | 183
    —Amos Yong

Afterword: What's Next? | 196
—Paul Louis Metzger

Appendix: Questions for Reflection and Discussion | 203
Bibliography | 215
Scripture Index | 239

Contributors

Brandon C. Benziger (ThM, MDiv, Denver Seminary), freelance editor and independent writer and researcher. His publications include "Emotions and the Bible: An Introductory Bibliography" and "From *Femme Fatale* to Fidelity: Affect, Rhetoric, and Character Ethics in the 'Strange Woman' Poems of Proverbs 1–9."

Craig L. Blomberg (PhD, University of Aberdeen), Distinguished Professor of New Testament at Denver Seminary. His publications include *How Wide the Divide? A Mormon and an Evangelical in Conversation*; *Contagious Holiness: Jesus' Meals with Sinners*; and *A New Testament Theology*.

W. Scott Cleveland (PhD, Baylor University), Assistant Professor of Philosophy at the University of Mary. His publications include "The Emotions of Courageous Activity"; "The Distinctiveness of Intellectual Virtues: A Response to Roberts and Wood"; and *Becoming Good: New Philosophical Essays in Aid of Virtue Formation*.

Elizabeth Agnew Cochran (PhD, University of Notre Dame), Associate Professor and Director of Graduate Studies at McAnuity College and Graduate School of Liberal Arts, Duquesne University. Her publications include "The Moral Significance of the Religious Affections: A Reformed Perspective on Emotions and Moral Formation"; *Receptive Human Virtues: A New Reading of Jonathan Edwards's Ethics*; and *Protestant Virtue and Stoic Ethics*.

Thomas A. Fergus (PhD, Northern Illinois University), Associate Professor of Psychology at Baylor University. His publications include "The Potentiating Effect of Disgust Sensitivity on the Relationship between Disgust Propensity and Mental Contamination" and "The Attention Training Technique: A Review of a Neurobehavioral Therapy for Emotional Disorders."

Rosemond T. Lorona (PhD, Baylor University), Assistant Professor of Psychology at Point Loma Nazarene University. Her publications include "Self-Stigma and Etiological Attributions About Symptoms Among Individuals Diagnosed with an Anxiety Disorder: Relations with Symptom Severity and Symptom Improvement Following CBT" and "Assessing State Mental Contamination: Development and Preliminary Validation of the State Mental Contamination Scale."

Paul Louis Metzger (PhD, King's College, University of London), Professor of Christian Theology and Theology of Culture at Multnomah Biblical Seminary/Multnomah University. His publications include *Connecting Christ: How to Discuss Jesus in a World of Diverse Paths*; *Evangelical Zen: A Christian's Spiritual Travels with a Buddhist Friend*; and *Beatitudes, Not Platitudes: Jesus' Invitation to the Good Life*.

John W. Morehead (MA, Salt Lake Theological Seminary), Director of Multi-Faith Matters and the Evangelical Chapter of the Foundation for Religious Diplomacy. His publications include *Encountering New Religious Movements: A Holistic Evangelical Approach*; *Beyond the Burning Times: A Pagan and Christian in Dialogue*; and *The Paranormal and Popular Culture: A Postmodern Religious Landscape*.

Richard J. Mouw (PhD, University of Chicago), President Emeritus and Professor of Faith and Public Life at Fuller Theological Seminary. His publications include *Uncommon Decency: Christian Civility in an Uncivil World*; *Talking with Mormons: An Invitation to Evangelicals*; and *Adventures in Evangelical Civility: A Lifelong Quest for Common Ground*.

Terry C. Muck (PhD, Northwestern University), cofounder of the Society for Buddhist-Christian Studies. His publications include *Christianity Encountering World Religions: The Practice of Mission in the Twenty-First Century*; *Handbook of Religion: A Christian Engagement with Traditions, Teachings, and Practices*; and *Why Study Religion? Understanding Humanity's Pursuit of the Divine*.

Adam C. Pelser (PhD, Baylor University), Assistant Professor of Philosophy at the United States Air Force Academy, Colorado. His publications include "Reasons of the Heart: Emotions in Apologetics"; *Eyes of the Heart: Emotions in the Christian Life*; and *Becoming Good: New Philosophical Essays in Aid of Virtue Formation*.

Bob Robinson (PhD, University of London), Senior Research Fellow at Laidlaw College, New Zealand. His publications include *Christians Meeting Hindus: An Analysis and Theological Critique of the Hindu-Christian Encounter in India*; *Jesus and the Religions: Retrieving a Neglected Example for a Multi-Cultural World*; and *"Without Ceasing to Be a Christian": A Catholic and Protestant Assess the Christological Contribution of Raimon Panikkar*.

Wade C. Rowatt (PhD, University of Louisville), Professor of Psychology at Baylor University. His publications include "Religion, Prejudice, and Intergroup Relations"; "Patterns and Personality Correlates of Implicit and Explicit Attitudes toward Christians and Muslims"; and "Differences in Attitudes towards Out-Groups in Religious and Non-Religious Contexts in a Multi-National Sample: A Situational Context Priming Study."

Karen L. H. Shaw (DMin, Gordon-Conwell Theological Seminary), Assistant Professor of Cross-Cultural Ministry at Arab Baptist Theological Seminary, Lebanon. Her publications include "Divine Heartbeats and Human Echoes: A Theology of Affectivity and Implications for Mission" and *Wealth and Piety: Middle Eastern Perspectives for Expat Workers*.

Michael L. Spezio (PhD, Cornell University; PhD, University of Oregon), Associate Professor of Psychology and Neuroscience at Scripps College and visiting faculty at California Institute of Technology. His publications include *Theology and the Science of Moral Action: Virtue Ethics, Exemplarity, and Cognitive Neuroscience* and *Habits in Mind: Integrating Theology, Philosophy, and the Cognitive Science of Virtue, Emotion, and Character Formation*.

Amos Yong (PhD, Boston University), Professor of Theology and Mission and Director of the Center for Missiological Research at Fuller Theological Seminary. His publications include *Beyond the Impasse: Toward a Pneumatological Theology of Religions*; *Hospitality and the Other: Pentecost, Christian Practices, and the Neighbor*; and *The Spirit, Affectivity, and the Christian Tradition*.

Foreword

Richard J. Mouw

When I started to type these comments, I committed a typo even before I wrote my first sentence. For the heading, I wrote "Forward" instead of "Foreword." Actually, that was a fitting error—it might even be that my subconscious was giving me a good prodding. As I had read the essays for this volume, I was struck by the fact that we Evangelicals are making some excellent progress in exploring interfaith topics. We are clearly at a new stage in this exploration. So this volume is very much about moving "forward"!

Of course, some observers might say that it is about time that we Evangelicals start doing some creative thinking about interfaith matters. Already five decades ago, post-Vatican II Catholicism began producing some significant documents about the relationship of Christianity to other faith communities. And in the broader Protestant world, scholars have been at the topic of world religions for a long time. By comparison, our Evangelical patterns of productivity on interfaith topics has been quite meager.

Well, meager at least if we focus mainly on the dialogue variety of engagement. When it comes to evangelizing people of other faiths, though, we Evangelicals have been quite passionate. We have also produced considerable literature in the category of what we can label "interfaith apologetics."

In the pages that follow, however, we are given excellent insights about how to engage persons of other faiths in ways that go beyond evangelistic strategies and defenses of Christianity. Here we have well-informed, and often quite winsome, reflections on the benefits of participating in mutually edifying conversations with persons of other faiths. And the scholarly quality here is impressive. Having read widely in the writings of Catholics and mainline Protestants about such matters, I can testify to the fact that these essays are up to the highest intellectual standards.

I am impressed and pleased to see the orthopathy theme woven throughout these contributions. It is exactly the emphasis that is essential to an Evangelical approach to other religions. The "right thinking" (orthodoxy) emphasis has always been there for us. The teachings of other faiths have been a major focus in our past—even though we have frequently been less than fair in how we have represented those teachings. Nor have we been opposed to cooperative action—of the orthopraxy variety—with non-Christians. Francis Schaeffer made much of the need for Evangelicals to find "co-belligerents" on an ad hoc basis in the public arena, to say nothing of how this took shape in Jerry Falwell's "moral majority" alliances.

What has been lacking for us, though, has been sufficient attention to the affective dimension—particularly the qualities featured in these essays: compassion, empathy, humility, and the like. Evangelicals have made good progress in the past few decades, moving from generic preachments on the need for daily "quiet times with the Lord" to carefully laying out substantive patterns of spiritual formation. These essays can be seen as now carrying those newly refined insights, along with recent advocacies of a "virtue ethic," into the arena of interfaith engagement.

In my own interfaith journey, I have come to appreciate in new ways the element of mystery that surrounds God's dealings with people who are outside the boundaries of the Christian community. I have come to see that this sense of mystery is not something that we hold *in tension with* our deepest Christian convictions, but that the mystery of the workings of divine grace is *itself* one of the essential convictions. The Westminster Confession puts it nicely: "Christ through the Spirit . . . worketh when, and where, and how he pleaseth." This fine book is for me yet another testimony to the marvels of the sovereign grace that sent the Savior into the world!

Acknowledgments

ANY PUBLISHING PROJECT OF this kind warrants grateful acknowledgment at the outset of others who have helped shape its contents and encouraged its progress. First and foremost, we would like to express a heartfelt thanks to each of our contributors for their gratuitous commitment and enlightening contributions to this book: Richard J. Mouw, Bob Robinson, Elizabeth Agnew Cochran, Rosemond T. Lorona, Thomas A. Fergus, Wade C. Rowatt, W. Scott Cleveland, Terry C. Muck, Michael L. Spezio, Craig L. Blomberg, Karen L. H. Shaw, Adam C. Pelser, Amos Yong, and Paul Louis Metzger. Thanks also go to Edward Collins Vacek, Bob Robinson, Matthew Richard Schlimm, and Donald Fairbairn for helping us think through various issues related to the volume; the Louisville Institute for supporting much of John's research on emotions and multifaith engagement these last five years; Pickwick Publications for its partnership in bringing this timely project to fruition; and Brent Adams, Darin Brush, Charles Randall Paul, Loren Sickles, and Edgar L. Stone for helping fund our typesetting fee. Our respective families deserve special mention as well, specifically for their longsuffering love and support during the three years it took to develop, edit, and write portions of the book—namely, John's wife, Wendy, and granddaughter Rose, and Brandon's wife, Stephanie, and children, Evelyn, Oliver, and Theodore. Finally, thanks are due in double measure to Terry Muck for his inspiration of the present volume. In many ways, his contention in recent decades that interreligious dialogue involves, to a significant degree, "an emotion or attitude toward people of other religious traditions" has fueled this project from its inception.[1] For this reason, we dedicate the volume, in gratitude and admiration, to him.

1. Muck, "Interreligious Dialogue and Evangelism," 140.

Introduction

Orthopathy, Evangelicals, and Multifaith Engagement

JOHN W. MOREHEAD AND BRANDON C. BENZIGER

IN JULY 2014, THE nonpartisan fact tank Pew Research Center published a survey entitled "How Americans Feel About Religious Groups." Intriguingly, the study used a "feeling thermometer" to determine how various segments of the American population felt about select religious groups, including Jews, Catholics, Evangelicals, Buddhists, Hindus, Mormons, Atheists, and Muslims.[1] Scores of 0 to 33 comprised the cool and negative end of the scale, 34 to 66 were midrange, and 67 to 100 represented the warm and positive feelings. The section of the report on how religious groups rate each other—especially how Evangelicals both rate and are rated by others—is most interesting.[2] While Evangelicals rated Jews and Catholics

---

1. Atheism, of course, is not technically a "religion," according to many definitions of that term. Atheists themselves usually reject the association as well (see, e.g., Buckner, "Atheism," 602). For the purposes of this essay, however, we will simply note the issue and allow the Pew report to speak on its own terms.

2. Not surprisingly, the report assumes a generous, phenomenological definition of *Evangelicalism*: Evangelicals are "people who describe themselves as born-again or evangelical Christians" (Pew Research Center, "How Americans Feel," 2). It should also be noted at the outset that the present volume does not seek to define Evangelicalism prescriptively. Rather, while aware of its difficulties, we assume a broad sociological definition based on David Bebbington's well-known "quadrilateral": *conversionism, activism, biblicism,* and *crucicentrism.* These refer, respectively, to a belief in the necessity of spiritual regeneration, an emphasis on proclaiming and living out the gospel, a high view of Scripture as the primary source of truth, and a focus on Christ's atoning death

1

fairly highly on average (69 and 63, respectively), they rated other religious traditions much less favorably. "When asked about other non-Christian groups, evangelicals tend to express more negative views. White evangelicals assign Buddhists an average rating of 39, Hindus 38, Muslims 30 and atheists 25."[3] Curiously, these were the lowest-reported ratings for all four of these groups. Moreover, while Evangelicals were rated warmly by other Christian groups, they received colder mean ratings by Jews (34), Atheists (28), Agnostics (37), and adherents of "nothing in particular" (45).[4] The report, unfortunately, says nothing of Buddhist, Hindu, Mormon, or Muslim ratings of Evangelicals; however, we might reasonably speculate, given both our knowledge of Evangelical relations with these groups and the consistently negative ratings of Evangelicals by non-Christian groups, that such ratings would have fallen on either the cooler side of midrange or the chilly end of the spectrum altogether.

On the heels of a contentious election year in which Americans became increasingly divided on politics, Pew released an updated version of this survey data in February 2017.[5] In the almost three years since the previous report, the American public in general expressed warmer feelings for religious groups. Although "Americans still feel coolest toward Muslims and atheists," the report asserts, the mean ratings for these two groups nevertheless increased as well.[6] Somewhat anomalously, however, average ratings for Evangelicals stayed the same. In fact, "Evangelical Christians, rated relatively warmly at 61 degrees, are the only group for which the mean rating did not change since the question was last asked in 2014."[7] In addition, while mean Evangelical ratings of Buddhists, Hindus, Muslims, and Atheists all rose since the previous report (47, 47, 37, and 33, respectively),

---

on the cross. For the classic formulation, see Bebbington, *Evangelicalism in Modern Britain*. For additional proposals, see, e.g., Marsden, "Introduction," xii–xix; Stackhouse, "Generic Evangelicalism," 116–26; Olson, "Postconservative Evangelicalism," 168–78. Note, however, Trueman, *Real Scandal*.

3. Pew Research Center, "How Americans Feel," 5.
4. Pew Research Center, "How Americans Feel," 4.
5. Pew Research Center, "Increasingly Warm Feelings."
6. Pew Research Center, "Increasingly Warm Feelings," 3.
7. Pew Research Center, "Increasingly Warm Feelings," 3. Note, however, the singular, drastic uptick in Jewish ratings of Evangelicals: from 34 in 2014 to 59 in 2017 ("How Americans Feel," 4; cf. "Increasingly Warm Feelings," 8). This is likely related to the return of the heavily Evangelical Republican party to the US presidential office in early 2017, coupled with its strong political support of the Jewish nation of Israel. See, e.g., Kress, "Jewish-Christian Relations Today," s.v. "Evangelical Protestants."

they continued to be the coldest among the surveyed groups, with Evangelical ratings of Mormons tied for second to lowest (52).[8]

Briefly removing Atheists from our analytical purview, it is noteworthy that Evangelical sentiments for other religions are at their lowest with respect to Islam. As Harold Netland has observed, "In American Christians' eyes, especially after September 11, 2001, Islam is not simply another religion: it is the Diabolical Other. Images of Muslims provoke intense passions among many American Christians that are absent when considering Buddhists, Hindus, or Mormons."[9] Evangelicals, in fact, have had a long history of conflict and hostility with Islam, extending even to Evangelicalism's emergence in the Great Awakening (ca. 1720–1750).[10] Such adversity was only exacerbated by the rise of Islamic terrorism and suicide bombings in the 1970s and 1980s, culminating in the attacks of 9/11,[11] which American Evangelicals have often interpreted as Islamic attacks on Christianity.[12] Key terrorist incidents in the past, together with recent and ongoing attacks by ISIS, Boko Haram, and other Islamic groups, have fueled fear, anger, and even hatred among Christians. Thus, it is no surprise that Evangelicals and other conservative Christians tend to have little interest in—indeed, are adamantly opposed to—hospitable, conciliatory engagement with Muslims. As scholar of Islam John Azumah has recognized, "In our post 9/11 world, Islamic militancy seems to have become the main driving force or determining factor for Christian responses to Islam. The trauma of the attacks as well as the almost daily headlines of violence involving Muslims have had far reaching psychological and even theological impact on Christians as it has on the general non-Muslim world."[13] Azumah finds this *deeply* problematic, arguing, in fact, that Christian responses to Islam in our day represent a struggle for the soul of the faith itself:

> Some Evangelicals are very close to allowing radical Islam to not only define and drive their missions, but also their attitude towards Muslims and even other Christians who think differently. . . . The main casualty in the collateral damage of

8. Pew Research Center, "Increasingly Warm Feelings," 8.

9. Netland, *Christianity and Religious Diversity*, 231; cf. Bhatia, "American Evangelicals and Islam."

10. See esp. Kidd, *American Christians and Islam*.

11. The relationship between religion and terrorism is a contentious subject, but for a scholarly analysis of suicide terrorism since 1980, see Pape, *Dying to Win*.

12. Cf. Kidd, *American Christians and Islam*, 144; Bhatia, "American Evangelicals and Islam," 27. For a study of Evangelical discourse on Islam after 9/11, see Cimino, "'No God in Common.'"

13. Azumah, "Christian Responses to Islam," 84.

radical Islam is the fruit of the Spirit described in Galatians 5:22–23, expressed in qualities such as love, peace, compassion, gentleness, kindness, etc. These biblical characterisations of Christ-likeness have, unfortunately, become virtually dirty words in some Christian circles as far as engaging with Islam and Muslims is concerned.[14]

As Pew's surveys and Azumah's observations begin to illustrate, it is clear that Evangelicals and other conservative Christians of the twenty-first century face enormous challenges in the pluralistic public square, not least with Muslims. Contrary to biblical injunctions to "keep in step with the Spirit" (Gal 5:25b) and to love our neighbors as ourselves (e.g., Matt 22:37–40; Luke 10:25–37)—both of which involve not only behavioral but also important affective elements[15]—we often harbor deep-seated antipathies toward our religious neighbors.[16] While such feelings are at times justified and help us cope with conflict-related tragedies, they are also often baseless, misconstrued, and counterproductive, priming us to avoid adherents of other religions, to support discriminatory policies against them, and even to confront or attack them in verbal or physical ways.[17] In more extreme contexts, such as the intractable religious conflicts in Nigeria and the Middle East, the effects of such emotions can be much more serious.[18] As social and political psychologist Eran Halperin writes in a concise overview of the relevant literature,

> Research suggests that negative emotions lead to the rejection of positive information about the opponent . . . and lead individuals to oppose renewal of negotiation, compromise, and reconciliation. . . . Other studies have suggested that emotions like fear and collective angst may result in higher sensitivity to outgroup threats, more right-wing inclinations . . . as well as strengthening ingroup ties . . . and promoting risk-aversive political

---

14. Azumah, "Christian Responses to Islam," 93. Of course, "compassion" is not explicitly listed as part of the "fruit of the Spirit" in Gal 5:22–23. However, as others have pointed out (e.g., Dockery, "Fruit of the Spirit," 318), Paul's list there is more likely representative than exhaustive.

15. See esp. Roberts, *Spiritual Emotions*; Elliott, *Faithful Feelings*, 135–64; Elliott, "Emotional Core of Love."

16. Cf. chapter 5 in Knitter, *No Other Name?*; Bhatia, "American Evangelicals and Islam."

17. Cf. Smith and Mackie, "Intergroup Emotions," 414, 418–19; Beinart, "Conservatives Oppose 'Religious Freedom.'"

18. See Stark and Corcoran, *Religious Hostility*; Pew Research Center, "Religious and Ethnic Hatred."

tendencies.... Research also has shown that negative emotions, mainly anger and hatred, increase support for extreme aggression and military actions at harming or even at eliminating the opponent.... Furthermore, although recent studies show that anger can sometimes promote conflict resolution ... in most cases anger leads to the appraisal of future military attacks as less risky and more likely to have positive consequences.[19]

With such inhibiting and destructive tendencies, then, emotions such as disgust, fear, anger, and hatred can make conflict resolution, peacemaking, and civic cooperation between any opposing groups—Evangelicals and other religious groups included—particularly challenging, a reality that augurs very poorly in an increasingly globalized and pluralistic world.

A Charitable Orthopathy

Perhaps nowhere is it clearer than in their engagement of competing religious and theological traditions that Evangelicals have a passion for articulating and defending the truths of Christian orthodoxy. *Orthodoxy* can be defined as a biblically and theologically sound set of beliefs, usually with an emphasis on a core set of doctrines (e.g., bibliology, Christology, soteriology) and more freedom for disagreement on less central issues (the age and process of creation, views of the millennium, etc.). Related to this is the concept of *orthopraxy*—viz., biblically and theologically responsible practices, actions, and behaviors, ranging from the various rituals we perform (e.g., baptism, the Lord's Supper) to the values we live out in the realm of social ethics (justice, mercy, prudence, etc.). While Evangelicals in general have valued orthodoxy very highly and are becoming better known for their commitment to matters of orthopraxy,[20] they have paid comparatively little attention to a crucial third component of the well-known "ortho-" triad—namely, *orthopathy*. And this is especially true of orthopathy's social dimension, not least with respect to our religious neighbors.[21]

Though introduced to theological discourse only in the late twentieth century,[22] the term *orthopathy* draws upon a longstanding, even if marginal,

---

19. Halperin, *Emotions in Conflict*, 5.

20. See, e.g., Rah and VanderPol, *Return to Justice*.

21. Noteworthy exceptions to the neglect of orthopathy's social dimension include Solivan, *Spirit, Pathos and Liberation*; Duke, "Peacemaking Left Behind." While many have rightly deemed Evangelicalism a "religion of the heart," it should be pointed out that this identification deals first and foremost with spiritual revival and personal piety. See, e.g., Coffey, *Heart Religion*.

22. According to Knight ("Wesley's Orthopathy"), Wesleyan and Pentecostal

Christian tradition—based on Scripture and the example of Christ, and represented by such major theologians as Augustine of Hippo (354–430), Thomas Aquinas (ca. 1225–1274), Jonathan Edwards (1703–1758), and John Wesley (1703–1791)—that takes seriously the moral significance of human affectivity (i.e., passions, affections, emotions, etc.).[23] Thus, as Thomas Dixon writes in a summary of classical Christian psychology, "In general a clear distinction was made . . . between *inappropriate passions* of the lower appetite directed towards worldly objects and *appropriate affections*, or movements of the will, directed towards goodness, truth and, ultimately God."[24] Or as Robert C. Roberts describes in more familiar and concrete terms, "Emotions take moral predicates just about as readily as actions do. Cruel joy or hope is morally corrupt; envy is often despicable; gratitude can be praiseworthy. Anger can be unjust or righteous; fear, craven or morally noble."[25] In a modern theological context, then, *orthopathy* refers to those forms or patterns of emotions, attitudes, desires, and so forth that, according to Scripture and the Christian tradition, are appropriate or praiseworthy or righteous or noble.[26] It is important to stress, too, that the appropriateness (i.e., the "ortho-ness") of these states and dispositions assumes that they are not irrational, involuntary impulses to be suppressed or trivialized, but rather rich cognitive and social phenomena that can be deliberately taught and formed.[27]

---

theologians first coined the term in the 1970s. However, Land, Duke, and Coulter all trace the origins of the term to Runyon's 1987 article, "A New Look at 'Experience'" (Land, *Pentecostal Spirituality*, 43; Duke, "Peacemaking Left Behind," 177; Coulter, "Introduction," 5).

23. For a classic study of the differences between the premodern taxonomy of the passions and affections and the modern taxonomy of the emotions, see Dixon, *From Passions to Emotions*. Note Clapper's observation, however, that recent evaluative theories of emotion—represented by the likes of Martha C. Nussbaum and Robert C. Roberts—are "now reconstruing 'emotions' in a way entirely consistent with the Christian tradition's view of the 'affections,' allowing Christians to recover the classical discourse of the heart and its affections" (Clapper, "Affections," 45). For other historically oriented surveys of Christian thought regarding affectivity, see Tallon, "Christianity," 111–24; Powell, *Impassioned Life*, 49–170; Coulter and Yong, *Spirit, the Affections*; Corrigan, *Oxford Handbook*, part 4.

24. Dixon, *From Passions to Emotions*, 29 (italics added).

25. Roberts, "Emotions Among the Virtues," 38.

26. Other such descriptors and expressions can be found in the titles of several recent studies of affectivity from a Christian perspective, the reading of which would provide a well-rounded foray into the subject: Harak, *Virtuous Passions*; Gilman, *Fidelity of Heart*; Talbot, "Godly Emotions"; Elliott, *Faithful Feelings*; Roberts, *Spiritual Emotions*; Jensen, *True Feelings*. Also, note that *orthopathy* can refer more broadly to proper religious experience. See, e.g., Runyon, "Orthopathy and Criteria."

27. Elliott (*Faithful Feelings*, 143) rightly observes that while "emotions cannot be

It is our contention in this volume that in our concern for presenting and especially defending orthodoxy in multifaith contexts, we Evangelicals often end up neglecting—even violating—a balanced, biblical form of orthopathy, an element just as vital to Christian faith as the other standards we tend to emphasize as Evangelicals. Accordingly, it is crucial, perhaps now more than ever, that we not only examine the emotions and attitudes we harbor toward our religious neighbors, but also learn to engage such neighbors in a much kinder, humbler, and more loving, empathetic manner.[28] In short, we must form a *charitable orthopathy*. As we have already seen, there are not only pressing biblical and missiological reasons for this *éducation sentimentale*; there are also good social and political reasons. As Evangelical scholar of religion Terry C. Muck writes of empathy in particular:

> What happens in the world when this kind of empathetic attitude is displayed toward others' religions, not only by religion scholars but by anyone who comes in contact with a religious belief or a religious adherent with whom he or she disagrees? Put simply, the world's peace quotient among religions increases. When we realize that we have better ways to approach other religions than the ones most often presented in our histories—war, conflict, persecution, and hatred of the other—we find ourselves in a position to better our world by bettering ourselves, especially in the way we view [and, we might add, feel about and treat] other religions.[29]

---

forced or had on demand . . . one can change the emotion by dwelling on and changing the beliefs and evaluations that lie behind it." The Bible's apparent commands and prohibitions of emotion (see, e.g., Lev 19:17–18, 34; Prov 24:17; Phil 4:4) are perhaps best understood within this context. As Elliott further explains, "The fact that the command of emotion cannot be followed immediately is not to say that it cannot be commanded. In fact, a command of emotion . . . may be the paradigm of a command that cannot be acted on immediately. We might say that the command of emotion is indirect. That is, the cognition behind the emotion must be changed to change the emotion. Since these cognitions are under our control, emotion can be commanded" (*Faithful Feelings*, 143, citing Mark Talbot as aiding in the development of this argument). Emotions can be shaped in other ways as well, such as by acting or refusing to act in conformity with them. See Roberts, *Spiritual Emotions*, 27–29.

28. For similar appeals (though none developed as extensively as in the present anthology), see Muck, "New Testament Case," 13–15; "Interreligious Dialogue and Evangelism," 139–42, 148–50; Han et al., "Christian Hospitality," 21–24; Metzger, "Christian Interaction," 31–34; Stålsett, "From Dia-logos to Dia-pathos?" See also George and Woodbridge, *Mark of Jesus*, 151–72; Mouw, *Uncommon Decency*, 108–21; Mouw, *Adventures in Evangelical Civility*, 178–95; WCC et al., "Christian Witness."

29. Muck, *Why Study Religion?*, 47.

Purpose and Overview of Anthology

The purpose of this anthology is to offer an academically informed yet practically oriented collection of essays that encourages and helps shape orthopathic multifaith engagement among Evangelicals and other conservative Christians. Accordingly, we have assembled and edited eleven full-length essays, replete with a foreword, introduction, afterword, combined bibliography, reflection and discussion questions, and a Scripture index, on various aspects of emotions and attitudes in multifaith engagement. For a number of practical reasons (i.e., the general lack of Evangelical scholars of religion currently publishing on affectivity, scholarly availability, etc.), the international team of contributors we assembled represents a variety of Christian traditions, fields of expertise, and experience in multifaith engagement. Thus, while some have been involved in various modes of multifaith engagement for decades, others have relatively little such experience; while some are biblical, theological, and missiological scholars, others are psychologists, neuroscientists, and philosophers; and while some contributors freely identify as Evangelicals, others identify with mainline Protestant and Catholic traditions. Although our target audience is a broad, educated Evangelical readership, we hope that this openness to learning from scholars of other theological traditions only enhances the overall message and quality of the book.[30]

What remains is to introduce the structure of the volume and each of the ensuing essays. A quick perusal will reveal three main parts: Part I—Biblical, Theological, and Social-Psychological Foundations; Part II—From Heteropathy to Orthopathy in Multifaith Engagement; and Part III—Avenues of Orthopathic Multifaith Engagement. Part I consists of three orienting essays. First is Bob Robinson's survey of biblical attitudes toward religious outsiders, which focuses especially on the lessons that we can learn from Christ's encounters with Gentiles and Samaritans. Second is Elizabeth Agnew Cochran's analysis of the promises and challenges of orthopathy in the Christian life, which highlights Jonathan Edwards's conception of the religious affections as a model of orthopathy appropriately framed within the parameters of Christian orthodoxy. And third is Rosemond T. Lorona, Thomas A. Fergus, and Wade C. Rowatt's summary of recent theory and

---

30. Note Stackhouse's emphasis on *transdenominationalism* as a distinguishing feature of Evangelicalism since its inception—"recognizing authentic Christianity in other denominations sufficiently strong as to warrant working together on projects of mutual concern. Such an attitude made possible the cooperation of evangelicals in the eighteenth-century revivals, which were the defining moment of the emergence of evangelicalism . . . and the vast range of evangelical cooperation ever since" (Stackhouse, "Generic Evangelicalism," 121).

empirical research in the social psychology of emotion and intergroup dynamics, which introduces key concepts bearing upon interreligious relations, including social identity, moral foundations theory, threat-based theories of prejudice, and various models promoting healthier, more cooperative relations between groups.

Part II encompasses five essays concentrating on some of the most relevant emotions and attitudes in multifaith engagement, some heteropathic but most orthopathic in this setting.[31] In the first of these essays, John W. Morehead examines how Evangelical concerns for purity often lead to disgust for and fear of adherents of non-Christian religious traditions; accordingly, he underscores the challenge that Jesus's own approach to purity poses for Evangelicals today. In the second essay, W. Scott Cleveland discusses the virtue of courage and its associated emotions in multifaith contexts—namely, fear, despair, hope, and daring. Closely related is Terry C. Muck's essay on hope, which emphasizes this ubiquitous affective-cognitive phenomenon as an underused yet ideal point of common ground in multifaith interactions. Michael L. Spezio then contributes an essay on the cognitive science of compassion and empathy, arguing that these "active, rational affectivities," contra a number of recent public intellectuals, can be deliberately matured and even extended to outgroup members. And in the final essay of the section, Craig L. Blomberg reflects on Scripture and his twenty-five years of experience in Mormon-Evangelical dialogue to explore what it means for Christians to love their religious neighbors while retaining both their Christian convictions and their rejection of other (irreconcilable) religious tenets.

---

31. By labeling emotions and attitudes *ortho-* and *heteropathic*, we do not intend to suggest that they are "positive" or "negative" in and of themselves. As others have rightly pointed out, emotions are evaluated positively or negatively on the basis of their objects, among other things. Thus, as Christine Roy Yoder writes:

> Many biblical texts speak about emotions not as innately "positive" or "negative," but as faithful or foolhardy *depending on their objects*. Proverbs, for example, sketches persons of serious moral defect by, in part, pointing to their emotional confusion; they loathe the "right" objects (e.g., "fools despise wisdom and instruction," 1:7b) and esteem the "wrong" ones (e.g., the wicked "rejoice in doing evil and delight in the crookedness of evil," 2:14). . . . Conversely, the emotions of the faithful are directed to "right" objects. Proverbs describes the wise as loving wisdom and discipline (4:6; 8:17, 21; 12:1), rejoicing in their life companion (5:18–19), hating deceit, bribes, and unjust gain (14:17; 15:27; 28:16) and most notably . . . "fearing the LORD"—a fear that inspires ethical conduct and promotes happiness and wellbeing (e.g., 1:7). (Yoder, "Shape and Shaping of Emotion")

Moral philosopher W. Scott Cleveland identifies time, duration, construal, and concern as other evaluative bases of emotion as well. See his essay in this volume below.

Part III comprises three final essays focusing on various modes of multifaith engagement: evangelism and mission, apologetics, and hospitality, respectively. The first of these essays, by Karen L. H. Shaw, underscores six affective qualities that pervade the apostle Paul's theology and practice of evangelism and mission, which should pervade ours as well: grace, humility, peace, zeal, power in weakness, and anger rechanneled into expressions of love. The second essay, by Adam C. Pelser, contends that orthopathy offers a healthy corrective to current trends in apologetics—namely, approaching apologetics with a concern more for winning arguments than winning hearts and minds for Christ, exhibiting defensiveness and argumentativeness rather than a humble confidence in the truth, and viewing emotions as obstacles, rather than as aids, to thinking rationally. Finally, Amos Yong explores the benefits and drawbacks of an orthopathic approach to hospitality, inviting focus on an affective repertoire that not only facilitates the practices of hosting and being guests of our religious neighbors but also enables a dialogical sojourning with them in a critical yet empathetic way. At the conclusion of the volume, Paul Louis Metzger offers a fitting afterword that summarizes the book's key contributions and sketches several promising lines of further development.

With the publication of this insightful and stimulating collection of essays, it is our hope that Evangelicals and other conservative Christians will learn to engage their religious neighbors in a much more loving, compassionate, hopeful, and courageous manner—whether in the context of their homes, neighborhoods, schools, or churches; in debate and conference venues; on the mission field; or in the realm of politics. In line with classical Christian psychology as briefly discussed above, perhaps the most significant implication of this volume is that Christians *can*—indeed, *should*—work to shape their emotions and attitudes toward religious others in Christlike ways. Such formation, of course, is rarely easy, usually requiring a prolonged and prayerful reorientation of our evaluations and perceptions of religious others and how we should interact with them. As Matthew A. Elliott writes of emotional regulation in general, "People are fantastically complex and our emotions reflect this. . . . The road to emotional health can be difficult, sometimes requiring years to relearn harmful responses. There can be much to overcome, and perhaps a change is not even possible for some of us without radical intervention from the Holy Spirit."[32] But change *is* possible for most of us, especially with the aid of the Spirit, and we offer this volume in the hope of that possibility. The biblical call to keep in step with the Spirit and to love our neighbors as ourselves endures.

---

32. Elliott, *Faithful Feelings*, 267.

Part I

Biblical, Theological, and Social-Psychological Foundations

1

"He Had Compassion for Them"

A Key Biblical Foundation for Interreligious Relations

BOB ROBINSON

THIS IS A VOLUME whose writers aspire to enhance the way Christians relate to people of other faiths in today's world, a world in which the place and role of "outsiders" can provoke a wide range of responses. But this is also a volume that begins not in our contemporary context but in another place, by appealing to something old—Christian Scripture, from which biblically derived attitudes and examples might, with contextual care, be transposed into contemporary settings—to provide something new: a fresh approach to interreligious relations.

A Summary Survey of the Biblical Attitudes (Beyond the Gospels) to Outsiders

Constraints upon space allow no more than a summary survey of the biblical attitudes to non-Jewish outsiders.[1] The prevailing response in the Old Testament is negative in tone: Gentile religion and religions are usually seen

---

1. One helpful starting point is the comprehensive listing by Muck and Adeney of "Biblical Interreligious Encounters" (Muck and Adeney, *Christianity Encountering World Religions*, 379–85). They detail 239 such encounters, 178 in the Old Testament alone. This writer believes the number should be set a little higher by the inclusion of Jesus's encounters with Samaritans, given that, in Jewish eyes, Samaritanism is functionally equivalent to Gentile religion.

as rebellious and idolatrous; there is no avoiding the condemnation of idolatry and other forbidden praxis[2]—a disapproval that inevitably diminished Jewish openness to those called *nokrîm* ("foreigners"). Nonetheless, these same Gentiles are made in the divine image and are the beneficiaries of the providential care and "general revelation" of the God who declares his intention to bless *all* peoples. And there are also two notable sets of exceptions to the generally negative assessment of Gentile "aliens."

Firstly, there is the way in which the Old Testament acknowledges some Gentiles as believers in and followers of Yahweh in some significant and tangible way; for example: Melchizedek, Abimelech, Jethro, Balaam, Rahab, Naaman, Ruth, the Ninevites, Job. These appear to be "people who already know and are faithful to God within the borders of their existing religions."[3] Or as Gerald McDermott puts it, there is "surprising knowledge of God among Bible people outside Israel and the church."[4] Secondly, there are practices and attitudes that might be called inclusive in tone. In a helpful and well-documented discussion entitled "Hospitality, the People of God, and the Stranger," Amos Yong offers what he calls a revisiting of the history of ancient Israel "through the lens of hospitality." He draws attention to "the God whose redemptive hospitality was first made known to Abraham and his descendants," to the multiple obligations of the people of Israel toward "aliens," and to what Yong calls "the multicultural character of ancient Israelite hospitality" as seen in the Wisdom literature.[5]

The New Testament introduces the teaching of Jesus by means of the Sermon on the Mount (Matt 5–7). It prescribes attitudes and forms of behavior that remain central to the way in which Christians are still called to live, including in a religiously conflicted world: the need for non-selective greeting of people, the avoidance of hypocrisy, and, especially, directives

---

2. These are reminders of what Ida Glaser calls the ambiguous and potentially "dangerous triangle" of people, land, and power—a dynamic that displays the characteristics of human rebellion when the living God (the creator of people and land and the source of all power) is neglected or spurned (Glaser, *Bible and Other Faiths*, 98–105). See, for example, the biblical book of Joshua and Firth, "Models of Inclusion."

3. Heim, "Scriptural Paths," 65. See also the discussion in Pinnock, *Wideness in God's Mercy*, 22–27, 93–95, and the comments in Yong, *Hospitality and the Other*, 109, 116–17, in which he carries this discussion into the New Testament.

4. The subheading for the title of chapter 2 in McDermott, *God's Rivals*.

5. Yong, *Hospitality and the Other*, 108–17 (quotes from 109, 111). See also the discussion of Wisdom in Glaser, *Bible and Other Faiths*, 120–24, who, like Yong, relates her findings to contemporary religious plurality. For wider and more detailed surveys of Old Testament attitudes, see, for example, Glaser, *Bible and Other Faiths*, esp. 47–133; Gerstenberger, "Sensitivity towards Outsiders"; and the various entries in part 1 of Hagelia and Zehnder, *Interreligious Relations*.

for dealing with those seen as adversaries: do not kill; do not return evil for evil; love one's enemies, along with a frequent emphasis on forgiveness (a plea that is later repeated from the cross). The book of Acts records multiple encounters with both Jews and Gentiles. In Acts 4, there is the forceful reminder to the Jewish Sanhedrin that salvation is found only in "the name of Jesus Christ of Nazareth." But that exclusive and apparently excluding attitude seems somewhat muted in further encounters. There is the example of Cornelius, the Gentile and Roman soldier described as devout, God-fearing, generous, and prayerful (Acts 10:2), who is reassured by the apostle Peter that God is impartial and "accepts people in every nation who fear him and do what is right" (v. 35).[6] In Paul's Areopagus speech in Acts 17, he appears to begin with affirmation of the religious quest of his listeners with their altar to an "unknown god" (vv. 22–23). Paul goes on to describe God as the universal creator who "is not far away from each one of us" because "in him we live, and move, and exist"—the reason why all humanity is made in order to search for God "and perhaps grope for him and find him" (vv. 27–28). Gerald McDermott, after a survey of what he calls "The New Testament on Other Real Supernatural Powers Besides God," nonetheless concludes—mainly because of this Areopagus speech—that despite Greek religious ignorance, "the religions had *some* access to *some* true notions of the living God" and that despite the way in which fallen intermediary powers "have taken what is good and holy and used it for unholy ends . . . in the process, some truth emerges. Human beings under their thrall still learn something of God's truth and law."[7] Acts 19 (an account of Paul's two-year stay in Ephesus) also deserves comment because of its description of a four-fold range of interfaith encounter. In it, Luke employs the verbs *dialegomai* and *dialogizomai* (from which the English "dialogue" is derived) to describe one dimension of Paul's method of engagement in both synagogue and beyond, although there are some decidedly negative features also on display as well. One of Mark Heim's conclusions from these encounters in Ephesus is that "respectful dialogue with those in other religions, acceptance of their prior knowledge of God, and even shared religious practice with others (as Paul surely exhibits in the synagogue) do not rule out confrontation and critique with some religious groups, in some settings."[8]

Concerning the rest of the New Testament, two implications of its "high," universal, and even cosmic Christology for interreligious engagement

---

6. The author's own translations are employed throughout the chapter.

7. McDermott, *God's Rivals*, 82–83.

8. Heim, "Scriptural Paths," 67–69, quote from 69. For further discussion, see Stenschke, "Interreligious Encounters." For further discussion of the New Testament, see Glaser, *Bible and Other Faiths*, part 3; Kok et al., *Sensitivity towards Outsiders*, part 2.

deserve comment.⁹ (1) In the Pauline letters, it is clear that Jesus Christ is Lord. Nonetheless, there is no record of Paul explicitly adding the negative (though warranted) inference that, for example, "Christ is Lord, but not Caesar." This is because, as the British academic John Barclay argues, "Paul's gospel is subversive of Roman imperial claims precisely by not opposing them within their own terms, but by reducing Rome's agency and historical significance to just one more entity in a much greater drama. To oppose the Roman empire as such would be to take its claims all too seriously."¹⁰ Those who might want to frame a contemporary confession along the lines of "Jesus is Lord, but not Krishna, or Buddha, or Islam" might also consider omitting the negative inference—for the reasons advanced by Barclay. (2) A high Christology is also asserted by means of the divine, universal, and cosmic Logos ("Word"), especially as described in John 1:1–5, 9, 14, and in cosmic terms in Colossians 1:1–15 and Ephesians 1:9–10 (and elsewhere). Because this Word has been at work in the world through the one who is the "true light that enlightens [or 'shines upon'] *everyone*" (John 1:9a), it is but a small step to suggest the presence of *Christ* where *Jesus* is not known. Although conservative opinion can and does use these high Christology texts to reinforce a dismissive or triumphalist attitude to the religious faith of others, the passages cited above may point in another direction. McDermott, for example, concludes from the prologue to the Fourth Gospel that "it is Christ . . . who is responsible for whatever knowledge of the true God is found outside of Judaism and Christianity."¹¹ And Mark Heim persuasively argues from these same Logos texts that

> they affirm that the God who is uniquely, incarnationally present in Christ is the God who is and has been universally present. Their effect is not to narrow down the presence of the one God into the dimensions of one human life, but to make the extraordinary claim that Jesus is one with all of God's actions across time and space. . . . No one has ever come to the Father, except through the Word. . . . These texts are saying that anywhere the Word was, is, or will be, there also Christ is present, one with that Word. . . . The risen Christ, who is the constant

---

9. Discussion toward the end of the chapter will return to this high Christology (and its implications) as also found in the Gospel encounters of Jesus with Gentiles and Samaritans.

10. Barclay continues: "From Paul's perspective, the Roman empire never was and never would be a significant actor in the drama of history: its agency was derived and dependent, co-opted by powers (divine or Satanic) far more powerful than itself" (Barclay, *Pauline Churches*, 386).

11. McDermott, *God's Rivals*, 33.

presence behind these New Testament texts, is not so limited as to be unknown beyond the small circles of these first Christians. ... Exaltation of the incarnation encourages an openness to the work of God in the world, including in its religions.[12]

Might we then conclude that although Jesus is *the way* to the Father (John 14:6),[13] there might be multiple and even unexpected ways to Jesus given what we have called (because of the universal and cosmic Logos) "the presence of *Christ* where *Jesus* is not known"?

This chapter now pays particular attention to the compassionate attitudes and actions of Jesus toward two groups of "outsiders": Gentiles and Samaritans. His encounters with them feature in some of the most poignant passages in the Gospels:

- Jesus's Nazareth synagogue address and its dramatic consequences (Luke 4:16–30);
- Jesus's healing of a centurion's servant in Capernaum (Matt 8:5–13; Luke 7:1–10);
- Jesus's encounter with a Syrophoenician/Canaanite mother (Mark 7:24–30; Matt 15:21–28);
- Jesus's dialogue with a Samaritan woman (John 4:4–42);
- the parable of the compassionate Samaritan (Luke 10:25–37).

Although these encounters are relatively few, each of them, together with the conclusions Jesus seems to draw from them, is significant because of their display of genuine engagement and discussion, compassionate response, and even some forms of affirmation by him. Jesus transforms the received understanding of the possibility and place of Gentiles and Samaritans within the coming Rule of God, and he does so in striking contrast with the prevailing attitudes of the Second Temple Judaisms of his day.[14] He either ignores or barely critiques the inadequate theology and faulty religious praxis of Gentiles and Samaritans. Rather, he reveals himself as the fulfillment of their religious hopes, affirms aspects of their faith, includes them in the present in-breaking of the kingdom, and—in a word—models the divine orthopathos, or orthopathy, that is the subject matter of this volume.

---

12. Heim, "Scriptural Paths," 69–70.

13. It is important to remember that the context of the verse is the offering by Jesus of reassurance to puzzled disciples; in itself, the verse says nothing decisive about wider interreligious relations or the exclusion or inclusion of outsiders.

14. For a fairly detailed survey, see Robinson, *Jesus and the Religions*, 41–53.

Rather than offering a detailed exegesis of these encounter passages, what follows in this chapter offers some principles and conclusions that might be drawn from the encounters as a whole. The exegesis that has led to these principles and conclusions has assumed readers who are embedded in or inquiringly aware of what it means to live Christianly in the midst of religious plurality.[15] What the example of Jesus seems to suggest for the interreligious encounters of our own day may be summarized under a number of headings.

The Compassionate Jesus Responds to Gentiles and Samaritans

Jesus is reported as commending examples of faith, humility, and right praxis, which he meets in some Gentiles and Samaritans. Some of these individuals receive healing as a result, and some are the object of comment (both positive and negative) in a number of places in his teaching as well. His negative comments about Gentile religiosity, while not unexpected from the lips of a Jewish person of the time, cannot be ignored, but neither should they displace the commendations that he also offers.[16]

In the Nazareth story in Luke 4, Jesus appeals to Yahweh's active presence in the life of a Gentile widow in "pagan" Zarephath, and he also deploys Naaman the Syrian as an example of humility. In both stories, Jesus implies that Israel receives *from Gentiles* rebuke for what it was blind to: its religious and nationalist insularity. The dynamics of faith and humility that Jesus affirms in Luke 4 are also met by him in the stories of the centurion and the Syrophoenician mother. Faith and humility are seen in the attitude of the centurion who calls Jesus "Lord" and who expresses unlimited confidence in the authority of Jesus to heal. It is, as David Garland writes, a "display of exemplary faith by a complete outsider."[17] When ten leprosy sufferers are healed, they remain ungrateful except for the gratitude and praise displayed by another outsider, a Samaritan (Luke 17:12–19).

The healing of the centurion's servant has the New Testament's first explicit mention of "faith," and Jesus is willing to contrast such faith favorably with what he finds "in Israel" and, by implication, with the "little faith" of

---

15. See this author's *Jesus and the Religions* for such detailed exegesis, as well as an explanation of the reader-centered hermeneutic and theological interpretation employed.

16. These negative features are reminders of the ambiguities found in all religious traditions and faith communities, past and present. For a summary and brief comment, see Robinson, *Jesus and the Religions*, 229.

17. Garland, *Reading Matthew*, 94.

his own disciples. The Synoptic Gospels rarely offer explicit comment on the apparent emotions of Jesus, but Matthew does so here (8:10) with the recollection that Jesus "marveled" (or "was amazed" or "was astonished") at this display of faith.[18] The faith shown by the Syrophoenician mother is full of humility and insight; it might even be called extravagant and tenacious in its display of an unconditional confidence and trust. Even in the face of Jesus's reminder of the gulf that separates Jews from Gentiles, it becomes clear in the stories both of the woman and the centurion that what determines God's blessing is neither Jewishness nor conventionally appropriate behavior, but receptive faith. The faith of these Gentiles leads Donald Baillie to comment that "it is plain that Jesus came to single out this faith-attitude as a very vital one and to attach unlimited importance to it."[19] Wendy Cotter even concludes that the examples of persistent petitioners who are affirmed by Jesus demand of disciples "the abandonment of usual criteria of what is 'worthy,' to focus on the quality of faith, regardless of status or class."[20]

The Nazareth incident also sounds a note that is heard in all four canonical Gospels: some Gentiles and Samaritans respond to Jesus or display behaviors of which he approves, while the chosen people hesitate or even reject him. At times, outsiders comprehend what insiders do not. The Samaritan woman repeatedly raises the key issues that divided Samaritans from Jews—as Muslims can sometimes do today because of their differences with Christians—but, nonetheless, she does comprehend what privileged insiders fail to understand. Over against the attitude and actions of a priest and a Levite, Jesus commends the attitude and the actions of a compassionate Samaritan, a compliment that would function as a startling oxymoron in the minds of his Jewish hearers. Samaritans were, in Jewish eyes, the religious and moral equivalents of Gentiles and—at least with respect to the Second Temple Judaisms of the time of Jesus—shared a relationship with Jews that was characterized by reciprocal slander and even occasional violence.[21] In the parable, the Samaritan is the defining actor in the story; he knows and acts out the heart of the Law better than the two Jewish religious leaders. The compassionate heart of the Samaritan beats

---

18. Craig Keener comments that "so palpably quantifiable a nonverbal expression would have had to have made a profound impression on the earliest disciples from whom the tradition stems" (Keener, *Gospel of Matthew*, 268n22). New Testament scholars have long been wary of attempts to probe the inner emotions of Jesus, but among recent attempts, see Voorwinde, *Jesus's Emotions*; Gibson, "Whose Tears?," 113–40; Cha, "Anthropology in Jesus's Emotions," 373–98.

19. Baillie, *Faith in God*, 78.

20. Cotter, *Christ*, 7.

21. See further in Robinson, *Jesus and the Religions*, 204–5.

in conformity with the divine will. Although Jesus's intention was hardly to endorse or promote Samaritanism as such, the parable does imply continuity of some kind between the Samaritan's instinctive action and the divine intent of love that is the heart of covenant law.

Despite reminders of the enmity between Samaritans and Jews in John 4 (some of them suggested by the Samaritan woman herself), Jesus does not denigrate Samaritanism but clearly assumes a degree of continuity; he assumes the woman understands, from her own faith, what he is claiming. The examples might even stand as a rebuke for some of the Christian community's attitudes toward people of other faiths, given that Jesus is seen to affirm at least some dimensions of the faith of these outsiders—challenging though it can be to translate what he affirms into contemporary contexts. At the very least, the encounters suggest that these marginalized outsiders "actually provide a model for the virtues to be sought by followers of Jesus"[22]—and what this present volume calls "orthopathy" is among them.

Jesus and Respectful, Non-Condescending Dialogue

A rereading of the Gospels might also suggest a somewhat neglected asset for the contemporary Christian church: the example of Jesus himself as a model for dialogue with people of other faiths. The opening words of the account in John 4 imply a theological reading of the story as a whole: it is "necessary" for Jesus to pass through Samaria (John 4:4). This is not simply a necessity of convenience or geography but an implication of both the divine necessity of Jesus's presence among the Samaritans and also its method: humble encounter framed in contextually sensitive categories and respectful (yet culture-transcending) dialogue as well. In the encounter, Jesus is both alert to and connects with the religious interests and desires of the woman. There is genuine, extended dialogue; he treats the woman with non-condescending respect. A patient and respectful attitude is also seen in the way that Jesus allows, and perhaps even encourages, the woman's concerns to lead the dialogue, at least to some extent. The two dynamics—a willingness for extended dialogue and the display of genuine respect—have constructive implications for the interreligious encounter today. They surely suggest that Christians can and should pursue respectful, constructive, and practical dialogue with people of other faiths.[23]

---

22. Cotter, *Christ*, 254.

23. For a not uncritical defense of such dialogue (and with a mainly non-theistic religious tradition in mind), see Robinson, "Christian-Hindu Dialogue."

Care must be taken not to exaggerate the place of dialogue as a means of communicating the gospel in the New Testament. However, there is often the assumption among many Christians that proclamation—in the sense of monologue—is the only biblically based or biblically endorsed means of communicating the Christian message. However, both principled and pragmatic reasons can be advanced for multifaith engagement and discussion (both informal and formal), and the consequences are tangible: enhanced understanding, the avoidance of defamation and social conflict, the bridging of communal divides, and even the multiplication of the social capital that exists within and between diverse faith communities.[24] The orthopathos that cares enough to converse can and does lead to such fruitful consequences; well-informed understanding and a willingness for patient dialogue almost always result in improved interreligious relations.[25]

The Example of Jesus and Its Implications

The *example* of Jesus has a significant place in the Gospel passages under discussion. Jesus teaches not only by his words but also by his example and symbolic actions. This exemplary dimension has received rather little scholarly attention, but one major suggestion of this chapter is that disciples today, by reflecting on the Gospels, can discern something of the attitude of Jesus—especially his sensitivity, respect, and compassion (orthopathos)—toward the religious others he encountered or spoke about. One distinct advantage of such an exemplary Christology is that it advocates a Christ-centered approach to the interreligious encounter as it draws attention to the considerable openness of Jesus in his reported meeting with Gentiles and others. This "imitation of Christ" has always been the Christian way. It is certainly found in the apostle Paul: "imitate me as I imitate Christ" (1 Cor 11:1).

The implied call to imitate Jesus the Christ is deeply embedded in the Gospels. In fact, one reason *why* there are Gospel accounts of Jesus's encounters is to provide such an example for his would-be followers. The analysis by Wendy Cotter of the healing miracles of Jesus is particularly

---

24. See chapters 2, 3, 4 in Robinson, *Christians Meeting Hindus*; "Christian-Hindu Dialogue."

25. One of the distinguishing features of Muck and Adeney, *Christianity Encountering World Religions*, is the emphasis they place upon the careful acquisition of knowledge of other faiths and cultures. See esp. chapters 16 and 17, respectively titled: "The Spiral of Knowledge Acquisition" and "Encountering: Learning from a New Culture and Religion." A similar point is made in Robinson, *Christians Meeting Hindus*, 60–61, 77–78, 82–84, 94–97.

instructive. She begins her study by measuring the behavior and speech of the petitioners for healing against conventional good manners as understood in the Greco-Roman world, in which most of the first hearers and readers of the Gospels lived. From her comparisons, she concludes that while some of the petitioners are said by Jesus to be examples of faith, they generally "provide a very challenging ideal to the ordinary person"[26] because the Gospel narrators seem to have chosen petitioners who are: "bold, brash, outrageous, rude" (7), "forward, pushy, and insistent" (8), "spunky, noisy . . . and outrageous" (256) in their approaches to Jesus. She points out that the stories are written in such a way as to show that they are "not simply a vehicle to hurry us to the amazing miraculous action at all. Rather, . . . the narrator, having caught the listener's attention with the presence of these bold petitioners, now illustrates Jesus's view of them and his response" (7). Jesus's reaction to these persons—who, according to social convention, deserve a strong rebuke and could hardly be considered as desirable models of faith—is remarkable and certainly surprising. "Jesus does not seem to pay any attention to their behavior, but he rather sees past it to the desperation that brings them to him, and to the unshakeable confidence that explains their determination, a confidence that astonishes Jesus" (8).

According to Cotter, the healing stories reveal Jesus's loving concern for others, his humility, and a graciousness that Cotter describes as "a 'sweetness,' a 'gentleness,' in his astonishment at the confidence that these petitioners have in him" (255). She concludes that "these stories reveal how the virtues of Jesus are profound expressions of the *agapē* enjoined on all his followers" (13). The portrait of Jesus in the miracle-story encounters calls for the abandonment of judgment, rejection, reproof, and denial on any grounds; it also calls his followers "to look beneath the externals to the desperate need, the anxiety, the shame, the abuse, and the social rejection that explain their externals. It calls on the followers to feel compassion, understanding, and more" (9). Moreover, even when Jesus appears to attach blame to his petitioners,[27] he displays "the humility which allows him to see things in another way and grant generously what had been withheld" (256). If the followers of Jesus *then* were "to feel compassion, understanding, and more" (9), then nothing less should be expected in today's interreligious encounters, which can also have their share of robust,

---

26. Cotter, *Christ*, 6–7. Further page references to Cotter's volume are in parentheses in the text.

27. Cotter has in mind the parents of demonized children, "for it is clear that Jesus holds them responsible for permitting a climate devoid of faith to allow the demon access to the child" (*Christ*, 255). She explains this in more detail in Cotter, *Christ*, 179–80.

insistent, and even harsh dialogue and unfair polemic. Christian responses, past and present, to supposedly harsh, unfair, and even aggressive behavior from some Muslims and Hindus (for example) have not always followed the example of Christ when he encountered similar behavior. The contemporary disciple who encounters such an atmosphere is offered, in the encounter stories, a reminder of the orthopathos that undergirds the response of Jesus. In fact, with interreligious encounter in mind, it is helpful to emphasize that it is the person of Jesus that, more effectively than any other aspect of Christianity, enables the Christian "word" to be apprehended across a range of religious contexts because—to employ the helpful metaphor of Mark Heim—"people cross the membranes between different cultures more effectively than ideas or concepts do."[28]

Some Further Implications for a Religiously Plural World

Universal Compassion

In the parable of the compassionate Samaritan (Luke 10:25–37), the behavior of the Samaritan reflected "a compassion with few limits, as shown in the rich and loving detail which Jesus . . . supplies."[29] The conclusion to the parable appeals simply and directly to behavior that reflects the divine character of mercy (v. 37)—mercy that both extends across ethnic/religious boundaries and is found in the surprising example of the Samaritan. Given that the miracles of Jesus, "performed for Gentiles, and for a Samaritan, bear witness to the inclusion within the people of YHWH of those who had formerly been outside,"[30] Jesus's encounters with Gentiles and Samaritans amount to an announcement of the restoration of Israel that includes an opening for Gentiles and Samaritans to join the reconstituted people of God and to experience the blessing of Israel's salvation by means of healing, exorcism, and other signs. In the Nazareth episode, Jesus exegetes two Old Testament incidents in which it becomes clear that the living God has a compassionate concern for at least some of those who reside—geographically and spiritually—outside the borders of Israel. The stories offer the reassurance that Yahweh is able to reveal himself to people outside Israel and to heal and guide them. This is the same divine guidance that brings Jesus to his encounter with the Samaritan woman and her fellow Samaritans.

---

28. Heim, "Pilgrim Christ," 119. See also 123.
29. Esler, "Jesus and the Reduction," 343. Esler has vv. 34–35 in mind.
30. Wright, *Jesus and the Victory*, 192.

The principle of universality is also demonstrated in the encounter with Samaritans. In the one figure of the Samaritan woman are found many of the characteristics of the marginal persons with whom Jesus regularly deals in the Synoptic Gospels. Social-science analysis plausibly suggests that she is what Jerome Neyrey calls "an amalgam of cultural deviance," a person who embodies most of the social liabilities that would marginalize her in both Samaritan and Jewish society[31]—and yet her status is transformed from that of outsider to insider because of the encounter with Jesus. The universality and centrality of the love command over against any notion of ethnic or religious superiority is asserted by Jesus—as the parable of the compassionate Samaritan also makes clear. And, if Michael Bird is correct, the encounter between Jesus and the centurion has a dimension that is usually missed: Jesus performs an act of compassionate healing for someone who was a potential enemy, an insight that transforms the story into a living parable of loving one's enemies.[32] Although the inclusion of *some* Gentiles need not imply the inclusion of all, exegetes have usually attached considerable importance to Matthew 8:11–12 with its assurance that *many* will come from East and West to join the patriarchs in the eschatological banquet at the end of the age—and the centurion context clearly implies that many Gentiles will be among them.

One condition for positive interreligious relations is surely the "seeing heart" of the compassionate Samaritan, which is modeled in the teller of the story, Jesus himself. What, then, might Christians conclude when Muslims (or other outsiders) display the principles of the love commandment that Jesus so strongly affirmed (thus keeping the religious Law—however that might be defined—more scrupulously than they themselves might do)? Might they conclude, with N. T. Wright, that the story of the compassionate Samaritan "dramatically redefines the covenant boundary of Israel" and explicitly shows that "there was a way of being Israel which would be truly and radically faithful to the very centre of Torah" even if it "would involve the redrawing of Israel's boundaries, to include those normally reckoned beyond the pale"?[33]

---

31. See Neyrey, "What's Wrong." The Syrophoenician woman, the widow of Zarephath, and Naaman the Syrian also embody many of the same social liabilities, at least in Jewish eyes.

32. Bird, *Jesus and the Origins*, 120–21.

33. Wright, *Jesus and the Victory*, 307.

Eschatology and Reversal of Confident Expectation

Jesus attaches eschatological significance to the responses of Gentiles and Samaritans to his prophetic word. They are exemplary confirmation of the Word that is heard "today" (Luke 4:21); they foreshadow and even illustrate aspects of a new eschatological age. As Jacques Dupuis points out, "the miracles worked by Jesus for 'foreigners' have the very same meaning that he gives to all of his other miracles. They mean that the Reign of God is already present and at work."[34] This is particularly true of the healings: "When Jesus heals, his act has eschatological significance and is always the sign and pledge of the breaking in of the Messianic Age, an anticipatory participation in its blessings."[35] Moreover, alongside the principle of universality, the theme of reversal is also prominent in many of the passages considered. The reversal provides warnings to the first Jewish and Gentile hearers and readers of the Gospels about the dangers of religious presumption and assumptions of assured privilege. Jesus signals the extraordinary significance of Gentiles and Samaritans by his employment of their example as signs and affirmations of the eschatological inversion of the coming-yet-present Rule of God. In Luke 4, he employs this principle of eschatological reversal when exegeting what might seem to be two rather minor and insignificant incidents centering on Gentiles to characterize the new eschatological age being inaugurated in him. The theme of reversal offers warning (and even reprimand) to those whose attitudes today display indifference to the faith of outsiders, or whose self-assured confidence attempts triumphantly to exclude or denigrate others. The example of Jesus offers repeated warnings that religious appraisal of the other is not to be based on external markers such as unconventional behavior and certainly not on those of gender or ethnicity.

The principle of reversal is also seen in the encounters of Jesus with the centurion and the Syrophoenician mother. They, like the widow in Zarephath and Naaman the Syrian, become models of faith by comparison with recalcitrant Israel and even his own disciples. Outsiders who display faith and humility are declared to be included; insiders who presume upon their privilege find themselves excluded. If Jesus can so strongly affirm the faith of a Roman centurion and a Gentile woman, and contrast such faith with both the faith of his fellow Jews and his own disciples, what are the implications for a comparable assessment today? Such a question is more easily (and less often) asked than answered as Christians (and perhaps others)

---

34. Dupuis, *Christianity and the Religions*, 24.
35. Jeremias, *Jesus's Promise*, 28.

look at a contemporary multireligious world. But that is no reason not to go on asking such questions when comparable examples of faith and humility are visible among neighbors near and far. It is not difficult to discern temptations toward forms of Christian presumption that seem immune to challenge from the example of Jesus himself. In all such cases, the forceful challenge of Gaventa and Hays might be heard: "Wherever Jesus is invoked as the guarantor of an established order, we may rightly suspect that identity fraud is being perpetrated."[36]

The Renunciation of Vengeance and Violence

The exclusion of vengeance is also presented as one consequence of God's universal compassion. In Luke 4, the message of hope from the opening verses of Isaiah 61, originally intended to console returned exiles, is exegeted by Jesus as good news of reversal, freedom, and Jubilee-release for *all* who are oppressed. It becomes a message of universal hope that excludes retribution. Jesus rejects the notion of eschatological vengeance on Israel's Gentile enemies by stopping short of the threat of vengeance in his appeal to the text of Isaiah 61. Instead, he will offer healing and even inclusion to them. If Jesus's healing of the centurion's servant is an example of love of enemy, then it is also an example of a refusal to see Gentiles as objects only of God's vengeance. Jesus's praise of Naaman (a notable military enemy of Israel) in Luke 4 also implies a refusal of vengeance or retaliation; instead, an insistently forgiving spirit becomes one of the distinctive features of Jesus's ethical teaching. The principle of the renunciation of vengeance and violence certainly relates to the Christian-Muslim encounter, where retaliation, past and present, has often been an item on the agendas of the aggrieved—or projected into assurances about the eschatological future.

In Luke 9:51–56, immediately after the positive affirmation that "whoever is not against you is for you" (v. 50), Luke recounts Jesus's rebuke of his own followers. The disciples want to call down fiery retribution on inhospitable Samaritan villagers who reject them, apparently on religious grounds. Jesus's attitude toward Samaritans includes a refusal to respond to provocation. The response is a revealing indication both of his impatience with ethnic and religious bias and also the refusal of vengeance that characterizes his teaching about Samaritans and Gentiles and his call to love enemies (Matt 5:44). As Ida Glaser puts it, the Samaritans "raise issues most likely to spoil relationships with people of other faiths, the issues of prejudice and

---

36. Gaventa and Hays, "Identity of Jesus," 21.

hostility."[37] But she also adds that it is with the Samaritans that we have the best example of Jesus interacting with people of a different faith.[38]

Compassionate Reconciliation–Even of Enemies

The parable of the compassionate Samaritan has relevance for the Christian evaluation of the faith of others. The parable clearly implies and commends discernment about the other based upon an internal orientation that Jesus identifies as an embodiment of the love commandment, rather than judgment based on membership of, or identification with, a particular group. This theme of compassionate reconciliation has obvious and important implications for conflict reduction in a religiously divided world. One telling and even provocative contemporary application of the principle is found in the advocacy of "forgiveness as foreign policy."[39] The principle of compassionate reconciliation might even extend to the vexing question of contested locations for worship, for which Jesus offers an eschatological answer (John 4). Is it possible that both Christian and Muslim might find in this affirmation a reminder of the *temporary* nature of all preferred worship locations? Nonetheless, disputes over a divine agenda for worship locations are items in a larger set of long-standing and deep-seated emotional grudges held by Jews and Samaritans toward each other. Parallel misgivings have a long and continuing history in Christian-Muslim relations as well.[40] But grudges are never healed by means of a frontal assault, verbal or otherwise; the key, if the example of Jesus is to be followed, is forgiving love and reconciling praxis toward those on the other side of the grudge.

Recognition of Particularity

Our discussion of the affirmations offered by Jesus is not, of course, intended to overlook the religious distinctiveness and differences that are apparent (and not avoided or ignored) in some of the encounter stories discussed. In the meeting with the Samaritan woman, substantial and long-standing divisions are on display although Jesus refuses her implied offer to discuss some central Samaritan claims. As already noted, Jesus does offer a critical

---

37. Glaser, *Bible and Other Faiths*, 162.

38. Glaser, *Bible and Other Faiths*, 162.

39. See Rae, "Ethics of Jesus," 47–64. Another writer offers a reading of the Gospel stories about Jesus and Samaritans in the light of present-day conflicts in Israel-Palestine. See Durber, "Political Reading."

40. On Jewish-Samaritan relations and their parallels with Christian-Muslim relations, see chapters 4–5 in Robinson, *Jesus and the Religions*; Neely, "Jesus at the Well."

appraisal of some dimensions of Gentile religiosity. Perhaps the initial silence with which he responds to the Syrophoenician mother derives from a disapproval of some of her past choices. Undeniable and divisive particularities are also apparent in today's multireligious world. The Christian appraisal of Islam certainly seems to require a willingness to acknowledge some substantial differences. Any embrace of compassionate dialogue is an embrace of the listening and understanding that should leave no doubts about the deep-seated nature of the distinctive particularities of the world's religious traditions—even where undoubted continuities are also discernible.

Compassion, Dialogue, and Risk

There is a theological necessity (John 4:4) that leads Jesus to the Samaritan woman and his dialogue with her. Such an imperative suggests not only divine approval for mission into Samaria but also an endorsement of its method: humble encounter framed in contextually sensitive categories and respectful, non-condescending (and yet culture-transcending) dialogue as well. In Luke 4, however, hearers and subsequent readers know that Elijah is led into the company of a Gentile woman (a lowly and vulnerable widow) in which his actions—in the eyes of many or most Second Temple Jews—are suspect: he not only associates but also eats and lodges with a woman who, nonetheless, is seen both to recognize and to accept a prophet sent by God. The way that this Gentile-favoring behavior is endorsed by Jesus is, in part, the reason for the hostile reaction after his synagogue address in Nazareth. The disclosure that Jesus himself deliberately goes to the notoriously "pagan" region of Tyre and Sidon (Matt 15:21) will have prompted disquiet, including among his disciples. The compassionate Samaritan of the parable is said to stay at least one night at the inn, doubtless to the discomfort of at least some other travelers. Jesus deliberately disregards cultural norms—shared drinking vessels and a stay of two days in Sychar with Samaritans (John 4:40)—in order to bring the Samaritan woman into the equivalent of his kinship circle. At the same time, one consequence of these purity issues is brought out by an observation by Tom Holmén about Jesus and purity: the impurities of those considered unclean do not transfer to Jesus; instead, Jesus's purity can transform them.[41] This transformation should have (reassuring) implications for those Christians whose response to religious others is one of anxiety because of fears of spiritual contamination.

The command to love one's neighbor is difficult to obey without conversational dialogue, but such conversation requires a proximity that can

---

41. Holmén, "Contagious Purity."

invite misunderstanding, risk, and even accusations of purity-compromising sympathy. Such anxiety may be one reason why Jesus is accused of being a Samaritan (John 8:48; cf. 9:16, 24). Is this simply a term of abuse, or is the accusation grounded in the suspicion that Jesus was a Samaritan sympathizer? In commenting on John 4, Gail O'Day points to the setting in the Fourth Gospel that shows Jesus "leaves the land and the people who are 'clean,' to enter a land that is 'unclean.'"[42] If the Son of God journeyed to "a far country" (to employ Karl Barth's poignant wording),[43] his followers today have an example to follow as they face the risks and discomfort of encounters across cultural and religious boundaries.

The Challenge of the Person and Identity of Jesus

Christian faith has always drawn attention to the unique and irreplaceable position occupied by Jesus the Christ in Christian self-understanding. The powerfully significant relation and challenge of this centrality to the world of religious claims might become apparent by means of some questions that are provoked by the interreligious encounters that we have looked at in the Gospels. From those encounters, we might ask: Who is this one who heals by a word and at a distance, and who lives under the authority of the inaugurated Rule of God? Who is it who can redefine the borders of Israel to accept some of those who are assuredly excluded by his compatriots? Who is it who can rearrange priorities within the Torah as he diminishes the importance of purity rules in order to promote the supremacy of the love command? Who is it who accepts address as *kurie* ("Lord") with its implied associations of divine authority and even divine identity? Who is it who offers "living water" and announces, in his own person, a settlement of contested worship locations, including the obsolescence of the Temple? Who is this in whom history is broken into by a now-present future age, and who is recognized by those who have come from the nations? Traditional Christian conclusions and assertions about the uniqueness, finality, universality, and authoritative example of Christ derive from answers to such questions. The appeal to orthopathos cannot be separated from an understanding of the person and identity of this Jesus, who best embodies it.

---

42. O'Day, "Surprised by Faith," 115.

43. The title of the relevant section in Barth's *Church Dogmatics*, in which he begins his discussion of the incarnation, is "The Way of the Son of God into the Far Country."

Some Conclusions

The model we have advocated in this opening chapter calls for *engagement* with the religions based on the example of Jesus disclosed in the pages of Scripture. This example becomes a transforming model as Jesus inspires new perspectives, fresh insights, and a willingness to look with new eyes at a religiously plural world. Jesus deploys a hermeneutical method that enables hearers—then and now—to see that the "weight" to be attached to his encounters with Gentiles and Samaritans far exceeds the actual number of their occurrences. Like the mustard seed of the parable, the kind of faith, humility, and behavior displayed by some Gentiles (and some Samaritans) is elevated by Jesus to assume theological and missional significance beyond what might have been imagined. Considerable transformative and relational implications might flow if the Christian community were to scrutinize its own evaluation of the religions along the lines of this principle, which is apparently embraced by Jesus himself. Such an evaluation could helpfully employ Steven Koskie's suggestion that one "theological way of reading would be to allow Scripture to change our questions and challenge us, bringing to our attention something other than the agenda we bring to it."[44]

Jesus never met Hindus, Buddhists, or Muslims. But he did meet and engage with (and comment on) those who might be regarded as their near religio-cultural equivalents in his own world. By contrast with the continuing temptation among Christians toward triumphalism, the humanity and servant spirit of Jesus challenges such attitudes and offers a better path. One finding of the "Identity of Jesus Project" is that *"Jesus is a disturbing, destabilizing figure. . . .* And it has remained true across time that Jesus's teachings and presence have a way of unsettling things, challenging privilege."[45] Disciples are still called to measure their fears, insecurities, prejudices, and indifferences against the example of Jesus; our attempt to find a better way has involved looking at his example of sensitivity, respect, and compassion—his model of orthopathos. We have, then, heard something of what it means to "have the same attitude of mind that Christ Jesus had" (Phil 2:5) and to hear that "whoever claims to live in him must live [literally 'walk'] as Jesus did" (1 John 2:6).

---

44. Koskie, "Seeking Comment," 247.
45. Gaventa and Hays, "Identity of Jesus," 21.

2

Orthopathy in the Christian Tradition

Promises and Challenges

ELIZABETH AGNEW COCHRAN

CHRISTIAN THEOLOGIANS, PARTICULARLY THOSE who specialize in theological ethics, have over the last thirty years increasingly come to recognize the importance of the emotions to the moral life. This recognition coincides with and complements the emergence of the field of "virtue ethics," an approach to ethics that emphasizes the character and formation of moral agents, the importance of intention and context for evaluating moral actions, the notion that goodness is linked to human flourishing, and the retrieval of historical texts for contemporary reflection on what it means to live a good life. A focus on moral character as central to Christian theology and ethics prompts questions about the role emotions should play in the Christian life—whether certain emotions should be pursued and others resisted, and whether the pursuit of right emotions, or orthopathy, should be considered essential to Christian faith and practice. This essay defends the importance of orthopathy within the Christian life by identifying two Christian theological convictions—namely, the Christian view of faith and a Christian understanding of Jesus as a moral exemplar for human beings—that require prioritizing the emotions as part of Christian moral experience. I then briefly recognize potential risks in accounts of ethics that emphasize the emotions. Because of these risks, contemporary theologians should look for models of an appropriately framed orthopathy within the historical tradition as a starting point for reflection on the emotions' place in the Christian life. The writings of eighteenth-century Puritan theologian Jonathan Edwards offer one compelling starting point for an ethic that maintains a positive and central role for the emotions in the Christian life. Edwards's account of the religious affections preserves the theological convictions important to a positive view of the emotions but simultaneously avoids at least some of the risks of such a position. I conclude this essay by considering how this vision of orthopathy, though rooted in the particulars of Christian theology, offers a promising avenue through which to engage other religious traditions.

Orthopathy and the Christian Life

While the term *orthopathy* was coined relatively recently,[1] reflection on the proper role of the emotions in the Christian life has much earlier roots. An examination of arguments from across the Christian tradition indicates that orthopathy can and should be embraced as part of the Christian life for at least two theological reasons. The first is that right emotions are essential to the practice of faith. The second is that right emotions are exemplified in the life, death, and ministry of Jesus Christ.

Historical and contemporary discussions of the nature of faith demonstrate the inadequacy of a faith that is expressed as mere cognitive belief. To be sure, adherence to specific intellectual beliefs is a part of Christian faith, and certain accounts of faith stress its intellectual or cognitive dimension in a manner that implies that faith is largely a matter of right belief. For example, Martin Luther associates faith with belief and with a confession of the truth of the Gospel narratives, so much so that a failure to express belief in portions of these narratives undermines the very character of faith.[2] But it is simultaneously clear that authentic faith results in the embodiment of particular dispositions that can best be conceptualized as at least partly related to the emotions. Many views of faith stress that faith itself couples cognitive belief in God with a second disposition of intentional *trust* in God, a disposition that goes beyond accepting cognitive propositions and that instead is an expression of a person's overall being, including his or her emotional being.[3] John Calvin explains that faith is an exercise of both

---

1. For a helpful introduction to the term, see both the introduction to the present volume and Vacek, "Orthodoxy Requires Orthopathy," 218–41.

2. Luther, "Freedom of a Christian," 362; *Lectures on Romans*, 237–39.

3. Samuel M. Powell argues that medieval Christian thought presents an integrated view of the human person that allows for a more integrated picture of the workings of reason, emotion, and will. He affirms that Thomas Aquinas's view "of will, following

the "mind" and the "heart,"[4] suggesting that faith is lived out not merely through our intellect but through our overall character. Even as he notes that the Christian Scriptures associate faith with intellectual knowledge,[5] Calvin stresses that faith goes beyond mere belief or the "bare simple assent of the understanding."[6] Instead, faith "is more a matter of the heart than the head, of the affection than the intellect."[7] Faith requires "inwardly embracing" God's promises of mercy.[8] Twentieth-century scholar James Gustafson argues that faith should be defined in terms of "believing" rather than "belief" in order to describe the ways in which faith involves dimensions of experience that are not merely cognitive; faith is "an experiential and affective component of life."[9]

In addition to helping secure the fullness of faith as exercised in trust, the emotions' importance to faith is also made clear in recognizing the close and necessary relation between faith and love in Christian thought. Thomas Aquinas closely aligns faith, which he conceives as a virtue that primarily resides in the intellect,[10] with charity or love. Charity "quickens" faith and, indeed, perfects it; Aquinas explains that it is proper to view love as the "form of faith" insofar as "the act of faith is perfected and formed by charity."[11] Calvin and Edwards likewise link faith closely to love. Calvin argues that love for God necessarily follows from faith.[12] Edwards closely aligns "true and saving" faith (which he opposes to mere cognitive belief in God) with consent,

---

the lead of Aristotle, shows us that the Christian tradition was able to produce a moral psychology in which reason is not utterly opposed to emotion, passion, and desire. . . . This is an improvement over the rationalistic approach of classical philosophy, with its simple opposition of reason and emotion" (Powell, *Impassioned Life*, 384). As I read them, Calvin's understanding of the heart and Edwards's account of the affections reflect a similarly integrated view of the workings of reason, will, and emotions.

4. Calvin, *Institutes* 3.2.7 (360).
5. Calvin, *Institutes* 3.2.14 (365).
6. Calvin, *Institutes* 3.2.33 (377). See also 3.2.10 (361).
7. Calvin, *Institutes* 3.2.8 (360).
8. Calvin, *Institutes* 3.2.16 (365). Phillip Cary argues that this emphasis on internalizing faith distinguishes Calvin and his followers from Luther. See Cary, "Sola Fide," 273–76.
9. Gustafson, *Can Ethics Be Christian?*, 45, 64.
10. Aquinas, *Summa Theologiae* II.II.4.2.
11. Aquinas, *Summa Theologiae* II.II.4.3. Luther criticizes the Scholastic conception of "faith" as "formed by love," expressing concern that this position gives love too much primacy over faith in the Christian religion (Luther, *Lectures on Galatians*, 269). However, at points in his writings he also upholds a close relation between love and faith, affirming, for example, that faith is made "active through love" in the Christian life (Luther, "Freedom of a Christian," 365).
12. Calvin, *Institutes* 3.2.41 (382).

or "love of the heart," for Christ. The moment of salvation is simultaneously an act of "choice" (the soul choosing "God and Christ") and an act of love.[13] Edwards later clarifies more explicitly that love and faith mutually reinforce and sustain each other as virtues within the Christian life. He affirms, on one hand, that "faith promotes love, and love is the most essential ingredient in a saving faith. And love tends to promote and cherish faith"; and simultaneously, on the other hand, that "Love is dependent on faith. For a being cannot be truly loved, and especially loved above all other beings, which is not looked upon as a real being."[14] The mutual relation between love and faith indicates that the Christian life cannot be simply a life that is characterized exclusively in terms of adherence to particular doctrines. Its core commitments must be lived out and embodied in a manner that involves the exercise of the affective dimensions of human being.

A second theological reason that Christians should embrace the notion of orthopathy is that a number of Scripture passages suggest that the incarnate Christ exercised emotions, or at least some form of the emotions, in his human nature. This argument is not uncontested in the Christian tradition as a whole. Classical philosophical traditions, particularly those of the Stoics, are known to view the emotions with great caution, and parts of the Christian understanding of God reflect an influence from these traditions. Classical conceptions of God affirm that God's being is immutable and unchangeable and that "impassibility," or an absence of passions or emotions, is thus a hallmark characteristic of God. Some Christian thinkers, heavily influenced by this tradition, are highly cautious about ascribing true emotions to Christ. Richard Sorabji provides a helpful overview of thinkers, such as Philo of Alexandria, Origen, and Jerome, whose nuanced theological positions associate both Christ and other scriptural exemplars with the exercise of a sort of "pre-passion," or first movement, that differs from fully experiencing an emotion or passion.[15] Thus, for example, Origen affirms that Jesus "began to" feel emotions such as sadness and fear, but did not experience "anything more of sadness or fear than just its beginning."[16] These efforts presume that Christ's sinlessness and divine nature are incompatible with the full-fledged influence of a passion.

Yet Sorabji notes that Augustine marks a shift in affirming that Christ experiences emotion in a true sense, as a corollary to a conception of the

---

13. Edwards, "Charity and Its Fruits," 139.
14. Edwards, "Charity and Its Fruits," 329.
15. Sorabji, *Emotion and Peace*, 344–56.
16. Sorabji summarizes Origen's account of Christ's "beginning to be sad" in *Emotion and Peace*, 349–50.

incarnation according to which Christ is fully human and fully divine.[17] At many points, Augustine's defense of the emotions as part of human experience implies that emotions are appropriate to this life but were probably not part of human nature prior to the Fall. This position suggests that Augustine sees the emotions as having moral value (for example, his grief at a friend's death helped lead him to God), but not necessarily that emotions should be actively sought out.[18] However, Augustine is also clear that the emotions attributed to Jesus in the Scriptures are fully authentic and not "falsely ascribed" to him. He affirms that this is the case even as God is sinless; God's act of condescending to become human also involved choosing to assume particular emotions when he saw it as appropriate. The authentic character of these emotions corresponds to and reinforces the genuine nature of the incarnation: "For as there was in Him a true human body and a true human soul, so was there also a true human emotion."[19] Augustine stresses that the exercise of emotion does not undermine Christ's divine nature or God's omnipotence, but he nevertheless affirms that Christ fully assumes the emotions, and he likewise maintains that the emotions are appropriate to the Christian life.[20] Later thinkers such as Calvin assert this position even more strongly; Calvin contends that Christ exercised emotions such as sadness and grief, providing an "example" that shows the moral appropriateness of certain emotions.[21]

The argument that Christ exercises emotions is crucial for Christian ethicists, particularly those who focus on questions of virtue and character, because an understanding of Christ as a moral paradigm or exemplar is central to the Christian tradition. Christ is not merely an exemplar, of course; orthodox Christianity affirms that his life, death, and resurrection more radically accomplished salvation and ensured a reconciliation between God and sinful humanity. But Christ is nevertheless the embodiment of God's perfections, and so many strands of Christian theology emphasize the ways in which the incarnate Christ radically embodies these perfections in a manner that reveals the nature of goodness to human beings.[22] Augustine,

17. Sorabji, *Emotion and Peace*, 398.
18. Sorabji, *Emotion and Peace*, 397–99.
19. Augustine, *City of God* 14.9.
20. Powell argues that the centrality of the emotions in Augustine's account of the Christian life is even more clearly evident in the *Confessions*, in which Augustine consistently and decisively depicts "the path to God" as "emotionally varied," "an affair of the heart, with its full panoply of emotions and not simply a matter of knowledge" (Powell, *Impassioned Life*, 157–59; quote from 159).
21. Calvin, *Institutes* 3.8.9 (461–62).
22. This understanding of Jesus Christ as moral exemplar is broadly consistent with

for example, indicates that human beings can seek life with God in part through imitating Christ's humility. As Albert Verwilghen puts it, the path of humility is for Augustine "the model and the secret for walking in the only path, the *via humilitatis*, which will lead to the Father."[23] A conception of Christ as moral exemplar, whose character traits we should work to emulate, is important to historical authors such as Erasmus[24] and Jonathan Edwards,[25] as well as more recent treatments of the virtues, including Catholic theologian Livio Melina's interpretation of the path of virtue upheld in John Paul II's *Veritatis Splendor*.[26] According to this way of thinking, particularly emphasized in the Augustinian tradition, the incarnate Christ embodies those character traits that are to be emulated. Because Christ embodies certain emotions, it would seem to follow that these emotions should be incorporated, at least in some manner, into the Christian life.

The Risks of Pure Orthopathy: Ordering Emotions Rightly

While there are theologically compelling reasons to take orthopathy seriously, two cautions need to be made about the potential risks that could arise from stressing emotions as a hallmark of Christian moral experience. These concerns by no means undermine the value of recovering orthopathy as a necessary complement to orthodoxy, but they do suggest the importance of maintaining a balance between the two. The first concern relates to the risk of hypocrisy that accompanies any account of the moral life that emphasizes qualities internal to a moral agent—virtues, emotions,

---

orthodox Christian theology as a whole, though elsewhere I have noted ways in which it particularly characterizes Augustinian thought and Protestant Augustinian positions. This distinction is significant in virtue ethics because Thomas Aquinas, following Aristotle, defines virtues as perfections characteristic of human nature, but I have suggested this position stands in a certain kind of tension with Christian views of God as radically aligned with virtue (such that the virtues are properly perfections of God rather than of human nature). For thinkers such as Jonathan Edwards, virtue and goodness are properly qualities of God, and human beings take part in virtue either through participating in God's virtue or through seeking out qualities that themselves reflect or participate in God's virtue. For more on these distinctions, see Cochran, *Receptive Human Virtues*, esp. chapters 2–4. Nevertheless, it is appropriate to speak of the notion of Christ as exemplar as broadly a commitment that reflects the Christian tradition more generally.

23. Verwilghen, "Jesus Christ," 302–3.

24. Jennifer A. Herdt emphasizes the role of the mimesis of Christ in Erasmus's understanding of the moral life. See Herdt, *Putting on Virtue*, 6–8, 101–24, 344.

25. See chapter 4 in Cochran, *Receptive Human Virtues*.

26. Melina, *Sharing in Christ's Virtues*.

and intentions. How can we determine whether an agent truly possesses or exercises internal qualities? There is a risk that a moral agent practices deception, and even self-deception, about her motives and intentions for performing particular actions; likewise, deception could be exercised about the emotions one feels. Anxiety about the authenticity of conversion experiences characterizes many moments in early modern Christian thought, particularly moments of revival in which a perceived conversion could take place as a result of an emotional fervor that was in a sense detached from reality. At points, eighteenth-century Puritan theologian Jonathan Edwards, a central figure in the Great Awakening, writes about the revivals both as a testimony to their magnitude (and to God's impressive and extensive work of salvation made evident in the authentic conversions associated with these events) and as an effort to offer guidelines for distinguishing true religious experience—and, in particular, true religious experience of the emotions—from false experience.

A second concern about elevating orthopathy in the Christian life relates to the risk of encouraging a kind of anti-intellectualism. While certain forms of pure orthodoxy may be prone to generating a problematic, intellectual elitism, orthopathy might just as easily foster a devaluing of theological studies and a dismissal of efforts to work through complex doctrinal disagreements. Luther's stress on the need for Christians to adhere to belief in the particular teachings of Scripture might seem at odds with a certain kind of ethic that elevates love above intellectual belief. But a stress on orthodoxy as a necessary complement to orthopathy grounds our exercise of the emotions in a particular object and a particular narrative. An ethic that stresses a complementary orthodoxy and orthopathy stresses love not as a general commitment or value, but as a particular mode of living out and embodying faith in the incarnate Christ. Christian love is a universal ethic of self-giving love, in some ways akin to philosophical views of altruism. But the nature and character of Christian love cannot be understood apart from God, who is love itself and who reveals the character of love in the person and work of Christ described in the Scriptures.

These concerns do not negate the overall importance of orthopathy, but they do indicate that efforts to speak of the emotions in the Christian life must retain a connection to the particulars of Christian teaching. Likewise, these efforts should in some way acknowledge that accounts of ethics that prioritize internal qualities raise questions about how we determine and assess particular moral experiences, or the exercises of particular emotions, as authentic. When negotiating possible models for recovering the emotions in keeping with other particulars of the Christian faith, it is helpful to turn to historical thinkers who present the emotions as central to the Christian life. The work of Jonathan Edwards in particular provides a compelling starting point for recovering a view of the emotions as central to the Christian life.

Jonathan Edwards's "Religious Affections" as a Model for Contemporary Orthopathy

Jonathan Edwards's notion of religious affections offers a Christian account of the emotions in the moral life that attends to the varied concerns I have noted above. In some ways, a "purer" orthopathy could be derived from a different historical author, such as Gregory of Nyssa or Thomas Aquinas, who works explicitly with the "passions" or "emotions."[27] Technically, Edwards's "religious affections" are not identical to the emotions or passions as these are conceived in some traditions of thought. Diana Fritz Cates argues that "affections" are more characteristic of Reformed authors, such as Edwards and the twentieth-century Protestant ethicist James Gustafson, than of thinkers like Thomas Aquinas.[28] But Edwards's account of the affections intersects with considerations of the emotions to a degree that makes its retrieval appropriate for Christian efforts to articulate a defense of orthopathy,[29] and Edwards's view of the affections helpfully anticipates both the positive potential of orthopathy and the potential risks in it.

Edwards's account of the religious affections reflects a commitment to understanding virtue and goodness as divine perfections, qualities that are characteristic of God's triune being and essence.[30] God, Edwards affirms, is "the original good, and the fountain of all good."[31] As part of his theology of redemption, Edwards maintains that Christ uniquely reveals this goodness to us because in the incarnate Christ, divine and human excellences coexist and align perfectly.[32] Edwards particularly emphasizes Christ's exemplarity when discussing a set of virtues that are excellences proper to human nature but that are not, strictly speaking, appropriate to God's nature. Humility and meekness are examples of such virtues that reveal and demonstrate the spiritual beauty and holiness of Christ's perfect human nature.[33]

---

27. Recent scholarship on these thinkers points to the promise of exploring their views as part of a more expanded exploration of orthopathy in the Christian tradition. See, among other works, Smith, *Passion and Paradise*; Lombardo, *Logic of Desire*.
28. Cates, *Aquinas on the Emotions*, 8–9, 41–50.
29. For more on this, see Cochran, "Moral Significance," 150–62.
30. See Danaher, *Trinitarian Ethics*.
31. Edwards, "Dissertation One," 424, 433–34.
32. Edwards, *Work of Redemption*, 320.
33. Edwards, *Work of Redemption*, 320.

Because Edwards stresses the moral perfection of Christ's human nature, it is significant for interpreting the place of emotions in his ethic to note that Edwards staunchly contends that the affections are central to Christ's nature and consistently at work in his life and ministry. Edwards's *Treatise on Religious Affections* expressly notes Christ's "affectionate heart" in the context of reminding his audience of the moral exemplarity of Christ's character:

> He whom God sent into the world, to be the Light of the World, and Head of the whole church, and the perfect example of true religion and virtue, for the imitation of all . . . the Lord Jesus Christ, was a person who was remarkably of a tender and affectionate heart; and his virtue was expressed very much in the exercise of holy affections.[34]

Edwards affirms here both that Christ's affections are exemplary in the Christian life and that Christ's exemplary virtue is lived out in particular affections. He goes on to depict Christ as embodying particularly intense and strong love for God and human beings.

Strikingly, whereas we saw above that some Christian thinkers are cautious even to attribute emotions to Christ, Edwards is comfortable not only attributing emotions to him, but also depicting a conflict among these emotions. The strength of Christ's love ensured that love prevailed within this conflict, but Christ nonetheless experienced a barrage of emotions that caused him pain and struggle. Edwards explains that love "got the victory, in that mighty struggle and conflict of [Christ's] affections, in his agonies, when he prayed more earnestly, and offered strong crying and tears, and wrestled in tears and in blood."[35] Edwards goes on to enumerate scriptural examples that present Christ not only as an exemplar for particular affections central to the Christian life (such as love and zeal), but also as a being subject to natural affections that are more mixed parts of human experience (and aligned with traditional views of the passions); these qualities include "fear," "grief," and "sorrow."[36] Edwards's depiction of Christ presents him both as an exemplar of affections appropriate to the Christian life and as someone who, in his humanity, experienced the emotional dimensions of human existence as a source of genuine personal struggle and wrestling. In suggesting even that Christ struggled with competing emotions, Edwards allows for a conflict of emotions to be compatible with Christ's perfection and sinlessness.

34. Edwards, *Religious Affections*, 111.
35. Edwards, *Religious Affections*, 111–12.
36. Edwards, *Religious Affections*, 112.

Also departing from thinkers such as Augustine, who acknowledges that Christ experiences the emotions but resists imagining the emotions as characterizing the life of human beings prior to sin, Edwards argues that the religious affections are central to the "religion of heaven" practiced by the saints. Affections are not merely appropriate to embodied, earthly humans who have "blood and animal spirits," but they are appropriate to the existence of the souls of the saints in heaven. Edwards stresses that the "love and joy of the saints on earth" is "the same in nature" (though not in "degree") as the love and joy experienced by the souls of saints in heaven.[37] Affections are not a concession to human embodiment or a means of accommodating human sinfulness, but are instead central to the enterprise of religion itself. The religious affections of love and joy characterize "true religion" in its "highest perfection."[38] Religious practices, such as prayer and sacraments, are designed to foster and support these affections.[39]

Edwards clearly prioritizes the emotions in religious experience. He also anticipates the concerns I noted above and begins to offer resources to address them. The first concern relates to how we can discern the authenticity of particular religious affections, a question that also arises when reflecting on other forms of religious experience that are largely internal. Edwards works overtly to address this question and recognizes its urgency, observing that even the "true saints" are unable to discern other people's internal godliness. Even those who are under the influence of God's salvific grace can only make judgments based on external observations, which can very well be misleading. People "can neither feel, nor see" true religious affections "in the heart of another. There is nothing in others, that comes within their view but outward manifestations and appearances; but the Scripture plainly intimates that this way of judging what is in men by outward appearances, is at best uncertain, and liable to deceit."[40] Edwards identifies a number of signs that an affection is a true reflection of grace, and he likewise rejects several possible signs. He devotes a section to characteristics that could apply to a true religious affection or a false affection,[41] noting, for example, that intense affections are at work not only in scriptural exemplars, such as Paul, but also in the fervor of the multitude urging Pontius Pilate to crucify Jesus.[42] A large portion of *Religious Affections* lays out qualities that can mark authentic

---

37. Edwards, *Religious Affections*, 113.
38. Edwards, *Religious Affections*, 114.
39. Edwards, *Religious Affections*, 115.
40. Edwards, *Religious Affections*, 181.
41. Edwards, *Religious Affections*, 127–90.
42. Edwards, *Religious Affections*, 127–31.

religious affections, and Edwards's effort to offer such guidelines underscores his awareness of the complexity of elevating internal qualities, such as the emotions, within one's account of the moral life.

The second concern that Edwards anticipates relates to whether an ethic that prioritizes the affections tends toward anti-intellectualism. Edwards addresses this concern less directly and seems to find it less pressing. But his account of the affections presumes a unity in the human person that guards against a detachment of intellectual knowledge from the pursuit of right emotions. Edwards argues that the soul has "two faculties": the "understanding" that perceives and makes judgments and a second faculty that is inclined or disinclined toward these objects. This second faculty, Edwards explains, is at times called the "heart" or "will," and the affections are particularly intense ("vigorous and sensible") exercises of this faculty. The will and affections are thus a single faculty.[43] Even as Edwards differentiates this faculty from the understanding, his overall picture of the mind ensures that this faculty is responding to and building on intellectual judgment. Michael J. McClymond and Gerald R. McDermott note that Edwards's position rejects a dichotomy between mind and heart that many other thinkers of the Great Awakening adopted.[44] In this sense, too, Edwards's account of the affections resists some of the problematic conclusions one might draw from an ethic that overly emphasizes orthopathy.

Christian Theology, Orthopathy, and Multifaith Engagement

This essay has laid out a view of the emotions derived from the particulars of the Christian tradition, including a particular understanding of Jesus Christ as both savior and moral exemplar. Moreover, I have argued that a right conception of the emotions requires coupling orthopathy with orthodoxy, so that particular cognitive beliefs ensure the groundedness and coherence of an account of right emotions. It is appropriate to conclude this essay by considering very briefly what the implications of these commitments might be for Christian efforts to engage other religious traditions. Does an account of right emotions, as derived from the narratives of Christian Scripture, require restricting the capacities of non-Christians to exercise emotions as part of the moral life? If not, how can we begin to

---

43. Edwards, *Religious Affections*, 96–97.

44. McClymond and McDermott, *Theology of Jonathan Edwards*, 313–14. See also Lewis, "Springs of Motion," 275–97.

make sense of the possibility of "good" emotions in other religious and philosophical traditions?[45]

It is true that the deeply christocentric understanding of right emotions I lay out here has necessary roots in a specific religious tradition. But it need not follow that this tradition cannot enter into meaningful dialogue regarding the emotions with other traditions. Indeed, I would argue that developing an understanding of the particulars of one's own tradition is an essential precursor to taking part in meaningful dialogue about the good life. Alasdair MacIntyre's *After Virtue: A Study in Moral Theory* argues that the virtues are made coherent only through their embodiment in particular traditions, which are "historically extended" and "socially embodied" through time.[46] In turn, although John Rawls largely adopts a Kantian framework at odds with MacIntyre, his *Political Liberalism* recognizes that political structures marked by religious neutrality cannot answer moral questions about the highest good for humanity. Instead, citizens need to seek answers to these questions by pursuing the moral goods of particular "comprehensive philosophical doctrines," including religious traditions. The task of political liberalism is to constitute a political order that protects the existence of multiple moral traditions, even those whose beliefs seem incommensurable, because it recognizes that reasonable persons may adhere to varying visions of the good.[47] Within such a vision of the political order, religious and philosophical traditions provide a starting point for discerning and advocating particular views of the good. Building on Rawls's political liberalism, Catholic philosopher Paul Weithman argues that society benefits when participants in religious traditions use explicitly religious language to

---

45. Presenting Edwards's theology as a starting point for developing a Christian view of the emotions in some ways intensifies these questions. Edwards restricts true virtue to the elect and indicates that because of the exhaustive effects of original sin, human beings lack capacities to pursue genuine moral goodness unless they undergo justification. These commitments indicate that in a certain real sense, Edwards does not allow for actions and dispositions to be called morally good, although he develops a category of "natural goodness" that encompasses both justice and forms of love inferior to true virtue. Allowing for morally good emotions on the part of non-Christians is therefore a departure from Edwards. At the same time, dimensions of Edwards's thought (including Edwards's view of natural goodness) suggest that Edwards remains so committed to divine goodness and to its evidence in the created order that evidence of this goodness is not restricted to the Christian faith. In this sense, it is not fully out of keeping with Edwards's thought to explore possible points of intersection between Christian accounts of virtue and the moral life and the perspectives of other faith traditions.

46. MacIntyre, *After Virtue*.

47. Rawls, *Political Liberalism*, xviii.

contribute to public discourse, rather than attempting to make use of more publicly generic and "accessible" language.[48]

An account of the emotions grounded in a specific religious tradition can make a meaningful contribution to multifaith conversation precisely in its particularity and the starting point that this particularity offers for dialogue across religious traditions in a pluralistic society. Many recently published scholarly works point toward ways in which the emotions serve as a promising point of entry both for conversation among religious traditions and, in particular, for exploring points of convergence in the conceptions of the moral life advanced in varied traditions.[49] Edwards provides one possible model for considering how Christians might enter into this conversation by articulating an understanding of the emotions' place in the moral life that attends to the affective life exemplified in Christ. In turn, further scholarship exploring the nature of virtue and orthopathy in Christian thought and practice will deepen theologians' understandings of the Christian tradition and will simultaneously open new avenues for engaging in dialogue on the emotions and the moral life across religious traditions.

---

48. Weithman systematically defends the position that in a liberal democracy, citizens may allow their religions (or any other "comprehensive moral view") to guide how they vote and speak in the public sphere, without having to provide supplemental "accessible" reasons, as long as these citizens sincerely believe that the religious reasons they put forth can serve to justify government action. Weithman, *Religion and the Obligations*, 121–24. Weithman does not follow Rawls entirely in this text but nevertheless explicitly defends Rawls's view as allowing a greater role for religious language than is sometimes thought (with limits that Weithman argues are appropriate and helpful for public discourse). See Weithman, "Rawlsian Liberalism," 3–28.

49. For works that focus specifically on the emotions across religious traditions, see, for example, Roberts, *Tastes of the Divine*; Wilson, *Emotions and Spirituality*; Corrigan, *Oxford Handbook*, part 1.

3

The Social Psychology of Emotions and Religious Intergroup Relations

Rosemond T. Lorona, Thomas A. Fergus, and Wade C. Rowatt

Orthopathy and multifaith engagement are often based on theological and faith premises, but they can also be informed by social psychology. Myers and Twenge define social psychology as "the scientific study of how people think about, influence, and relate to one another."[1] Social-psychological theories of emotion and group dynamics can inform multifaith engagement because they provide lenses through which to understand how people tend to behave in groups and tend to emote in social contexts.

Social psychologists do not necessarily study orthopathy, or "right emotion," nor do they study people from a religious angle. However, social psychologists do study how emotions influence social groups or are influenced by social groups. Social psychologists sometimes refer to "positive" and "negative" emotions, although this refers to categories of emotions based on subjective feeling (e.g., happiness as a positive emotion and anger or disgust as a negative emotion) and not the moral rightness of the emotion. Emotions can serve social functions or reflect social needs, and sometimes negative emotion can serve a constructive purpose for a group. It may seem counterintuitive to examine negative emotion when trying to cultivate

1. Myers and Twenge, *Social Psychology*, 4.

positive emotion for multifaith engagement. However, understanding the social-psychological underpinnings and consequences of all types of emotion will give a more well-rounded perspective to group dynamics and one's own feelings in a multifaith context.

This chapter primarily focuses on theories of group relations and how emotion factors into group dynamics. Specifically, we will discuss the social identity approach to group relations, moral foundations theory and worldview, and threat-based theories of prejudice. We will also discuss how differences in individual traits, such as individual motivations and emotionality, may impact group dynamics and emotion. Lastly, we will discuss social-psychological theories of how prejudice between groups may be changed for the better. Our discussion of psychological theories related to group dynamics is not exhaustive, but we hope to offer a clear introduction to a few of the theories that we think show empirical support and the most promise when understanding orthopathy and multifaith engagement.[2]

Social Identity

When considering the subject of this book, it is critical to acknowledge that *multifaith* and *engagement* imply that people from different religious groups are coming together and interacting. As people label themselves and others into religion-based identity groups (e.g., Atheist, Buddhist, Christian, Hindu, Muslim, Scientologist), one can expect social consequences. Recognizing how humans view themselves in terms of religion-based identity groups is important, as these identities shape perspectives and behavior. For example, people use religious-identity information when forming judgments and deciding whether to trust others,[3] in hiring decisions,[4] and in deciding whether to give up a bus seat or excuse immoral behavior.[5] The social identity approach, which encompasses social identity theory and self-categorization theory,[6] is helpful when determining the social effects of social categorization and how to navigate intergroup relations.

People effortlessly categorize humans into social groups. Social groupings include but are not limited to gender, ethnicity, fan base, field of profession, and religion. The social identity approach suggests that people

---

2. For an in-depth review of theory and research about intergroup relations, see Brewer, "Intergroup Relations."

3. See, e.g., Gervais et al., "Believe in Atheists?," 1191–1200.

4. Van Camp et al., "Applicant's Religion," 462–63.

5. Różycka-Tran, "Love Thy Neighbor?," 9–10.

6. See Hornsey, "Social Identity Theory," for a review. See also Tajfel and Turner, "Integrative Theory"; Turner and Oakes, "Self-Categorization Theory."

categorize themselves and others based on salient information, or information found most important in any given context, which then helps people understand and predict the social environment.[7] For example, when a white Christian enters a room of diverse Buddhists and Muslims, she may feel very aware of her faith and cultural identity and the other identities represented in the room. The represented social groups may provide her with information on how to think and behave. Perhaps she will recognize that she represents a certain perspective in the group and so will say what she thinks best reflects her ingroup's perspective. While categorization is normal and serves a function for interacting with the social world, it can also create adverse divisions between groups.

The social identity approach highlights how group categorization leads to an "us" and "them" mentality. When people categorize themselves and others, they create a mental "ingroup" and "outgroup." The "us" and "them" creates separation and can foster stereotypes and group comparison.[8] Even seemingly innocuous distinctions, such as how "we" dress modernly while "they" dress traditionally, can become clear divisions and a basis for comparison. Internalized group norms and expectations from these social categories can also impact intergroup emotions and how groups feel about each other (i.e., intergroup emotions theory).[9] Thus, sometimes social identities or categories can create boundaries between groups.

Group categorization can also foster group bias. Being part of a positive and desirable group is rewarding; it makes people feel good to think that their ingroup is good and respectable. Therefore, when people are aware of group membership, they may be more motivated to see positive characteristics in their own social group in order to boost self-esteem and self-concept.[10] The same idea applies to religious groups. People may apply overly positive characteristics to their own faith group because it boosts self-esteem to be affiliated with a positive group. People may downplay their religion's weaknesses and emphasize their religion's positive qualities. People may also emphasize negative qualities in other faith groups and downplay outgroups' strengths in order to look better by comparison. In order to effectively approach multifaith engagement, it may be necessary to acknowledge the ways in which one's own faith group has been

---

7. Hornsey, "Social Identity Theory," 208; Turner and Oakes, "Self-Categorization Theory," 246.

8. Hornsey, "Social Identity Theory," 206; Tajfel and Turner, "Integrative Theory," 40. Interested readers should also see Greene, *Moral Tribes*.

9. See Mackie and Smith, "Intergroup Emotions Theory," for a review.

10. Tajfel and Turner, "Integrative Theory," 40; Hornsey, "Social Identity Theory," 207.

positively stereotyped (i.e., associated with positive characteristics) and ways in which individuals from other faith groups have been negatively stereotyped, perhaps inaccurately.

Although rapid social categorization into ingroups and outgroups based on salient features of social identity can lead to less desirable comparisons or biases, reframing social identity or identities can be a strength for individuals and groups. The social identity approach acknowledges that people have many social identities (e.g., gender, ethnicity, and fan base) and superordinate identities (e.g., American, human).[11] Recognizing these different levels of identity categorization could be a source of strength for multifaith engagement.

Considerable research examines the beneficial outcomes of recognizing multiple social identities.[12] Acknowledging multiple identities can reduce negative attitudes toward individuals who may be dissimilar in some identities (e.g., religion) but similar in others (e.g., ethnicity).[13] Acknowledging multiple social identities, and especially seeing one's many social identities as broad and inclusive, can also lead to more tolerance of others. For example, identifying as white and Christian could be seen as narrow (i.e., only identifying with other white Christians) or broad (i.e., identifying with all white people, regardless of religion, and all Christians, regardless of ethnicity).[14] Emotion also plays a role in whether people perceive more exclusive or inclusive social identities. Experiencing negative emotion can create more social exclusion, while experiencing positive emotion may reduce ingroup bias and increase group inclusivity.[15] Creating more inclusivity is important for multifaith engagement, and positive emotion may also aid the process.

Social identity theory is one social-psychological theory that captures multiple group and intergroup processes. Social identity impacts how people view themselves and others, mindsets that will likely surface during multifaith engagement. Other mindsets and concerns that may arise in multifaith engagement relate to moral perspectives and worldviews, discussed next.

---

11. Hornsey, "Social Identity Theory," 208; Turner and Oakes, "Self-Categorization Theory," 241.
12. See Crisp and Hewstone, "Multiple Social Categorization," for a review.
13. Hewstone et al., "Models of Crossed Categorization," 783–89.
14. Brewer and Pierce, "Social Identity Complexity," 433–35.
15. Crisp and Hewstone, "Multiple Social Categorization," 191–95.

Moral Foundations and Worldview

Moral values and worldviews are important aspects of human perspective, and they impact group relations and emotion. People from other religions and cultures may have different values and outlooks, and the perceived moral and value deviations can cause negative emotional responses. Therefore, understanding certain dynamics of moral foundations and worldview may inform one's practice of orthopathy in multifaith engagement.

Moral foundations theory frames morality into five major domains based on morals that appear to cross cultures and religions. The five morals seem to be "built into" human nature and universally acknowledged, although culture and individual experiences shape the morals.[16] The five morals are understood in terms of dimensions with extremes at either end. The moral foundations are care/harm, fairness/cheating, loyalty/betrayal, authority/subversion, and sanctity/degradation. The care/harm moral prioritizes caring for others and reducing suffering of others. The fairness/cheating moral fosters fair and reciprocal relations and discourages cheating and untrustworthiness. The loyalty/betrayal moral cultivates selfless and loyal relationships between individuals and minimizes disloyalty among group members. The authority/subversion moral foundation encourages social obedience and structure within hierarchies. The sanctity/degradation moral foundation prioritizes physical and moral purity and cleanliness.[17]

Morals are learned and developed through culture and individual experiences,[18] meaning that not everyone aligns with the moral foundations in the same ways. For example, religion may impact alignment with moral foundations. People from different religious perspectives may dissimilarly prioritize the moral foundations, and overall, as religiosity increases, agreement with the various moral foundations also tends to increase.[19] Additionally, within Christianity, specific beliefs are associated with the moral foundations. For example, more conservative beliefs and biblical literalism are related to more alignment with the loyalty/betrayal, authority/subversion, and purity/sanctity foundations, and conservative religious beliefs are associated with less alignment with care/harm and fairness/cheating.[20] A more outreach-based sense of faith (i.e., faith-motivated volunteerism and altruism) tends

---

16. Graham et al., "Moral Foundations Theory," 61–65.
17. Graham et al., "Moral Foundations Theory," 69–71.
18. Graham et al., "Moral Foundations Theory," 63–65.
19. Krull, "Religiosity and Moral Foundations," 42–45.
20. Johnson et al., "Moral Foundation Priorities," 59.

to relate to greater alignment with the care/harm moral.[21] Although it is also possible that moral concerns impact one's engagement with religion, such as through seeking out religious groups that validate one's prior moral views,[22] it appears that religion and culture can shape basic moral concerns. Differences in moral values would likely be noticed in multifaith engagement, where people represent different cultures and religions.

Each moral foundation also relates to specific emotions.[23] Care/harm promotes compassion for others and anger toward those who harm. Fairness/cheating promotes gratitude toward those who are fair, anger toward those who cheat, and guilt toward one's unfair self. Loyalty/betrayal encourages feelings of pride toward group members and anger toward disloyal people. Authority/subversion inspires respect and fear for those in authority. Sanctity/degradation promotes disgust toward physical dirtiness and immorality. Therefore, the morals that individuals value, in combination with perceived conformity or divergence from these morals, impact emotion.

The moral foundations theory gives insight into multifaith engagement and emotion. People may seem dissimilar in terms of alignment with morals and values, and this perceived deviation from morals may elicit particular negative emotions, depending on the moral misalignment or transgression. Different moral perspectives between groups can also explain disagreements, group polarization, perceived differentness, group stereotypes, and hostility between groups.[24] The potential adverse consequences of moral disagreement could taint multifaith engagement and emotional experience; therefore, it is important not only to recognize that people in a multifaith context will have differing amounts of moral concerns and emotions, but also to work against the divisiveness that could follow.

Worldview differs from morals and encompasses existential beliefs and beliefs about reality and meaning, in addition to beliefs about morality.[25] Overall, worldviews may function to help us cope with human mortality. When faced with the idea of mortality, people tend to like those who conform to their own worldview and feel threatened by those who do not conform to it. The threat of worldview disconfirmation can lead to aggression toward and punishment of those who deviate in worldview.[26] Therefore, humans seem to be motivated to associate with others who share

21. Johnson et al., "Moral Foundation Priorities," 59.
22. Johnson et al., "Moral Foundation Priorities," 60.
23. Graham et al., "Moral Foundations Theory," 68.
24. Graham et al., "Moral Foundations Theory," 71–97.
25. Koltko-Rivera, "Psychology of Worldviews," 4–5.
26. See Pyszczynski et al., "Terror Management Theory," for a review.

similar worldviews. Moreover, worldview often intertwines with religion, which can put religious groups at odds with each other. A more religious worldview relates to more prejudice toward religious outgroups.[27] As we will describe later in this chapter, differences in group values and norms can lead to prejudice and negative emotion, especially disgust, anger, and fear.[28] Thus, multifaith engagement challenges the human desire to confirm one's own worldview and avoid worldview threats.

In a multifaith context, people can expect to encounter some dissimilar moral priorities and worldviews. These differences in values and beliefs could be perceived as threatening, which also coincides with social-psychological theories of prejudice. Next, we will focus more on threat-based theories of prejudice and the role of emotion in prejudice.

Theories of Prejudice and Emotion

While the goal of this book is to promote orthopathic and positive multifaith engagement, it is important to acknowledge that prejudice often exists between groups and could impact multifaith engagement. Prejudice involves negative attitudes, feelings, and beliefs directed toward individuals on the basis of group affiliation.[29] Prejudice reflects generalizations that are not necessarily based on fact, although people will often try to rationalize and justify their prejudices.[30] Prejudice can also lead to discrimination, which is differential treatment of, or an action with social penalties to, the target of prejudice. Discrimination can range from verbal derogation and avoiding certain people to actively harming or aggressing toward people based on group membership.[31] Overall, prejudice ranges from relatively undetectable to overtly hostile, but all forms of prejudice are important to recognize and minimize in healthy intergroup contact. Understanding potential causes and consequences of prejudice can help individuals manage the difficulties that may arise with multifaith engagement.

Much social-psychological research has been done on prejudice between various groups, including religious groups.[32] Religious groups are not immune to prejudice, even though many religions preach messages

---

27. Goplen and Plant, "Religious Worldview," 1476–83.

28. Cottrell and Neuberg, "Different Emotional Reactions," 773; Matthews and Levin, "Dual Process Model," 570–71.

29. Myers and Twenge, *Social Psychology*, 309.

30. Allport, *Nature of Prejudice*, 6–9.

31. Allport, *Nature of Prejudice*, 14–15.

32. See Rowatt et al., "Religion, Prejudice," for a review.

of love and acceptance. When approaching multifaith dialogue, it is imperative to identify prejudices held between religious groups and how that prejudice may impact dialogue and emotion. Next, we will describe some specific conflict and threat-based theories of prejudice and how prejudice functions in terms of emotion.

Realistic Group Conflict and Integrated Threat Approaches

Realistic group conflict theory suggests that when groups compete for resources, there will be conflict and prejudice between the groups. Even very simple competitive situations, such as competing in a sports game, can result in negative feelings between groups.[33] Many religious groups compete, which taints group relations. For example, some religious denominations compete for congregants, as some denominations are faster growing than others. Alternatively, some churches may perceive competition with Atheism, which grows and threatens church membership. Other religious group conflicts are more obvious. Jews and Muslims compete for land and political power in Israel/Palestine, which exemplifies intense hostility and violence that arises with extreme group competition.

Integrated threat theory furthers realistic conflict theory and suggests that intergroup attitudes are impacted by both realistic threats and symbolic threats.[34] Realistic threats are concerns that a different group may threaten one's physical safety or security of economic resources, whereas symbolic threats are concerns that another group holds values and beliefs that are different and threaten one's own value system.[35] Neither realistic nor symbolic threats have to actually be "real," or actually have a high probability of occurring; rather, realistic and symbolic threats simply need to be perceived as *possible* dangers in order for prejudice to occur.[36] In later examples, we will discuss how these perceived threats manifest in religion-based prejudice. First, we will discuss another threat-based theory of prejudice that focuses on the social functions of emotions.

---

33. See Sherif et al., *Intergroup Conflict and Cooperation*, for a review.
34. Stephan et al., "Intergroup Threat Theory," 44.
35. Stephan et al., "Intergroup Threat Theory," 44.
36. Stephan et al., "Intergroup Threat Theory," 45; Stephan and Stephan, "Predicting Prejudice," 418.

Sociofunctional Approach

The sociofunctional approach to prejudice is a threat-based evolutionary theory.[37] The theory posits that emotions experienced toward groups serve an adaptive purpose, which leads to the survival of the group and, therefore, the survival of the individual. The sociofunctional approach to prejudice suggests that emotion-based prejudice toward outgroups arises out of specific group threats and motivates individuals to respond to those group threats, fostering group survival. Therefore, certain emotions may be seen as functional or adaptive because they can work in favor of one's own group needs.[38] Emotion serves other purposes than simply enhancing group functioning,[39] but the sociofunctional approach to prejudice can help explain why people tend to experience emotions in similar ways and why it seems natural to experience certain emotions in intergroup contexts.

According to the sociofunctional theory, specific emotions occur due to group threats and encourage people to respond to threats.[40] Accordingly, fear arises when humans feel that they or their group are physically threatened. The fear then motivates the individual to avoid the source of threat (e.g., run away). Anger tends to arise out of threats to resources or group cooperativeness and motivates individuals to change the situation to restore the balance of resources or group cooperation. Envy closely relates to anger, since envy also arises when resources are threatened, specifically when one group has limited resources that another group desires. Envy may encourage people to take or earn more of the limited resources for their own group. Another negative emotion, disgust, arises out of concerns for contamination. Contamination may be symbolic, such as contamination of group values or norms, or physical, such as contamination through bodily infections. The threat of contamination elicits disgust, which then motivates avoidance of the potential contaminant.[41] Fear, anger, envy, and disgust are examples of "negative" emotions, which can serve positive purposes in responding to social threats.

The sociofunctional approach to emotion also accounts for the social emotions of pity and guilt. For example, pity may arise out of threats that individuals may be unable to reciprocate help or resources, but not due to

---

37. Cottrell and Neuberg, "Different Emotional Reactions," 771. See also Neuberg and Cottrell, "Intergroup Emotions."
38. Cottrell and Neuberg, "Different Emotional Reactions," 771–74.
39. Cottrell and Neuberg, "Different Emotional Reactions," 771–72.
40. Cottrell and Neuberg, "Different Emotional Reactions," 773.
41. Cottrell and Neuberg, "Different Emotional Reactions," 773.

their own choice.[42] One may have pity on a begging orphan and provide that child with some money or food without expecting anything in return, since the child is likely unable to reciprocate—and probably not by choice. The emotion of pity may help to maintain positive relationships between individuals and groups. Guilt arises when someone is concerned that their social group will look tainted or immoral, and so guilt motivates individuals to make a situation right in order to restore relationships.[43] For instance, if someone knows that her social group cheated another person or group and feels sorry about it, she may feel threatened that her group's reputation will be tarnished. Then perhaps she would confess to the cheating and pay retribution, repairing the perception of her and her group as moral and trustworthy.

Because these emotions, especially the negative emotions, are often highly rewarded (e.g., fear may lead to successful avoidance of a dangerous situation, leading to survival), it can be difficult to work against these emotions. It appears that functional emotions are so adaptive that they may be overreactive, because overreactivity may lead to better overall survival.[44] For example, if someone notices a bad-smelling food (eliciting disgust), it is better to experience high disgust and not eat it, even if it might be safe to eat. If he or she takes a risk and eats the food when it is, in fact, rotten and dangerous, he or she may get sick and die. Therefore, it is better to respond earnestly to threats, even if the threat may be harmless, to enhance one's chance of survival. Hence, humans' emotional reaction systems may be somewhat overreactive, for better or for worse.[45]

Integrated threat theory and the sociofunctional approach to prejudice are similar in their foundations of threat appraisals and consequences of social threats. Outcomes of these threats may include negative emotions and other forms of prejudice or discrimination, which may impact multifaith engagement. Social-psychological researchers have studied some examples of threat-based prejudice between religious groups. In the United States, people who see Muslims as a symbolic threat may experience more anger and disgust toward Muslims, which may lead to distancing, less tolerance, or more prejudice.[46] Atheists can represent threats to values, which may lead to moral disgust and general negativity directed toward Atheists.[47] Atheists are typically

---

42. Cottrell and Neuberg, "Different Emotional Reactions," 773–74.
43. Cottrell and Neuberg, "Different Emotional Reactions," 773–74.
44. See Neuberg and Schaller, "Evolutionary Threat-Management Approach," 2.
45. Neuberg and Schaller, "Evolutionary Threat-Management Approach," 2.
46. Wirtz et al., "Negative Attitudes toward Muslims," 78–80.
47. Cook et al., "No Good without God," 220–24.

distrusted because religious people cannot assume that Atheists follow similar morals and norms.[48] Realistic threats, or threats concerning physical and economic well-being, also impact prejudice between religious groups, such that resource deprivation is associated with more prejudice toward religious outgroups.[49] Perceived threats and consequential emotions can affect engagement with individuals from different faith backgrounds.

Research has also examined threats and prejudice that relate to the dehumanization of certain groups. Dehumanization reflects assigning less human characteristics to people of another group, demeaning them into a less-than-full human status.[50] For example, Americans generally tend to blatantly dehumanize Arabs and Muslims, and this dehumanization is associated with prejudice and support for discriminatory or aggressive behaviors against them. However, dehumanization is also heightened by perceptions of threat and conflict; Arabs are more dehumanized after terrorist attacks.[51] Therefore, perceived threats can also lead to negative and hostile reactions through dehumanization.

Overall, the social-psychological theories outlined above attempt to account for reasons why people experience certain emotions in social contexts or when responding to specific groups. The realistic group conflict, integrated threat, and sociofunctional theories emphasize potential causes of prejudice and emotion, especially perceived group threats, and consequences of human prejudice and emotion. Understanding emotion can help to recognize why people sometimes feel negatively or apprehensively when dialoguing with members of different faith groups. As the above theories suggest, certain negative emotions give insight into threat appraisals and can serve an adaptive purpose. Identifying one's own emotions toward other people can help that person consider the reasons why he/she feels threatened and evaluate the validity of those concerns in particular situations.

Individual Differences

Certain aspects of personality, or individual differences, also influence group dynamics, prejudice, and emotion. Individual differences inform intergroup relations and emotion because individuals bring their own unique beliefs and ways of thinking to social situations, and not all people act the same way in social contexts. Two commonly studied individual

---

48. Gervais et al., "Believe in Atheists?," 1191–1200.
49. Tripathi and Srivastava, "Relative Deprivation," 315–17.
50. See Kteily et al., "Ascent of Man," 902–4.
51. Kteily et al., "Ascent of Man," 906–923.

differences in relation to group dynamics are *social dominance orientation* (SDO) and *right-wing authoritarianism* (RWA). SDO is an individual attitudinal and motivational preference focused on beliefs about how different social groups should relate to one another. Specifically, people with high SDO prefer social hierarchy and believe that certain groups, especially one's ingroup, should be superior and control other, inferior groups.[52] RWA is an individual attitudinal and motivational characteristic based on a preference for traditional values and authorities who preserve those values, as well as a desire to punish those who violate traditional values and worldviews. RWA is also characterized by more disliking of outgroups, especially those who are perceived as value-violating.[53] SDO and RWA represent dimensional features that range from very low to very high.

RWA and SDO are similar in some ways, such that they share moderate-to-high positive correlations with prejudice.[54] However, SDO and RWA show uniqueness in important ways. Pursuant to the social threat-based theories of prejudice previously discussed, SDO and RWA differentially associate with perceived social threats. Higher RWA may make people more sensitive to symbolic threats, leading to more prejudice, whereas higher SDO may make people more attuned to realistic threats from competitive groups, leading to more prejudice.[55] Similar results are seen in prejudice toward Muslims. RWA predicted perceptions of value (symbolic) threats, while SDO predicted more perceived economic (realistic) threats, and both types of threats lead to more disgust and anger.[56] Therefore, individual levels of SDO and RWA may also indirectly impact emotion experienced between groups.

Emotionality can also be conceptualized as an aspect of personality. We typically think of emotions as situational states or situationally caused; however, emotionality can also be trait-like and consistent over time. Certain people may be more or less prone to experiencing positive emotions, such as happiness, and others may be more or less prone to experiencing negative emotions, such as anger and fear, over time.[57] Personality traits related to emotionality also impact how positively or negatively a person responds and feels in situational contexts,[58] which becomes relevant when

---

52. Pratto et al., "Social Dominance Orientation," 741–42.
53. Altemeyer, *Right-Wing Authoritarianism*, 147–55.
54. Sibley and Duckitt, "Personality and Prejudice," 257.
55. Duckitt and Sibley, "Right-Wing Authoritarianism," 291–94.
56. Matthews and Levin, "Dual Process Model," 570–71.
57. E.g., Costa and McCrae, "Influence of Extraversion," 671–75.
58. E.g., Larsen and Ketelaar, "Personality and Susceptibility," 135–37.

considering emotion in multifaith engagement. Certain emotions may come more naturally than others due to personality, potentially impacting the practice of orthopathy and multifaith engagement.

Emotion tendencies (traits) also impact relationships between both SDO and prejudice and RWA and prejudice. For example, more trait anger, combined with more RWA, is associated with more prejudice, whereas more trait fear, combined with high SDO, is associated with more prejudice.[59] A tendency to experience disgust in interpersonal contexts also relates to more SDO and RWA, which then promotes more prejudice.[60] Understanding individual differences in trait emotion can shed light on how people orient to group relations, such as through preferring social hierarchies (SDO) or through preferring groups that conform to traditional values (RWA). Individual differences can also shed light on how people tend to emote in social situations.

Bettering Group Relations and Reducing Prejudice

Joanna Burch-Brown and William Baker offer a good review of some ways that religion can help reduce prejudice. Among other ideas, they suggest promoting more inclusive theologies, emphasizing common and shared identities between groups, making more contact, and building cooperative relationships and friendships with people who seem different at first blush.[61] Psychological theories support some of these recommendations. The common ingroup identity model suggests that when people are recategorized by a superordinate identity, instead of narrower group identities, they exhibit more positive interactions.[62] In multifaith contexts, there may be many opportunities to view others as part of the collective "we," making identity in the group more inclusive. For example, the collective "we" in a multifaith context might be "community partners" or "peacemakers" seeking social justice or solving a neighborhood problem. Alternatively, the "we" might be "Americans" who want more civil political discourse and inclusive opportunities.

Gordon Allport's contact hypothesis also suggests that positive interactions and exposure to other groups help to reduce prejudice. More specifically, ideal contact situations would include people with established, equal status working with a common purpose and with the approval of the

---

59. Kossowska et al., "Impact," 746–48.
60. Hodson and Costello, "Interpersonal Disgust," 694–96.
61. Burch-Brown and Baker, "Religion and Reducing Prejudice," 785.
62. Gaertner and Dovidio, *Reducing Intergroup Bias*, 42.

community or culture.[63] Muzafer Sherif and colleagues also emphasized that creating a superordinate goal for all group members is an especially effective way to reduce prejudice.[64] Across research studies, contact appears to decrease prejudice between groups.[65] Beyond contact, building genuine friendships between group members also consistently improves attitudes between groups.[66] Thus, although religion paradoxically seems to foster prejudice in certain ways, religion also has the opportunity to foster inclusion.[67]

Conclusions

This chapter introduced several social-psychological theories of group dynamics and emotion. The social identity approach displays how individuals view group memberships and how acknowledging broader group memberships can help dispel the biases sometimes shown to one's own ingroup. Moral foundations theory presents common morals and emotions that arise out of each moral, but it also demonstrates that not everyone values all morals equally. Moral differences, along with differences in worldviews, can cause groups to clash. The threat-based approaches to prejudice offer insight not only into prejudice formation but also into how prejudice and negative emotion disclose perceived threats and frustrations between groups. Identifying the causes and implications of emotion and prejudice can help to understand group dynamics and perhaps minimize negative group interactions. Lastly, acknowledging individual differences provides insight into why certain emotions or approaches to the social world differ among individuals in social settings.

In closing, and to revisit the role of social psychology in informing orthopathy and multifaith engagement, it is important to note that while social psychologists do not study "right" and "wrong" emotion, this does not mean that emotions and their consequences are predetermined or amoral.[68] Most psychologists agree that prejudice is not right and not justifiable, even though the processes of prejudice and emotion may be understandable. Therefore, this chapter should not be taken as incompatible with the theology and moral assertions of the other chapters in this book. While social psychology attempts to explain group dynamics and emotion in ways not

63. Allport, *Nature of Prejudice*, 281.
64. Sherif et al., *Intergroup Conflict and Cooperation*, 159–83.
65. Pettigrew and Tropp, "Meta-Analytic Test," 757.
66. Davies et al., "Cross-Group Friendships," 335–39.
67. Allport, *Nature of Prejudice*, 444.
68. See Cottrell and Neuberg, "Different Emotional Reactions," 771.

intertwined with religious faith, theology can provide further interpretation, meaning, and a context for applying scientific knowledge. Partnerships between science and religion have much to offer,[69] as do partnerships between faith groups. Hopefully, this chapter has offered some significant insight into common human behavior and emotion in the social world, which can be applied to a variety of intergroup and multifaith contexts.

---

69. Interested readers should see Clayton, *Religion and Science*.

Part II

From Heteropathy to Orthopathy in Multifaith Engagement

4

Evangelicals and Gross Religions

Disgust and Fear in Multifaith Engagement

JOHN W. MOREHEAD

MANY AMERICAN EVANGELICALS DON'T have warm feelings when it comes to other religions, and this is accompanied by negative perceptions about them. A 2014 survey by the Pew Research Center, titled "How Americans Feel About Religious Groups," included some insightful statistics on Evangelicals.[1] Like those of other religious groups, Evangelicals felt most positive about their own members. Concerning other religions, Evangelicals had the most positive feelings toward Catholics and Jews, but the "feeling thermometer" rating system used by Pew—ranging from 0 to 100, with 0 representing the coldest emotions—dropped significantly when other groups came into view. Buddhists, Hindus, and especially Muslims elicited largely negative emotions, receiving an average rating of 39, 38, and 30, respectively. Only Atheists were viewed more negatively at 25. Pew returned to this survey in 2017, and while all other demographic groups showed warmer feelings about others since the initial survey, Evangelicals stayed the same, and the feelings others have about Evangelicals got cooler.[2]

---

1. Pew Research Center, "How Americans Feel."

2. Pew Research Center, "Increasingly Warm Feelings." These cool feelings toward other religions are not just an American Evangelical phenomenon. Pew surveyed international Evangelical leaders connected with the Lausanne Committee for World Evangelization, and the result was that "solid majorities express unfavorable views of Buddhists (65 percent), Hindus (65 percent), Muslims (67 percent), and atheists (70 percent). Interestingly, the leaders who live in Muslim-majority countries generally are

Not only do Evangelicals tend to feel less than warm about adherents of other religious groups; these frosty feelings seem to have a connection to negative perceptions about them. Perceptions of Muslims provide a good example. A LifeWay Research survey of Protestant pastors in the US asked them to describe Islam.[3] The data showed that "a majority of pastors considered Islam dangerous,"[4] and 45 percent of those surveyed stated that the ISIS terrorist group "gives a true indication of what an Islamic society looks like."[5]

These cool feelings and negative perceptions toward other religions are generally indicative of Evangelical approaches to other religions and the phenomenon of religious pluralism in America. As a result, many Evangelicals either ignore members of other religions around them or, when they do engage them, draw upon defensive and confrontational apologetic strategies as a means of response. In order to understand some of the reasons why, this chapter brings this Evangelical approach to multifaith engagement into conversation with social psychology. Consideration is given to the Evangelical emphasis on doctrinal purity, Evangelical fears of worldview contamination, and the ways in which these connect to disgust reactions as a protective mechanism. After considering the importance of purity and disgust to understanding Evangelical concerns about multifaith engagement, I briefly sketch other areas of research from social psychology and sociology to better understand these phenomena, and then discuss the implications of these psychological dynamics for multifaith engagement. Finally, given the significance of purity for Evangelicals, this chapter concludes with a consideration of both Jesus's approach to purity in his own socioreligious context and what this might mean for critical self-reflection by Evangelicals in an increasingly pluralistic world.

Moral Foundations, Heretical Disgust, and Spiritual Harm

Two significant features of Evangelical reactions to other religions are concerns for doctrinal purity and fears of contamination. Previously, I spent several years working within the Evangelical "counter-cult" community, a subculture devoted to an approach to analyzing "cults" or new religious

---

more positive in their assessments of Muslims than are the evangelical leaders overall" (Pew Research Center, "Evangelical Protestant Leaders," 14).

3. Green, "New Study."
4. Taylor, "Islam Is 'Dangerous.'"
5. Madhani, "Study."

movements that strongly emphasizes apologetic argumentation and refutation of these groups. In this regard, it is not uncommon to hear concerns about syncretism—the blending of Christian teachings with the doctrines of other religions—understood in theology and missiology as "the replacement or dilution of the essential truths of the gospel through the incorporation of non-Christian elements."[6] After moving outside of the counter-cult due to concerns about its approach, and shifting into a cross-cultural missions methodology and, more recently, multifaith engagement, I still encounter repeated concerns from Evangelicals about syncretism. In fact, such concerns often keep Evangelicals from relating to their religious neighbors in any way other than evangelistic proclamation or apologetic refutation.

This concern about syncretism plays a significant role among conservative Evangelicals, not only in their theology but also in the psychology that underlies their doctrine and praxis toward religious others. This became a focus of research for me in connection with a grant project funded by the Louisville Institute. I served as leader and academic member for a collaborative inquiry team of Evangelical pastors and scholars who conducted research as a means of understanding the psychological processes underlying Evangelical approaches to other religions.[7] An initial grant allowed us to compile case studies of Evangelical churches involved in hospitable forms of multifaith engagement in their communities. A supplemental grant was then undertaken to find out how these churches had worked through their concerns for syncretism, which often prevent most churches from pursuing a hospitable approach to their religious neighbors.[8]

Early in the research process, aspects of social psychology stood out as promising for shedding light on important dynamics in Evangelical approaches to multifaith engagement. Social psychology provides a number of important tools to help us understand the dynamics of multifaith encounters.[9] In particular, the study of moral psychology is especially illuminating. One approach to the study of moral psychology comes by way of moral

---

6. Moreau, "Syncretism," 924.

7. A summary description of the team's work can be found on the Louisville Institute's website. See Morehead et al., "Multi-Faith Matters."

8. The theological and psychological challenges posed by syncretism also play a part in the labeling of Evangelicals involved in hospitable multifaith engagement as "compromisers"—or worse. See Stetzer, "Rick Warren Interview"; Sataline, "Befriending Witches."

9. See Lorona et al.'s essay in this volume for a summary and discussion of various facets of social psychology and intergroup processes in application to multifaith engagement.

foundations theory,[10] which attempts to account for the psychological origins of morality and the similarities and variability of morality in groups and cultures. It puts forward the idea that human beings have various moral intuitions and innate modular foundations, and that these "are one powerful and largely unexplored psychological mechanism that underlies ideology in general and issue positions in particular."[11] Social psychologists have identified five moral foundations, including harm/care, fairness/reciprocity, ingroup/loyalty, authority/respect, and purity/sanctity.[12] According to the theory, while human beings share the same moral intuitions, conservatives and liberals emphasize different moral foundations. Liberals tend to draw upon two foundations, care and fairness, whereas conservatives tend to emphasize loyalty, authority, and purity. As this relates to multifaith engagement, given their concerns for fairness toward others, liberals more naturally gravitate toward interest in participation in interfaith activities, where the call is to care for and be fair to minority religious groups, as well as to coexist with and tolerate others. Commonality and fairness are emphasized, rather than religious difference and separation. But conservatives come at this from a very different set of moral foundations. Conservative Christians, particularly Evangelicals, emphasize ingroup/loyalty, which includes things like allegiance to the church and its teachings; authority/respect, which involves a recognition of religious authority in relation to their understanding of Scripture; and especially purity/sanctity, which includes notions of holiness and freedom from contamination. When it comes to an emphasis on particular moral foundations for Evangelicals in regard to other religions, ingroup/loyalty and authority/respect are certainly at play, but a good case can be made that the most significant concerns are for purity and safeguarding Christian doctrine and worldview from possible contamination by contact with other religions. Research in social psychology helps us understand this idea and the challenge it poses for Evangelicals in multifaith engagement.

The work of Ryan Ritter and Jesse Lee Preston is significant here in their exploration of "the role of disgust in the context of rejected religious

---

10. See Haidt and Graham, "When Morality Opposes Justice"; Haidt and Joseph, "Intuitive Ethics." For a popular exposition of this, see Haidt, *Righteous Mind*, and for an alternative perspective, see Greene, *Moral Tribes*.

11. Koleva et al., "Tracing the Threads."

12. Researchers have identified other candidates for additional foundations, including liberty/oppression (Dobolyi et al., "Moral Foundations Theory") and one with special significance to Evangelicals and concerns for purity: truth (Anderson, "Truth, a Potential Foundation").

belief."[13] They predicted "that people may become literally disgusted by contact with an outgroup religion," just as they would be by harm to the physical body (e.g., disease) and socio-moral violations (e.g., incest).[14] The moral process operating here is one wherein "contact with rejected religious beliefs may be perceived as a threat to one's spiritual self and so be rejected by the same intuitive emotional mechanism."[15] In order to test their prediction, Ritter and Preston set up three experiments involving prescreened, self-identified Christian volunteers from the University of Illinois at Urbana-Champaign. A consideration of their first experiment will suffice for us to make connections to multifaith engagement. Participants were told that they were going to be a part of a marketing study to rate two different kinds of drinks. In connection with the taste test, they were also asked to copy down a religious text as a task unrelated to the drink testing. The participants were then asked to sample two drinks (unknowingly the exact same drink each time) and, alternatively, to write down texts from the Qur'an, Atheist Richard Dawkins's book *The God Delusion*, and something from a dictionary (a control text). The result of this experiment relates to the discussion of religious purity:

> As predicted, participants in Study 1 showed an increased disgust response following contact with rejected religious beliefs (i.e., Islam and Atheism) but not a neutral text. Other ratings of the drink (e.g., sweetness, sourness) were not as strongly influenced by writing the passage, indicating that the effect was limited to disgust responses and not taste in general. . . . In sum, Study 1 provided evidence that contact with outgroup religions elicits disgust, by violating the symbolic spiritual purity of the self.[16]

Similar results were found in two additional experiments where slight modifications were made to the initial test. In their concluding discussion, Ritter and Preston note the connection between disgust and intuitive moral judgment, asserting "that contact with moral impurities or immoral actions may literally leave a bad taste in the mouth."[17] This is because interactions with such beliefs are understood to have the "potential to undermine a given sacred order."[18] In addition, Ritter and Preston reflect on whether the disgust was caused by simply thinking about another religious tradition, or whether

13. Ritter and Preston, "Gross Gods," 1225.
14. Ritter and Preston, "Gross Gods," 1225.
15. Ritter and Preston, "Gross Gods," 1225.
16. Ritter and Preston, "Gross Gods," 1227.
17. Ritter and Preston, "Gross Gods," 1229.
18. Ritter and Preston, "Gross Gods," 1229.

some action in connection with the experiments (e.g., writing the texts) was the trigger. The latter provides greater optimism for multifaith engagement than the former. As Ritter and Preston put it, "If purity is compromised upon merely contemplating ideas that conflict with one's own sacred beliefs . . . this suggests a bleak potential for peaceful intergroup relations. How can religious groups hope to overcome their differences in culture and beliefs if they are also divided by gut-level disgust that repels them further apart?"[19] Ritter and Preston go on to state near the end of their article that they "expect that the effect is moderated by the degree of perceived threat presented by the outgroup religions."[20] As we will see later in this essay, threat perception is another important consideration, particularly when connected to concerns for purity violations.

Ritter and Preston built upon their experimentation with additional work discussed in another article, where they are joined by Erika Salomon and Daniel Relihan-Johnson.[21] In a series of experiments involving Christian students, the researchers sought to discover whether "mere contemplation of heretical thoughts (i.e., ideas contrary to one's closely held religious beliefs) elicit[s] disgust."[22] As previously noted, their prior research presented this as a possibility, and in their quest to understand the connection of disgust to the spiritual purity of mind, these researchers argue that this continues to be a distinct possibility because "people treat the content of mind as contaminable and experience disgust when contemplating ideas that threaten spiritual purity."[23] After conducting their experiments and reflecting on the results, these psychologists concluded "that disgust produces harsher moral judgments [about contrary religious ideas] in part due to subjective feelings of *contamination*, suggesting that people actually conceptualize their thoughts as being unclean."[24] They go on to state, "For the strongly religious, heretical thoughts take on a special meaning, characterized by feelings of disgust, contamination and moral disapproval."[25] This research presents a great challenge to multifaith engagement in that it doesn't take physical interaction with someone from another religion to

---

19. Ritter and Preston, "Gross Gods," 1229.
20. Ritter and Preston, "Gross Gods," 1229.
21. Ritter et al., "Imagine No Religion."
22. Ritter et al., "Imagine No Religion," 779.
23. Ritter et al., "Imagine No Religion," 780.
24. Ritter et al., "Imagine No Religion," 786.
25. Ritter et al., "Imagine No Religion," 786.

trigger disgust. Instead, "people can feel *heretical disgust* by merely contemplating ideas contrary to religious beliefs."[26]

Dyadic morality is another psychological possibility for understanding disgust responses as a part of opposition to other religions. Where moral foundations theory presents various intuitions and "each represent[s] a distinct functional moral mechanism or *cognitive module*,"[27] dyadic morality suggests instead that moral judgments come from a cognitive template involving feelings of harm. From this perspective, "harm involves the perception of two interacting minds, one mind (an agent) intentionally causing suffering to another mind (a patient)—what we call the *moral dyad*."[28] In the view of some scholars, it is harm that moderates the connection between disgust and immorality, not a moral foundation of purity.[29] According to the theory of dyadic morality, "the link from harm to immorality means that perceived harm causes acts to be judged as immoral; when acts seem harmful, they seem morally wrong."[30] And it's not just acts that are viewed as harmful; ideas can be harmful too, including religious ones. The focus in this theory is the perception of harm, and studies have been done that include concerns about religious blasphemy. Building on their previous research on heretical disgust and purity of mind from the perspective of moral foundations, Schein, Ritter, and Gray conducted dyadic morality studies on "ostensibly harmless acts," including "sacrilegious ideas."[31] Participants were asked to rate how harmful certain statements were that conflicted with their religious worldview. The study showed a connection between disgust and immorality based on religious purity violations (as seen in other studies, such as Ritter and Preston's discussed above), but perceptions of harm made the connection. Interestingly, the "disgust-immorality link was also mediated by feelings of anger,"[32] an emotion that can be detected in many conservative Evangelical responses to other religions. Like the study on heretical disgust and the purity of mind, the process of Christians thinking about aspects of other religions was seen as compromising. In the case of the dyadic morality study, "simply entertaining sacrilegious thoughts may seem to have harmful effects."[33]

---

26. Ritter et al., "Imagine No Religion," 787.
27. Schein and Gray, "Unifying Moral Dyad," 1148.
28. Schein and Gray, "Unifying Moral Dyad," 1149.
29. Schein et al., "Disgust-Immorality Link."
30. Schein and Gray, "Theory of Dyadic Morality," 33.
31. Schein et al., "Disgust-Immorality Link," 867.
32. Schein et al., "Disgust-Immorality Link," 868.
33. Schein et al., "Disgust-Immorality Link," 868.

There are, then, two theoretical possibilities for understanding the psychological dynamics related to disgust in connection with other religions. Moral foundations theory is more frequently cited by scholars, but dyadic morality provides an alternative. If one wishes to accept dyadic morality over moral foundations as an explanatory theory, this does not mean that moral foundations theory is not helpful. As Schein and Gray state, rather than moral foundations as "deep and reified causal mechanisms," they can be understood as "genres" that "help catalog and describe the diversity of moral content across cultures and contexts, and hence still retain some 'pragmatic utility.'"[34]

Regardless of which theory one chooses in understanding the psychological dynamics involved, studies indicate that Christians feel disgust when contemplating other religions. The perception is that other religions are harmful, pose a threat, and may damage spiritual health.

Additional Psychological Possibilities

A study of the psychological dynamics involved in negative Evangelical feelings about other religions is not limited to consideration of purity and disgust. Other areas of research provide helpful insights as well, each related in some way to perception of harm. We will summarize two of them below.

Intergroup Threat Theory

Human beings are tribal, and we tend to form close bonds with those in our tribe. The corollary is that we then view those in other tribes as problematic. It's often us versus them, our tribe versus your tribe, our team versus your team.[35] From this perspective, those in the outgroup can be understood as potentially harmful. Intergroup threat theory helps explain how this dynamic works. As Stephan, Ybarra, and Morrison define it, "In the context of intergroup threat theory, an intergroup threat is experienced when members of one group perceive that another group is in a position to cause them harm."[36] Distinctions are also made with respect to the types of threats that groups may perceive. These include *realistic* threats and *symbolic* threats. Accordingly, Stephan and colleagues "refer to a concern about physical harm or a loss of resources as realistic threat, and to a concern about the integrity or validity of the ingroup's meaning system

---

34. Schein and Gray, "Theory of Dyadic Morality," 55.
35. Berreby, *Us and Them*.
36. Stephan et al., "Intergroup Threat Theory," 43.

as symbolic threat."[37] I believe that in most instances it is symbolic threat that is the primary form of concern for Evangelicals. Such a threat can be further defined as "threats to a group's religion, values, belief system, ideology, philosophy, morality, or worldview."[38] Given the Evangelical emphasis on doctrinal orthodoxy and worldview purity, other religious groups that present alternative belief systems and worldviews can be seen as a symbolic threat. It is not difficult to find examples of how this is expressed in Evangelicalism. Consider the amount of time and energy spent on refuting "cults" or new religious movements. Some Christian bookstores have whole sections devoted to this topic. Although there are a great number of new religions, counter-cult apologists tend to focus on a select few. In an analysis of counter-cult literature in the 1980s, Keith Tolbert found that Mormonism and Jehovah's Witnesses received the most scrutiny and that "the amount of disproportionate interested paid to them may very well be surprising."[39] These two groups, combined with the "New Age/Occult," made up about 83 percent of the focus. He goes on to note that "not one article on Islam or Judaism appeared in all of this literature in 1987. In fact, they become conspicuous by their absence."[40] We might wonder why such a small number of religious groups received such great attention. Tolbert wondered that as well, and he concluded that the reason for this high concentration on few religious categories was "the perceived danger of these groups."[41] This would seem to be an example of symbolic threat, particularly when we consider that researchers in intergroup threat theory state that an extensive history of conflict and perceptions of social deviancy are important predictors of perceptions of threat.[42] These characteristics are involved not only in the relationship between Evangelical Christianity and the new religions featured in counter-cult treatments, but in the historic relationship Evangelicalism has had with Islam as well.[43]

Islam provides another example of perceived threat for Evangelicals. In an article exploring anti-Muslim prejudice through the lens of intergroup threat theory, Fatih Uenal suggests that there is another form of threat that needs to be recognized, that of *terroristic* threat, understood as a type of

---

37. Stephan et al., "Intergroup Threat Theory," 43–44.
38. Stephan et al., "Intergroup Threat Theory," 44.
39. Tolbert, *ARC Cult Literature Index*, 21.
40. Tolbert, *ARC Cult Literature Index*, 22.
41. Tolbert, *ARC Cult Literature Index*, 22.
42. Stephan et al., "Intergroup Threat Theory," 46–47.
43. See Kidd, *American Christians and Islam*.

realistic threat.[44] Given the national trauma of 9/11, and given the ongoing attacks by ISIS, al Qaeda, Boko Haram, and other terrorist organizations around the globe, it is clear that terroristic threat is a part of twenty-first-century life. Whether associated fears are justified in light of the likelihood of being a victim of such an attack is another matter, but the threat perception itself is an important component of Evangelical fears and negative perceptions of Muslims. This is dramatically illustrated in the differing ways Evangelicals have written about Islam pre- and post-9/11. Richard Cimino conducted a content analysis of documents written by Evangelicals covering a period of ten years prior to September 11, 2001, and three years after. Cimino selected books listed in the Family Christian Bookstore, and the material was analyzed for how it portrayed Islam. Although negative portrayals of Islam did not represent all of Evangelicalism, the results of Cimino's study revealed a "pattern of anti-Islamic polemics that is found in much of the literature of evangelicals and charismatic Christians in the period after 9/11."[45] Prior to September 11, Evangelicals discussed Islam in the context of missions and evangelism, but after the attacks there was a shift to an apologetic approach with "the dual emphasis on Islam's inherently violent nature" and "the assertion that Muslims worship a false god distinctly different than the God of Christianity and Judaism."[46] Cimino also analyzed the conservative, newsweekly *World* magazine (covering the years 1996–2002) in order to understand not only changes in anti-Islamic sentiment but also concerns over "interfaith involvement and pluralism."[47] The study of *World*'s materials demonstrated that coverage of Islam was infrequent prior to 9/11, but afterward the coverage rose dramatically. Like the other materials by Evangelicals in Cimino's study, *World* featured negative portrayals of Islam but also included "alarm over religious pluralism and relativism."[48] Cimino characterizes this as significant in that "these articles frequently address Islam within the framework of a critique of pluralism and syncretism in American religion and society."[49] This indicates that for Evangelicals there is a close relationship between symbolic and realistic/terroristic threats. Indeed, fears of terroristic threats can be expressed in the form of fears of symbolic threats. In the case of Evangelical treatments of Islam after 9/11, fears of terrorist attacks were expressed in a greater interest

---

44. Uenal, "Disentangling Islamophobia."
45. Cimino, "'No God in Common,'" 163.
46. Cimino, "'No God in Common,'" 166.
47. Cimino, "'No God in Common,'" 165.
48. Cimino, "'No God in Common,'" 170.
49. Cimino, "'No God in Common,'" 170.

in countering symbolic threat, with syncretism and relativism representing "the new battlegrounds over heresy as well as the primary boundary marker for evangelical identity in today's pluralistic society."[50]

Religious Worldview Defense

The Evangelical interest in boundary maintenance and refutation of heresy is, of course, connected to a strong interest in apologetics. Historically, the Christian Church has always drawn upon various forms of apologetics,[51] and good cases have been made for the continued validity of apologetics in interreligious encounters.[52] So the concern as it connects to the subject matter of this chapter isn't the use of apologetics per se in relation to other religions. Instead, concerns arise as to the various functions that apologetics serves for Evangelicals, how Evangelicals use apologetic arguments with religious others, and what the underlying psychology is with respect to such approaches. In relation to adherents of new religious movements and world religions alike, Evangelical approaches to apologetics have been deeply problematic.

There are a variety of different types of apologetic approaches that Evangelicals use in relation to new religions, but a dominant type has been labeled the "heresy-rationalist approach."[53] This is a standard template in Evangelical apologetics. The heresy part of the template involves a comparison of key doctrines of Christianity and what is understood as corresponding teachings in another religion. Contradictions are noted, along with a citation of relevant biblical passages, and a refutation of the group's heresy is offered. For the rationalist part of the template, many times a series of arguments is offered for the irrationality or inconsistency of the competing worldview. Although this template is most often applied to the new religions, Evangelical apologists have also applied it to world religions.[54] John Saliba characterizes it as a "negative" apologetic that often involves monologue and

---

50. Cimino, "'No God in Common,'" 172.

51. Dulles, *History of Apologetics*.

52. See Griffiths, *Apology for Apologetics*; Netland, "Toward Contextualized Apologetics."

53. Johnson, "Aquarian Age and Apologetics," 52.

54. Perhaps the best example of this comes by way of *World Religions Made Easy*, edited by Paul Carden and published by Rose Publishing in 2018. Using the heresy-rationalist template, this book compares twenty-nine religious groups with "biblical Christianity" in a total of only ninety-six pages. The simple fact is: exploring complex and diverse new religions and world religions in this fashion is not only formulaic but also reductionistic and simplistic.

hurled abuses, as well as belligerent responses from those targeted.[55] Given the obvious problems associated with such approaches, and given that they more often than not build fences rather than bridges between Christians and adherents of other religions, it is helpful to consider studies in sociology and social psychology to understand why Evangelicals are so fond of these apologetic techniques in religious worldview defense.

Our globalized and pluralistic world means that religions and worldviews no longer exist in isolation from one another. When religions cross paths in the lives of adherents, this can present a credibility challenge in maintaining the uniqueness and truthfulness of a given religion or worldview. Evangelicals are not immune to this challenge. In a study of the Evangelical counter-cult community, Douglas Cowan explored how this takes place in response to new religious movements.[56] His research methodology draws in part from the sociology of knowledge and, in particular, Peter Berger's concept of the *sacred canopy*, the idea that the socially constructed worlds we create give our lives meaning. In his study, Cowan reminds us that "*perceived* reality is not inevitably congruent with *actual* reality. It may well be, but it is not necessarily so."[57] We work with others in social groups in order to develop and maintain our understanding of reality. The presence of other religious groups with competing truth claims clashes with our own conceptions of reality and, thus, represents a challenge to the viability of our religious convictions. This means that these threats must be dealt with, and that a defense of our worldview must be offered to counter alternatives. In Cowan's view, the Evangelical emphasis on apologetic approaches to new religions represents a form of "cognitive boundary support and worldview maintenance."[58]

Research in social psychology in the area of religious worldview defense, a part of terror management theory, discusses the process of reality maintenance in ways that sound similar to Cowan's sociological analysis. McGregor and colleagues state that "although treated by the individual as absolute reality, the cultural worldview is a fragile social construction in need of constant validation from others."[59] Of course, this validation is not forthcoming from adherents of other religions; instead, alternative religious worldviews are seen as a threat to the stability of a given perception of reality. As a result, "historically many have tried to neutralize a threat to their

---

55. Saliba, *Understanding New Religious Movements*, 217–20.
56. Cowan, *Bearing False Witness?*
57. Cowan, *Bearing False Witness?*, 5.
58. Cowan, *Bearing False Witness?*, 28.
59. McGregor et al., "Terror Management and Aggression," 591.

worldview by attempting to annihilate those who are different."[60] In the case of Evangelicals, this annihilation process takes place in the arena of ideas, where the emphasis on apologetic denunciation of non-Christian doctrine and worldviews reinforces the Christian worldview while simultaneously neutralizing the threat from religious others.

In light of this research on religious worldview defense, it is difficult to disagree with Van den Bos and colleagues when they write about personal uncertainty and religious worldview defense that "it could be argued that a challenge for people living in the world after 9/11 is how to respond to critical statements about one's own worldview."[61] As we have seen in the research above, it does not take personal encounters with adherents of other religions offering critical statements about Christianity for Evangelicals to feel challenged by other religious worldviews. The mere presence of these religions is threatening enough. As a result, Evangelicals tend to respond defensively to them, with an eye toward bolstering their worldview by discrediting their religious rivals as a form of reality maintenance and self-protection. The sad irony here is that the price we pay with such defensiveness is a "neglect of many of the compassionate values espoused by the very religious doctrine one is attempting to defend."[62] In our zeal to defend our doctrine, loving our religious neighbor, efforts at peacemaking, and attempts at persuasively sharing our message get trampled on in the process.

What This All Means for Evangelical Multifaith Engagement

This chapter began by noting that Evangelicals tend to have cool feelings toward those in other religions. At the same time, Evangelicals place a high premium on maintaining the purity of their doctrine and worldview, and they fear the syncretistic compromise of their faith. As a result, perhaps the majority of Evangelical churches keep those of other religions at arm's length, and many pursue various forms of apologetic opposition to their doctrine. Having discussed some of the most relevant social-psychological research in detail, we can now summarize it all in order to understand the psychological dynamics underlying Evangelical stances of opposition to other religions. This will also allow us to explore some pertinent implications for multifaith engagement.

---

60. McGregor et al., "Terror Management and Aggression," 591.
61. Van den Bos et al., "Psychology of Religion," 335.
62. Rothschild et al., "Peace Have a Prayer?," 826.

First, research in social psychology helps us better understand why Evangelicals have such strong negative reactions toward certain religious groups. Conservatives tend to value purity, and in Evangelicalism this is expressed in a concern for maintaining sound doctrine and a Christian worldview. The teachings of other religious groups are viewed as a potential source of contamination and are thereby a threat to spiritual health. Because of this, Evangelicals often experience a disgust reaction. Disgust is a protective response that distances us from threats to health. Disgust reactions cause us either to shy away from what is potentially harmful or to expel it by various means if we feel our integrity has been compromised via contact or possible absorption of problematic elements. For Evangelicals, a process of heretical disgust takes place in order to protect ourselves from ideas we perceive as harmful to spiritual well-being. We then either shun members of other religions or engage in various forms of contaminant "cleansing," including strong doses of apologetic refutation and doctrinal reinforcement.

Evangelicals also entertain negative feelings about other religions because other religious groups are perceived as a threat. Much of the time, our concern is for symbolic threats that pose a danger to our doctrine and worldview (which provide us with a sense of meaning). But there are also important fears posed by realistic or terroristic threats, whereby we believe our physical safety and resources are threatened. For Evangelicals, when realistic threats are manifested, as with the attacks of 9/11, these fears can often be expressed through a heightened concern for the symbolic threats posed by other religious groups. Changing Evangelical responses to Islam before and after the 9/11 attacks are a striking example of this.

Then there is the psychology connected to some of our apologetic efforts. We find safety and confirmation when we stay within our Evangelical social bubbles and hold on to the concept of a Judeo-Christian America, but our globalized and interconnected world guarantees that we will eventually encounter those with very different and contradictory conceptions of religion. In response to these alternative conceptions of reality, Evangelicals often draw upon apologetic approaches of negation in order to neutralize the ideas of religious competitors, and by engaging in this boundary maintenance, the threats of syncretism and relativism are kept at bay.

It is also worth noting that the psychological reactions Evangelicals have in relation to other religions, which in some manifestations may be forms of prejudice, can be understood as a worldview protection strategy.[63] Members

---

63. Goplen and Plant, "Religious Worldview." People with religious worldviews aren't the only ones engaging in prejudice as a form of worldview protection. Research indicates that dogmatic Atheists are just as likely as dogmatic religious believers to engage in such practices. See Kossowska et al., "Many Faces of Dogmatism."

of other religions are seen as violators of Evangelical Christianity's sacred values, and as a means of protecting what is held dear, we avoid contact with them or engage in various forms of worldview quashing. This observation is not to be understood as an approval of the negative ways in which Evangelicals relate to those in other religions. One of the aims of this book is to draw attention to the emotional aspects of these relationships, with an eye toward improving things. But we must understand psychologically why Evangelicals engage in such actions before we can facilitate change.

Second, a social psychology of multifaith engagement must be accounted for by Evangelicals and non-Evangelicals alike. Those working in peacemaking and interreligious dialogue tend to engage in their work without considering the psychological dynamics Evangelicals experience in regard to other religions. On the one hand, Evangelicals engaged in peacemaking set forth various biblical texts as scriptural foundations and rationales, and they also develop theologies of peace and practices of hospitality with members of other religions. Together, these are then presented as part of a pedagogical effort aimed at helping Evangelicals embrace the hospitality and neighbor love exemplified in Jesus's participation in table fellowship with social outcasts.[64] On the other hand, those in interfaith work wonder at times why more Evangelicals aren't involved in their movement. At the same time, they assume liberal values and appeal to the need for fairness, diversity, and the virtues of embracing pluralism. While both Evangelical peacemaking and interfaith approaches have merit, they often miss the mark with Evangelicals. Unless a conscious effort is made to understand and sympathetically work through the Evangelical multifaith psyche, no significant gains will be made in more positive directions in attracting more conservatives for involvement. Evangelicals must come to feel and believe that they can be good Evangelicals while participating, working through their values and convictions without compromise, and they must come to understand that they can let go of their fears of harm from religious others before more of them will become comfortable with loving forms of multifaith encounters.

Final Thoughts about the Priority of Purity[65]

This chapter has discussed the emphasis Evangelicals place on purity and related fears of syncretism. Having discussed the psychology underlying our

64. See Bob Robinson's discussion in this volume of the example of Jesus in application to multifaith encounters.

65. This final section is a reworking of my ideas previously discussed on the blog of the Evangelical Chapter of the Foundation for Religious Diplomacy. See Morehead, "Author."

theological approaches to purity and religious others, I will close with a consideration of these important issues by drawing upon a biblical text where similar concerns and fears are mirrored in the ministry of Jesus.

In Matthew 9, Jesus calls Matthew, a tax collector, to be his disciple. Jesus then goes to Matthew's house to eat with him. The following encounter and confrontation ensues:

> While Jesus was having dinner at Matthew's house, many tax collectors and sinners came and ate with him and his disciples. When the Pharisees saw this, they asked his disciples, "Why does your teacher eat with tax collectors and sinners?" On hearing this, Jesus said, "It is not the healthy who need a doctor, but the sick. But go and learn what this means: 'I desire mercy, not sacrifice.' For I have not come to call the righteous, but sinners."[66]

As this passage makes clear, the concern of the Jewish religious leaders is that Jesus was violating ritual purity and, as a result, defiling himself. The question of Jesus and purity has become a significant area of research in historical Jesus studies. As New Testament scholar James D. G. Dunn has noted, "It cannot be doubted that purity was a major preoccupation in the Judaism of Jesus's time."[67] For the Pharisees, Jesus's meal with "sinners" was a major concern. His response was an interesting one, with significant implications for how Evangelicals engage their religious neighbors. Faced with the tension in the Jewish tradition and the Old Testament between purity (or holiness) and mercy, Jesus comes down on the side of mercy. Rather than safeguarding purity, which might have been compromised by close proximity to social outcasts, Jesus embraces the ritually unclean as a practice of mercy. This is not to say that Jesus had no interest in maintaining purity in keeping with his religious tradition. According to Dunn, Jesus did recognize "the importance of purity concerns within the community,"[68] but it was not a defining or limiting aspect of how Israel was to serve God. Contrary to the Pharisaical emphasis on purity and separation, "Jesus evidently had no interest in making ritual purity a test case of covenant loyalty. The emphasis on matters of purity, so characteristic of the factional rivalries of the time, was for Jesus an overemphasis."[69]

With Dunn's analysis in mind, we can connect the dots from Jesus's example and practice of purity to contemporary Evangelical stances toward those of other religions. We are concerned for maintaining doctrinal purity,

---

66. All Scripture quotations in this essay are from the NIV.
67. Dunn, "Jesus and Purity," 450.
68. Dunn, "Jesus and Purity," 467.
69. Dunn, "Jesus and Purity," 464.

and we should be. After all, New Testament passages such as 1 Timothy 4:16 tell us to "watch your life and doctrine closely." The issue for conservative Evangelicals isn't a concern for purity per se, but rather avoiding religious neighbors on the basis of that concern, together with concomitant fears of contamination and compromise. There is the biblical command to love God and neighbor (Matt 22:36–40), and our neighbor is also the one we may regard as an enemy—one of the challenging implications of the parable of the good Samaritan (Luke 10:25–37). So, like Jesus in his disagreement with the Pharisees in Matthew 9, we too face a tension between purity and mercy. Our concern, often times, is that close proximity to those of other religions will contaminate us. But if we are to follow the example of Christ, we have to come down on the side of mercy. This involves active social engagement in things like the table fellowship Jesus participated in. If I'm understanding Jesus correctly, with whom exclusion in the interests of purity gives way to the embrace of mercy, I suggest that this can be expressed in a reworking of the quotations from Dunn above:

> Jesus has no interest in Evangelicals making doctrinal purity a test case of gospel loyalty. The emphasis on matters of purity, so characteristic of Evangelical concerns about relating to other religions, is for Jesus an overemphasis. . . . Jesus does not want us to regard purity concerns as central to an understanding of what constitutes the social practice of our faith among those of other religions.

With a fresh look at Jesus in confrontation with the Pharisees over purity, and with an examination of Evangelical concerns for purity and doctrine in regard to other religions, we might well ask ourselves what our Lord's example means for us today as we seek to be transformed by the renewal of our minds (Rom 12:2) and "take captive every thought to make it obedient to Christ" (2 Cor 10:15).

5

Courage to Engage

Fear, Hope, Despair, and Daring in Courageous Multifaith Engagement

W. Scott Cleveland

Engaging with people of other faiths can give rise to strong emotions. A Christian may experience fear of violence when he hears of a Muslim man moving into the neighborhood. A Christian may hope for the conversion of a person of another faith or unbeliever to Christianity but despair of success in the face of her own inadequacies in knowledge or communication. A Christian may boldly and daringly share her faith with a non-Christian person but end up alienating the other with her zeal.

The emotions of fear, hope, despair, and daring can arise in multifaith engagement, for we may perceive such situations as involving threats that are difficult to avoid and opportunities that are difficult to realize. These emotions are relevant to the virtue of courage, which concerns facing threatening situations and pursuing difficult opportunities. The virtue of courage is the virtue for enduring such situations and acting well in them by ordering these emotions. Hence, it is vital for proper multifaith engagement that we think about and seek to form these proper emotions. Under what conditions are these emotions of fear, hope, despair, and daring proper and reasonable or improper and unreasonable? To begin to answer this question, we need a deeper understanding of the emotions in general and of hope, despair, fear, and daring in particular. This essay aids multifaith engagement by discussing these emotions, courage, and some causes of and remedies to improper instances of these emotions.

The Emotions—Thomas Aquinas and Robert Roberts

Thomas Aquinas, the medieval philosopher and theologian, and Robert Roberts, the contemporary philosopher, each have fruitful reflections on the emotions in light of the truths of God's revelation in Christ.[1] I'll explain some of their insights here to set the stage for further discussion. More specifically, I'll briefly summarize Aquinas's and Roberts's accounts of emotions in order to help explain the views of hope, despair, fear, and daring that will receive more detailed treatment later in this essay.

Having systemized and brought order to the discussion of emotions in the thirteenth century, Thomas Aquinas provides a simple yet powerful account of the emotions. For Aquinas, emotions are movements of the sense appetite. Such movements incline us toward or away from something apprehended as good or bad.[2] The sense appetite is that by which we are drawn to what is sensibly pleasing to us or withdraw from things that are sensibly painful to us. This being drawn to or withdrawing from is the movement Aquinas has in mind. A slightly oversimplified way to make his point is that emotions "push" us toward something that we find pleasing and "pull" us from something that we find painful.

Given this definition of emotions as movements of the sense appetite, there are two primary ways to identify and distinguish emotions. The first is according to their intentional object. The object in this sense is what the emotion is about. But the emotion is about more than simply a person, thing, or event. It is about a person, thing, or event *in a certain way*. Emotions are about something *seen as* good or bad in some respect. Robert Roberts calls this a *construal*.[3] Roberts says:

> On the view of emotions that I endorse, [emotions] are concern-based construals. That is, they are perceptions, in the

---

1. Aquinas uses the term *passions* instead of *emotions*. These two concepts can be distinguished, but for the purpose of this essay I will just use the latter. For a historical treatment of the distinction, see Dixon, *From Passions to Emotions*. For a very accessible guide to the role of some emotions in the spiritual life, I recommend Roberts, *Spiritual Emotions*. I've benefited significantly from that book in thinking about the issues of this chapter.

2. Aquinas, *Summa Theologiae* I.II.22–48. The discussion that follows will draw from this section of the *Summa* widely. The discussion is also informed by two excellent secondary resources: Miner, *Aquinas on the Passions*; Lombardo, *Logic of Desire*.

3. Roberts, *Emotions*.

> construal sense of the word, in which one or more of the elements going into the construal is a concern. . . . The idea that emotions are concern-based construals is that, for example, you will never feel fear if you don't care about the thing that you see as threatened, nor anger if you're not concerned about the thing you construe as offended against, nor shame if you don't care about being worthy of respect. You come into a situation that has emotional potential for you with a dispositional (or possibly occurrent) concern or desire, or an attachment; you then construe the situation in the terms characteristic of some emotion type, and the situation emotionally appears to you as it does because the terms in which you see the situation impinge on, connect with, that concern.[4]

A construal is a value-colored perception. It is a "seeing as," such as seeing a bear *as* threatening or seeing food *as* desirable to eat or seeing an action *as* unjust and so on. Given the person cares about safety, satisfying hunger, and justice, she will experience fear, desire, or anger in the various situations because of her concern-based construals. For a further example, consider the difference between a person who sees a bear in the zoo versus one who sees a bear on the path before him while hiking in the woods. In the first case, the bear is not seen or construed as something bad. But in the second case, the bear may very well be construed as something bad—namely, *as a threat*. It is the seeing or construing of the bear *as a threat* that produces (or is) fear. A construal is essential to every emotion. So the intentional object of an emotion or the construal is the first way to identify and distinguish emotions.

Returning to Aquinas, the second way to identify and distinguish emotions is according to their affective movement. This movement is either toward or away from the object. If a Christian construes a non-Christian as a threat and feels fear, he will experience fear's characteristic affective movement away from the threat. Fear makes us slow down, take caution, and "pulls" us back. This is one reason why a person who experiences overpowering fear will run from the threat. The fear prompts them to get away as fast as possible, even if that is the wrong thing to do in the situation. In contrast, emotions like desire move a person toward the object of desire, as in the case of the Christian desiring to befriend a non-Christian.

---

4. Roberts, *Emotions in the Moral Life*, 46. Aquinas's view of emotions is similar, although Aquinas and Roberts disagree about whether the construal produces the emotion (Aquinas's view) or constitutes the emotion (Roberts's view). But I won't explore this disagreement here.

Given these two features of emotions—namely, that they involve the construal of the emotion's intentional object in a particular way and an affective movement either toward or away from the object—Aquinas distinguishes eleven basic emotions. The sources of all emotions are the emotions of love and hate, with love being fundamental. As noted above, Roberts makes a similar point in identifying emotions as based on *concerns*. Love and hate are different from the other emotions in that they are tendencies to give rise to affective movements. For example, the hiker who sees a bear feels some fear when seeing the bear due to both his construal that the bear is a threat to himself and those who are with him and his love for himself and his companions. It is because of his underlying love or concern, in part, that he experiences fear. As an aside, Aquinas's notion of love is far richer than merely this sense of love as an emotion. He also understands love to be an act of willing the good of another and a supernatural virtue that God gives us by grace in order that we may love him as his adopted children.

The eleven basic emotions that Aquinas distinguishes are love (which is the basis for the others), hate, desire, aversion, joy, sorrow, hope, despair, fear, daring, and anger. He divides these into two sets. The first set, called the *concupiscible emotions*, has as its general object what is sensibly pleasing (a sensible "good" in his language) or sensibly painful (a sensible "evil" in his language) in some way. Love, desire, and joy concern what we find sensibly pleasing and tend to move us toward it and give us pleasure when we have it. Hatred, aversion, and sorrow concern what we find sensibly painful and tend to move us away from it and bring us pain when we have it. For example, a person may love or hate a certain kind of music, feel desire or aversion at the prospects of listening to it, and feel joy or sorrow when listening to it. Below is a table summarizing this set of emotions.

Table 1. Concupiscible Emotions

Emotion	Appetitive Movement	Intentional Object
Love	An inclination to move toward	A good (as sensibly pleasant)
Hatred	An inclination to move away from	An evil (as sensibly painful)
Desire	A movement toward	A good not yet present (as sensibly pleasant)
Aversion	A movement away from	An evil not yet present (as sensibly painful)

Emotion	Appetitive Movement	Intentional Object
Joy or pleasure	A response to (resting that we usually do not want to stop)	A present good (as sensibly pleasant)
Sorrow or pain	A response to ("resting" that we usually do want to stop)	A present evil (as sensibly painful)

The second set of emotions, called the *irascible emotions*, has as its general object what Aquinas calls an arduous, or difficult, good or evil. Such emotions involve either opportunities to attain or protect a good or obstacles to attaining or protecting a good, the possession of which brings joy. A good or evil is arduous when it is attainable or protectable only with some difficulty and it has not yet been attained (i.e., it is a good or evil in the future). For example, winning a tough game, convincing an obstinate friend to make a good choice in life, and the conversion of a friend to Christianity are difficult goods. A threat to winning the game, a threat to convincing that friend, or a threat to the friend's conversion are difficult evils. This second set of emotions includes hope, despair, fear, daring, and anger.

Hope, daring, and anger move us toward their respective objects. Fear and despair move us away from their respective objects. But these emotions are more complex than emotions such as desire, aversion, joy, and sorrow, for in this set we can be moved toward a difficult evil and away from a difficult good. For example, hope and despair both have a difficult good as their object. But even though hope and despair concern some good that is difficult to attain, hope urges us *toward* the good while despair pulls us *away* from it. Hope usually precedes despair, such that we despair as we lose hope of attaining our desire. An athlete, for instance, may hope to win a race when he sees the finish line but then despair when another athlete comes flying by him and he has no response. It may seem odd that the emotion of despair would pull us away from a good. But the oddity makes sense when we realize that despair involves our "giving up" on attaining the good. Some kinds of despair are appropriate in a situation because there is a genuine lack of grounds for hope. Both hope and despair concern a good or evil that is not yet present. We hope that we might achieve the good that we don't yet have (even if that involves protecting something we do have—it has not yet been protected), and we despair that we may fail to achieve the good that we don't yet have. But once we have the good we hope for, our hope turns to joy. Once the object of despair is surely lost, our despair turns to sorrow.

Likewise, fear and daring both have a difficult evil as their object. "Evil" here is something construed as a threat of some sort. But fear pulls us away from the evil while daring urges us toward it. For example, a hiker may fear the threat of an impending storm given her distance from shelter or daringly face the challenge as a race to shelter. Or a person sees his friend's sin as an impediment to his friend's flourishing and wants to daringly confront the person about the sin out of love for the friend. It may seem odd that an emotion of daring pushes us toward an evil. But the oddity makes sense when we realize that daring pushes us to face the threat for the sake of some other good like safety or friendship.

Another difference between the two sets of emotions is worth mentioning. Emotions from the second set, including hope, despair, fear, and daring, cease when the difficult good or evil is present. The apostle Paul writes of hope, "For in hope we were saved. Now hope that sees for itself is not hope. For who hopes for what one sees? But if we hope for what we do not see, we wait with endurance" (Rom 8:24–25).[5] If it is a good that is now present, then hope turns to joy. If the good is lost, then despair turns to sorrow. If it is an evil threat now present, then fear or daring turns to sorrow and perhaps anger.[6] If the evil threat is averted, then fear or daring turn to joy. Ultimately, once the good or evil is no longer anticipated in the future but now attained or lost, present or averted, joy or sorrow results. Below is a table summarizing the second set of emotions.

Table 2. Irascible Emotions

Emotion	Appetitive Movement	Intentional Object
Hope	A movement toward	A future, attainable (even if barely), but difficult good
Despair	A movement away from	A future, unattainable, and difficult good
Fear	A movement away from	A future, difficult evil (threat) that is not suitably able to be avoided or overcome

---

5. Scripture quotations in this essay are taken from the NAB (rev. ed.).

6. Anger is a complex emotion. It results from sorrow and moves the person to confront and/or attack some object with the goal of vengeance. If vengeance is achieved, then anger turns to joy. If not, it turns to sorrow.

Emotion	Appetitive Movement	Intentional Object
Daring	A movement toward	A future, difficult evil (threat) that is suitably able to be avoided or overcome (even if barely)
Anger	A movement toward	A present, harmful, and difficult evil (the attack of which is useful to attain the good of vindication)

Courage

In order to introduce courage's role, I'll say a little more about the particular emotions that will be our focus: fear, daring, despair, and hope. Fear and despair are linked together, just as hope and daring are linked together. When a person construes the threat they fear as removing the possibility of getting what they hope for, despair results. In contrast, when a person has hope, they are enabled to daringly face the threat they fear. In an article on courage, I describe this relation between daring and hope in greater detail:

> Daring depends on hope. Hope concerns an end of action and is grounded in the agent's confidence in the means to attaining that end. Daring concerns a means (i.e., confronting the threat) to hope's end (e.g., safety from the threat) and so requires hope as a source. Without hope in attaining an end, the agent will not be moved by daring to confront the threat, which is a means to executing the plan. For hope, which is grounded in a plan of action (and some resource for accomplishing the end), is required in order to construe the threat as apparently surmountable. Since daring involves an affective movement toward the threat, it involves construing the threat, which is an evil *essentially*, as a good *accidentally* (i.e., as something to be pursued). In order for the object of daring to be so construed, the object must be seen in light of the agent's hope. This reveals daring's dependence on hope but does not reduce daring to hope. For hope is about a difficult good *essentially* (i.e., safety from the threat).
>
> To illustrate the difference between daring and hope, consider a boxing match. The object of hope is victory over one's opponent as attainable while the object of daring is one's opponent himself as beatable. There is a distinct phenomenology to the feeling of hope for the prize of victory and the feeling of daring toward the opponent. Hope involves a longing that is absent from daring and feels more like desire. Daring is

associated with narrowing of the eyes, clenching of the jaw, and an eagerness for aggressive action.[7]

While courage is paradigmatically evinced when one risks one's life for a noble cause, I employ a more expansive notion that applies to many sorts of cases involving navigating threats to good goals. Courage is the virtue for achieving a good in a threatening situation—namely, a situation made difficult by the (at least apparent) presence of a significant threat—by means of facing rather than fleeing the threat. As such, courage concerns the emotions of fear and daring principally but also hope and despair. The courageous person experiences these emotions properly and manages himself wisely with respect to them. How does he manage himself? He indirectly controls his emotions through controlling his thoughts, what he imagines, and what he chooses to attend to in the situation. The courageous person, for instance, pays enough attention to the threat to ascertain its significance, but he does not dwell unnecessarily on it lest he paralyze himself with fear and fail to wisely think through how to handle the situation. This explains why a discussion of these emotions should include a discussion of courage. Fear and daring are emotional responses to threats, and hope and despair are emotional responses to prospects of achieving or failing to achieve something. Courage does not involve the elimination of the emotions of fear and daring; instead, each has a proper place in courageous action.[8] To see why, it is helpful to distinguish three distinct phases of courageous activity. First is our initial response to the situation. Second is our choice of what to do (which often involves deliberation). And third is the execution of the action we chose to do. The emotions of fear, hope, and daring coordinate in service of reason through each phase. Courage is a virtue that aids the person in wisely pursing good and reasonable goals in threatening situations. Proper understanding of courage cannot be had without proper understanding of wise decision-making, which is the province of what is called the virtue of prudence or practical wisdom.

In the essay I quoted above, I summarize the contributions of each emotion to prudent action:

> Fear is a proper first response to a perception of an apparently significant threat. In the first phase, fear not only initiates bodily responses useful for rapidly dealing with the threat, but, in the courageous person, focuses the attention on gathering salient information from the situation and facilitates caution in

---

7. Cleveland, "Emotions of Courageous Activity," 875–76.
8. While the virtue of courage does not eliminate emotions of fear or daring, daring can replace fear over the course of the courageous action.

assessing the resources to handle the threat and deliberation about the best means to do so. The good of averting the threat is the object of hope. In the second phase, hope diminishes fear, aids deliberation, moves the agent toward the end, and produces daring. Complete courageous activity involves averting the threat by means of confronting the threat, which is the object of daring. In the third phase, daring moves the agent toward confronting the threat, energizes the execution of the plan of action, and eliminates fear. Daring utilizes the body's fight or flight response that was initiated by the fear. Proper fear, hope, and daring are necessary for the courageous person to act in a courageous manner for each emotion principally (though not exclusively) contributes during different phases of the courageous activity: fear at first response, hope during deliberative choice, and daring during execution.[9]

Improper despair is an obstacle to courageous activity because it undermines the emotion of hope, which gives confidence in pursuit of the goal and energizes daring for facing the threat. Improper fear and angst (which is a kind of fear without a specific object) can also hinder by paralyzing a person in action or preventing clear thinking about how to respond to the situation. Proper fear is a good thing, however, both because it is the proper response to a significant threat and because it is an aid to our attention and caution in responding to the situation. The courageous person's emotions generally fit the situation and aid her right response to it.

Proper Emotions

In multifaith encounters, Christians may wonder whether their fear toward another person of a differing faith or their despair over their failure to adequately overcome another's objections to their faith is proper. The two notions of a *concern* and a *construal* yield a helpful way to determine how to identify when an emotion is proper. An emotion is proper in construal or in the concern upon which it is based. An emotion is proper in construal only when its intentional object fits the real object it is about. For example, one person's fear of another person as a threat is proper only if the person is genuinely threatening. In this sense, an emotion's properness is akin to a belief's truth. Both depend on a correspondence between the person's belief or emotions and the way the world is. We can also identify emotions as

---

9. Cleveland, "Emotions of Courageous Activity," 877–78. While beyond the scope of this essay, in this cited essay I discuss non-paradigmatic cases of courage, such as when the threat is not faced but rightly fled.

reasonable in construal even if they are not strictly proper in construal. We make the same distinction in the case of belief when we say that a person has a reasonable but false belief. So too an emotion can be reasonable in construal, given what the person perceives, even if the construal doesn't actually fit the situation. But just as beliefs can be unreasonable, so too can emotions be unreasonable.

An emotion is proper in concern only when the concern is rightly ordered with respect to other concerns. Another way of putting this is that an emotion is proper only when the person's loves are rightly ordered. For example, a person who cares too much for bodily comfort will be subject to an intensity of fear at the prospects of bodily pain that is incompatible with courage. Such intense fear may paralyze the person and so prevent him from rightly facing the bodily pain that may result from the courageous action he is called to perform. The basis for this improper fear is too great a love for one's own comfort. Or a person who cares too much for being the instrument of another person's conversion may be subject to disordered despair when the other persists in unbelief. Or a person who construes conversion as simply a matter of being convinced of certain beliefs may be improperly hopeful at the means to promoting the conversion of another.[10]

Application to Multifaith Situations

With a basic understanding of emotion in general, the specific emotions of fear, daring, hope, and desire, and courage's relation to these emotions, let us explore some applications to multifaith engagement. What are some occasions for fear, angst, despair, hope, or daring (or boldness)? When are they disordered? How might courage help? I will consider two situations: the first involving fear and angst, the second involving hope, daring, and despair.

A Case of Fear

As we saw above, emotions can go wrong if they are based on an improper concern or if they involve a mistaken construal. In other words, if there is an error in the heart or mind, then an emotion will fail to fit the situation.

Fear can arise in relating to people who do not share one's faith. One source of fear or anxiety is the perceived threat that a person (or group of persons) of another faith may pose to oneself, one's family, or one's society

---

10. There are other components to an emotion's being proper, such as *time* (i.e., the emotion occurs at the proper time given the situation) and *duration* (the emotion occurs for the proper duration given the situation). But I'll focus on being proper in construal and concern.

and culture. Such fear is proper only when it fits the situation. Mistakes in reasoning can lead us to experience improper emotions, such as fear or anxiety, which inhibit right relationships with others. For example, if we make assumptions about what a person believes without adequate knowledge of their beliefs, then we can misconstrue the other and so experience improper emotions.

Consider this situation. James is an Evangelical Christian and Wadi is a Muslim. After learning that Wadi is a Muslim, suppose James were to reason as follows. Wadi is a Muslim and believes that anything is permissible if God commands it. But that includes killing innocent people in the name of religion. So Wadi is a threat to society! If James draws this conclusion, then he may feel fear toward Wadi (or angst toward all Muslims), since he construes Wadi as a threat.

Let's look at two mistaken ways of thinking that are at work in this case and lead to improper fear or angst. In their 2013 essay "Getting Our Minds Out of the Gutter: Fallacies that Foul Our Discourse," Robert Garcia and Nathan King identify two commonly fallacious ways of thinking that hinder right relationships with those with whom we disagree. I'm going to summarize their work and use it to shed light on some mistaken ways of thinking that can lead to improper emotions in multifaith interactions. They call the two mistaken ways of reasoning they identify *the assailment-by-entailment fallacy* and *the attitude-to-agent fallacy*. They explain them by use of the following fictional dialogue:

> **Frank:** Hey Judith, what's your take on abortion? Don't you agree that abortion on demand is morally wrong?
>
> **Judith:** Actually, no. I think that abortion is morally permissible.
>
> **Frank:** What!? I couldn't disagree more. I just can't believe—like you do—that it's okay to murder an innocent person!
>
> **Judith:** Whoa—who said I believe *that*? Besides, I just can't believe—like you do—that it's okay to curtail the rights of women![11]

Frank reasons like this:

1. Judith believes that abortion is morally permissible.
2. If abortion is morally permissible, then it is permissible to murder an innocent person.

---

11. Garcia and King, "Out of the Gutter," 192.

3. So Judith must believe it is permissible to murder an innocent person.

Judith reasons like this:

1. Frank believes that abortion is morally wrong.
2. If abortion is morally wrong, then it is permissible to curtail the rights of women.
3. So Frank must believe it is permissible to curtail the rights of women.

Do you see the mistake? The mistake is attributing to the other person belief in statement 2 in each case. But notice that neither Frank nor Judith express belief in the relevant statement. The fallacy is called "assailment-by-entailment" because statement 2 is an entailment (i.e., a claim about what entails what) and the other person is assailed because they are treated as if they hold it (when they may not). But there are alternative explanations. Frank or Judith may not have thought about the entailment, or they may not have made up their minds about it, or they may have rejected it. Frank and Judith should not jump to the conclusion that the other believes the entailment without sufficient evidence. But they do jump to the conclusion. A crucial part of their conversation is discussing the truth of these statements, but they rush past this by assuming the other person believes the entailment that they themselves believe.

Garcia and King have the fictional dialogue continue.

Frank: You're a moral monster!

Judith: You're a misogynistic pig![12]

Frank judges that because Judith believes murdering innocent people is permissible, she's a moral monster. Judith judges that because Frank believes curtailing women's rights is permissible, he's a misogynistic pig. Frank and Judith are angry with each other and insult each other, and the chance for productive discussion is gone.

This illustrates the attitude-to-agent fallacy. The mistake here is to reason from "he believes such and such" to "he is a so-and-so." But there is a gap between these claims. Garcia and King write, "An isolated claim about a person's attitude is poor evidence for a negative evaluation of the person herself."[13] Or at least it sometimes is. We can make exceptions. For example, you can make a reasonable negative judgment about a person if he tells you he's just committed murder. But this is not a typical case. Think about a

12. Garcia and King, "Out of the Gutter," 192.
13. Garcia and King, "Out of the Gutter," 192.

more typical example. If you saw a parent yell at a child in public, could you conclude that he was a bad parent? What if that parent had just lost his job or his spouse or the outburst was entirely uncharacteristic? A person should generally not draw a conclusion about the person's character on the basis of an isolated instance of attitude or belief.

Let's consider the application of these fallacies to the multifaith situation of James and Wadi from above.

> James: Hey, Wadi, what do you think is the basis for right and wrong?
>
> Wadi: The will of Allah.
>
> James: I couldn't disagree more. I just can't believe—like you do—that any action whatsoever might be the right thing to do, including the murder of innocent people!
>
> Wadi: Whoa—who said I believe that?
>
> James: You're a threat to society!

James is reasoning like this.

1. Wadi believes that the will of Allah is the basis for right and wrong.

2. If the will of Allah is the basis for right and wrong, then since God could command anything, any action whatever would be the right thing to do, including murdering innocent people. (This is the belief that James attributes to Wadi.)

3. So Wadi must believe that since God could command anything, any action whatever would be the right thing to do, including murdering innocent people. (This is the unsupported conclusion James reaches.)

4. If Wadi believes that since God could command anything, any action whatsoever would be the right thing to do, including murdering innocent people, then Wadi is a threat to society.

5. So Wadi is a threat to society (and so James construes Wadi as a threat and experiences fear).

While these emotions can be appropriate in cases of genuine threats, it is unreasonable for James to assume without additional evidence that Wadi is a threat to society simply by virtue of his belief that morality comes from God's will. Indeed, some Christians hold to a divine command theory of morality, and that belief alone does not imply that they believe God has commanded them to kill innocents. It is also unreasonable for James to assume that Wadi believes that God has commanded Wadi to kill innocents without evidence. Even if Wadi believed that God had commanded the killing of Islam's enemies in past situations, it wouldn't follow that he believes those conditions obtain now or that he would do so even if they did. It is this mistake that precipitates James's construal of Wadi as a threat and his resulting fear. Hence, James's fear is not reasonable because his construal of Wadi as a threat is a result of unreasonable thinking.

There are individuals who believe that God has commanded them to kill others. But it would be a mistake to assume that a person of any particular faith holds to such a view without sufficient evidence regarding that person's beliefs about morality, God's commands in the past, God's commands now, and the applicability of those commands to his or her own life. And such a mistaken way of thinking will likely lead to improper emotions, such as fear and anxiety.

The general solution Garcia and King recommend applies to the case of James and Wadi as well. Don't assume more than your evidence warrants, don't conflate logical entailment with belief attribution, and do strive for intellectual charity. Garcia and King write:

> A charitable person is disposed both to desire the good for others and to think as well of them as she reasonably can. When applied to an intellectual activity, such as reading or discussion, charity becomes intellectual charity. Thus, a person who is intellectually charitable is disposed both to desire intellectual goods for others and to attribute as much intelligence and good will to them as she reasonably can.[14]

Garcia and King go on to provide practical guidance that applies to multifaith engagement as well. Carefully consider what beliefs and character traits one attributes to a person of another faith. Ask if one has sufficient evidence to do so. Don't assume the person holds a repugnant entailment of their belief, but ask him if he does.[15] In this way, we act both reasonably and with love for our neighbor.

A Case of Hope, Daring, and Despair

Hope and despair concern the prospects of attaining something important. Hope involves construing a future, difficult good as having significant likelihood of being attained, while despair involves construing that future,

---

14. Garcia and King, "Out of the Gutter," 195.
15. Garcia and King, "Out of the Gutter," 204.

difficult good as not attainable. As noted above, loving one's neighbor requires attributing as much intelligence and good will to her as one reasonably can. Love of neighbor also implies willing what is good for the neighbor. The highest good for anyone, from a Christian perspective, is to enjoy eternal friendship with God in heaven, which is made possible by divine grace through the work of Jesus Christ. That friendship can begin here and now when one is converted by grace and turned toward God in love. If this is truly the highest good, then love for one's neighbor involves willing such a conversion for him or her. But conversion is difficult, for God does not *force* people to love and follow him but rather gently *invites* them. And if a person does not appreciate or recognize God's invitation, then God's invitation to relationship with him may be drowned out by the clamoring of lesser goods for one's attention. Or one may adopt false beliefs about God and what God has revealed that hinder one's rightly relating to God. Given the difficulty of conversion, my neighbor's ultimate good is a potential object of hope or despair in me. Threats to my neighbor's good, such as her disordered desires or false beliefs about God, are potential objects of fear or daring in me. An evangelist may daringly confront her neighbor's disordered desires or false beliefs in an attempt to remove obstacles to her having a friendship with God. Even if the neighbor chooses not to convert in the present, the Christian ought to continue to hope for the neighbor's future conversion based on her trust in the providence of God, who "wills everyone be saved and to come to a knowledge of the truth" (1 Tim 2:4).

Let's consider another case. Rachel is a Christian and Sophia is one who claims that science is her religion. Sophia will only believe what can be confirmed by science. Rachel hopes that Sophia finds the truth, lives a good life pleasing to God, and enjoys friendship with God for eternity. Rachel hopes Sophia becomes a Christian. But imagine that Rachel's hope is principally grounded in her confidence in her own understanding of arguments for Christianity and her general ability to engage in an apologetic defense of her faith. So in virtue of her self-confidence, Rachel boldly and daringly engages Sophia with arguments for Christianity. But Rachel ends up alienating Sophia with her zeal and method of engagement, for Sophia thinks they lack the right kind of relationship for Rachel to engage her in this way. Dejected by Sophia's rejection and by her own failure, Rachel despairs of Sophia's lack of conversion. Furthermore, Rachel's rejection by Sophia lowers her confidence in speaking to others about her faith, and she despairs of her ability to be an effective witness for Christ more generally.

What are we to say of the case? First, Rachel's hope that Sophia would find the truth should not have been based on her self-confidence in her apologetic skills. While apologetics has an important place, conversion is ultimately a work of the Holy Spirit and not a work of human rhetorical power. In this case, Rachel has an unreasonable expectation about the role of her apologetic skill in the conversion of another. She does not sufficiently recognize the multifaceted ways in which the Holy Spirit works for a person's conversion. Rachel thus *misconstrues* the situation and so has improper hope. Rachel's misplaced self-confidence leads her to daringly attempt to undermine Sophia's false beliefs, which she sees as a threat to Sophia's good, but she does so in a foolish and ultimately ineffective way.

What Rachel needs is practical wisdom, humility, patience, and courage that is based on trust in God and his providence. We can assume that Rachel does love Sophia and desires her good, which properly grounds her hope for her neighbor's conversion. But let us suppose that Rachel's hope is also founded on an exaggerated *concern* for and notion of her own role in the conversion of her neighbor and the power of her arguments, which serves as the basis for her improper hope, daring, and foolish action. Rachel needs practical wisdom to recognize when Sophia has enough trust in and respect for Rachel to listen to her and to believe in her being motivated by a sincere desire for Sophia's good rather than by something else. Rachel also needs a humbler desire for and understanding of her role in the conversion of another person, and she needs to recognize that she may play only a planting or watering role rather than one of harvesting.[16]

Rachel also needs patience and courage to endure the hardship of Sophia's separation from her with respect to faith. Why courage? Courage is a virtue that helps one to endure hardship, confront threats, and stay the course set by practical wisdom by means of the rightly ordered emotions of fear, hope, and daring. The courageous person endures pain and discomfort in pursuit of a real good. This can include the pain and discomfort that arises internally by virtue of the uncertainty of one's own or one's neighbor's attainment of a significant good. Hope concerning the attainment of the good, fear at a threat to its attainment, and despair concerning the loss of the good may intermingle and create an emotionally uncomfortable (if sometimes exciting) state in the person. Think of when a fan hopes for her team to win a game, but the score is close. Proper hope helps the courageous person to endure through the emotionally uncomfortable state until it is reasonable to act. They do not rashly seek to prematurely act in order to eliminate the discomfort, nor do they cowardly fail to act because of the increased potential for discomfort that may result. They wisely act at the right time. Rachel needs courage to endure the hardship of her separation from Sophia in faith, her own regret regarding her failures in engaging Sophia,

---

16. The apostle Paul makes this point (1 Cor 3:6–7).

and her discomfort resulting from her uncertainty about how Sophia will respond to her and to the Christian faith in the future.

Boldness and daring with respect to speaking about the Christian faith may have a place in Rachel's relationship with Sophia, but Rachel must wait for the proper time to speak. The daring of a courageous person energizes her action when she does confront threats. If the time is right (based on the context and the relationship), Rachel may rightly be energized by daring as she confronts the threats to Sophia's ultimate good that Sophia's false beliefs pose. Courageous persons manage their fear, hope, despair, and daring well rather than letting those emotions govern their actions and lead them to act foolishly. By virtue of their proper concerns and construals, courageous persons' emotions aid their action without ruling it. Ultimately, for the Christian, courage must be founded on trust in God and his providence. As Christ said, "In the world you will have trouble, but take courage, I have conquered the world" (John 16:33b). Rachel will be a winsome witness for Christ when she has a hope properly founded in trust in God and a humble acceptance of her proper place in evangelizing her neighbor. Proper love will help Rachel keep her desire for Sophia's good at the heart of their relationship. Practically wise and patient courage will help Rachel to navigate the discomforts that characterize her friendship with Sophia.

In summary, the emotions of fear, hope, despair, and daring may arise properly and reasonably or improperly and unreasonably in multifaith engagements. They are proper or reasonable when the object or construal of the emotion fits the situation and when the concern upon which the emotion is based is rightly ordered. But they fail to be proper or reasonable if one of these components is missing. The virtue of courage helps a person to act well when these emotions are present. In loving and serving our neighbor of another or no faith, we must ask God for courage and grace to form proper concerns and to construe our situations in accordance with the truth so that we can be his profitable servants and live out our love for God in love for neighbor.

6

Hope as an Affective/Cognitive Tool for Multireligious Understanding

Terry C. Muck

WHAT IS HOPE? A dictionary definition of hope is sufficiently general to include almost everyone's way of looking at it: "Hope is the feeling that what is wanted will happen."[1] It locates hope first of all in the affective domain of human nature—that is, as a feeling, as one of our emotions, loosely related to desire. Yet hope also has a cognitive element to it, especially in the part about speculation about what will happen and how it might happen. Finally, the definition gives it a bit of temporal specificity—we want *now* what might happen in the *future*.[2] It leaves open for a moment the question of whether hope is universal among all peoples and cultures, but still it is a good definition. It is where we will begin in this essay.

Yet we will want to go further in our understanding of hope, which means we will need to distinguish among various understandings of the contents of our hopes, particularly ones related to various intellectual disciplines—psychological hope, sociological hope, political hope, philosophical

---

1. Friend and Guralnik, *Webster's New World Dictionary*, s.v. "hope."

2. The temporality of hope is a bit tricky. In simple terms, it is about the future. But what we want we want now, and what we want now depends heavily on past experience. We would do well to remember C. G. Jung's caution that hope works only "if we live in the past, present and future simultaneously" (Jung, *Memories, Dreams, Reflections*, 237).

hope, and religious hope (and there are others we will not deal with in this essay). We will quickly discover that the "hopes" referred to in these discrete disciplines differ from one another. So in order to go deeper, we must first be specific about which discipline we want to explore more deeply (religion, in our case), and then ask a second question: Hope for what?—or in our case, *religious* hope for what? This second question adds important content in our quest to understand hope.

If one wants to get more specific still, one can disagree with, champion, edit, amend, and/or explain one or two "theological" understandings of hope, that is, specific religious conceptions of hope. For example, we might compare and contrast what the Buddha said about hope with what Jesus said about hope. Or instead of an interreligious comparison we could do an intrareligious comparison within a single religious tradition—how Calvin's understanding of hope compares with Aquinas's would be one example. We will do a bit of that, attempting a generic Christian understanding of hope in answer to the question, Hope for what, according to the Christian tradition?

Finally, it may be that one wants to attempt to add something new to our understanding of hope. We definitely want to do that. We want to test an understanding of hope that suggests its utility as an interreligious category. Here is the proposition we want to test: religious hope has been a perplexingly underused common ground when we engage in attempts at multireligious understandings.

What Is Hope?

As we mentioned above, the most basic definition of hope is "a feeling that what is wanted will happen." Hope is both an affect (of desire) and a cognition (discerning the possibilities and the ways and means of what might happen). We can say that hope is neither purely an affect nor a cognition. Or better yet, we can say that it is both. Hope is a complex state of mind.

In addition, hope is probably a universal human state of mind (appearing in the extant literature of all cultures, for example). Yet hope is not a universal good or a universal evil. To be sure, there is adequate empirical evidence to show that hopefulness in an individual can lead to better physical health, increased psychological well-being, sociological effectiveness, and growing religious meaning. Likewise, studies have clearly supported the idea that a certain optimism about life forestalls hope's hopeless opposites, dejection and despair. But hope can become a debilitating snare if it is applied to a negative goal, or if the goal is fantastical, or if hope is cherished in spite of a total lack of agency with which to achieve it. In other words, one can hope for good things like happiness, love, long life, or for bad things like excessive wealth or notoriety or hedonistic excess. Thus, hope, in addition to being a complex state of mind, has a complex moral status.³

One of the earliest references to hope in our Western tradition is in the Greek mythological story of Pandora's jar. It appears in several versions in early Greek literature and then is taken up by numerous Western philosophers to our current day. The original telling of the story by Hesiod in the eighth century BCE is simple in the extreme:⁴ The titan Prometheus stole fire from his superior, the chief Greek god Zeus, and gave it to humanity. This made Zeus angry and he vowed revenge. He ordered one of his underlings to create a beautiful, beguiling creature called woman and offer her as a gift to man. Despite warnings about accepting such gifts, man accepts. Before delivering the gift, Zeus gives Pandora (the name of the woman, meaning "all gifts") a jar with a lid and warns her never to open it. Out of curiosity, Pandora opens the jar—and all manner of evil spirits escape, the spirits of sickness, death, crime, hate, envy, and many others that man had never known before. When she sees what is escaping from the jar, Pandora slams shut the lid, but the only thing left trapped in the jar is the spirit of hope. Zeus had his revenge, and all that humankind is left with is hope.

What do we learn from Hesiod's version of the story, aside from his patent misogyny? Primarily, we learn Hesiod's explanation of how evil comes into the world. But more telling, perhaps, is what we don't learn from the story. We don't learn whether the hope that is left in the jar is a good thing or a bad thing. And we don't learn whether hope is trapped in the jar and thus unavailable to humanity or whether the jar is a positive repository for hope, keeping it safe for humankind's use. These two questions—Is hope good or bad, and is hope in a prison or a pantry?—have dominated attempts to interpret the parable ever since.⁵

And the interpretations have been frequent and varied. Because in its original version it is noncommittal in answering the two key questions, it has acted throughout subsequent Western history as a sort of moral palimpsest, a story capable of being told over and over again with a wide range of meanings.⁶ Scores of philosophers have read into the story meanings congenial to their ideologies. Erasmus, the sixteenth-century humanist philosopher, for example, changed the jar to a box and also changed who opened the jar, from

3. Or to put it a slightly different way, Joan Didion reminds us that "not all expectations are hopes" (Didion, *Year of Magical Thinking*, 27).

4. The following is my summary of Hesiod's story. I have used M. L. West's new translation (West, *"Theogony" and "Works,"* 38–40).

5. Beall, "Hesiod's Pandora Jar," 227–30.

6. Panofsky and Panofsky, *Pandora's Box*.

Pandora to her husband, Epimetheus. For Erasmus, the moral of the story of Pandora's box is this: "from experiencing trouble a fool is made wise."[7] For Erasmus, the escaped spirits are bad and hope is good.

One of Erasmus's contemporaries, the sixteenth-century renaissance poet Gabriele Faerno, argues the opposite—that all the spirits in the jar are good spirits, and all, except hope, have escaped from humanity. Hope is all that is left; hope is our only hope. Actually, Faerno draws on a tradition started by a contemporary of Hesiod, Theognis, who also believed all the spirits in the jar were good ones, and only hope remains.

In contrast, Friedrich Nietzsche, the nineteenth-century philosopher, thought all the spirits in the jar were evil spirits, including hope. In fact, in Nietzsche's view, hope "is the most evil of all evils because it prolongs man's torment."[8]

Current interpreters of the story of Pandora's box (Erasmus's edit has stuck) are also divided, although the more common view is probably the one represented by M. L. West, who has published a recent retranslation of the story in Hesiod's long poem *Works and Days*. West sees hope as a good thing, available for humankind's use.[9] Yet others, such as Mark Griffith, see hope as a blessing, but one withheld from us so that our lives should be drearier and more depressing.[10]

Most interesting, given the above, is what the story of Pandora's box has come to mean in common Western culture. It actually is not the story itself and its relationship to the meaning of hope that has become a common metaphor, but rather the simple statement "That will open Pandora's box." Most people, when asked about Pandora's box, do not know the story as related by Hesiod. But they do have an impression of what it means to say something like, "it was a Pandora's box and I didn't want to open it." What they mean by that is that getting involved in something is sure to make us all susceptible to multiple negative consequences. It is somewhat similar to other sayings, such as "opening a can of worms," "stir up a hornet's nest," or to say something about "borrowing trouble." In such situations, it is better, we think, to just not get into it, to "let sleeping dogs lie."

To summarize, hope is a feeling that what is wanted will happen, but whether hope is a good thing or a bad thing goes beyond essential definitional pronouncements and has to be determined by examining other contextual

---

7. Erasmus, *Adages of Erasmus*, 98.

8. Nietzsche, *Human, All Too Human*, esp. section 2, "On the History of Moral Feelings," aphorism 71.

9. West, "Introduction," xii–xiv.

10. Griffith, *Aeschylus*, 250.

factors that have to do with both the content of desire and the agency, or lack thereof, of hopeful (or hopeless) human beings and societies to bring about the desired outcomes. In order to answer these contextual questions, we must ask a second question about hope: hope for what?

Hope for What?

Asking and answering this question puts us on the road to deciding whether hope is a good thing or an evil thing. As we have seen, hope is a morally complex state of mind; that is, hope can be a good thing or a bad thing. Hope for what? is one of those questions that has multiple answers. The way to reduce the number of answers, of course, is to put two words in front of the question, as in "We should hope for x," thereby turning it from a question into a prescription. But I am going to suggest that there is a great deal of value in both delaying the making of that prescriptive move and simply looking at the various things that people do hope for—that is, making an inventory of hopes and dreams and visions of what different groups of people might like to see happen.

Let's begin our inventory by looking at four generic answers to the question, answers that are common to four disciplines of thought: psychology, sociology, philosophy, and religion. Let's begin with psychology. When psychologists use the term *hope*, they implicitly answer the question with this: psychological health. In a bit of circular reasoning, they consider being hopeful a positive human trait, as opposed to being despairing. For psychologists, hope is a good thing if it produces a constant state of hopefulness. One hopes for achievable things that we have at least some power to bring about; such hopes reinforce being hopeful, whereas hoping for things that we have no chance of achieving extinguishes hopefulness and creates despair.[11] Psychologist Charles Snyder created the Hope Scale, twelve questions that measure a person's determination to achieve their goals. We might call this an "instrumental" approach to hope.[12]

Closely related to this understanding of hope is the healthcare approach to hope. There is ample empirical evidence to support the contention that being hopeful lessens a person's exposure to disease in the first place and helps in battling illnesses when a person is afflicted.[13] Positive psychologists teach

---

11. Jonathan Haidt notes that hope in immortality enabled soldiers to die for country and comrades, and to my mind this raises the question as to whether our super-individualistic age is a natural inhibitor of hope (Haidt, *Righteous Mind*, 222).

12. Snyder et al., "Hope Theory," 257–76.

13. See Wiles et al., "Hope, Expectations, and Recovery," 564–73.

strategies to help boost a person's hope. I suppose you could call this psychological (and medical) view of hope "the science of hope."

As one might expect, the sociologists' views of hope are not unlike that of the psychologists', except that the sociological emphasis is on groups of people rather than individuals. Just as individuals can be helpfully hopeful, so groups of people and whole cultures can also be hopeful. And implied, of course, is that hopeful cultures are healthier than despairing ones.[14] Yet groups of people have different dynamics than individuals. One of the most interesting features of sociological hope is that in order to communicate and develop hope, groups need mythic stories that justify whatever hopeful cultural features they want to personify. Like any good myth, a cultural myth is both an explanation of who we are and where we came from and a prescription to its members on how to be.[15] The prescription includes a fairly detailed picture of what we hope for as a group. We want to be inclusive, empowering of minorities, a bastion of solidarity and wholeness. Or we want to be different, unique, appealing precisely because of what some would see as our weirdness.[16]

Clearly, closely related to the sociological understanding of hope is the way politicians use hope as campaigning rallying cries. In the case of politics, the content of hope is the politician himself or herself; it is as if they are saying "your only hope lies in me and my policies." President Barack Obama used the concept of hope very effectively in both of his campaigns for president. His campaign was based on the premise that he was our hope for the future.[17]

How do philosophers answer the question of the object of hope? Of course, philosophy's main concern is about meaning. Instead of beginning with discerning the practical outcomes of hope, as psychologists and sociologists do, philosophers are interested in what meaning and role hope has in a culture's overall approach to life (ontology), and whether or not they are able to successfully communicate that meaning through language and other thought forms (epistemology). In our Western culture, hope can be seen to develop in three distinct stages. The ancient Greeks saw hope in primarily negative terms—i.e., hope was/is the result of insufficient knowledge and thus results in wishful thinking. This is the reason ancient Greek writings about hope (as we have seen with Pandora's box) tend to be ambiguous and

14. Bennett, "Manufacture of Hope," 115–30.

15. Sociologists writing today emphasize knowledge that is local and particular rather than global and universal. Hope needs to be rooted in specific situations and among certain people. See Seidman, "End of Sociological Theory," 131–46.

16. See also Rorty, *Philosophy and Social Hope*.

17. This was also the premise of Barack Obama's campaign book, *Audacity of Hope*.

hope, a minor character in the play of life.[18] The second stage, the Christian stage, brought hope front and center in a leading role, and gave it the character of theological promise. We will discuss the pros and cons of this move in the next section. Finally, the post-Christian era in which we now live emphasizes hope as understood through the eyes of pragmatism: hope is as hope does. Hope is good to the extent that it brings about desired ends, bad to the extent that it doesn't. For moderns, hope can just as easily be personality-building as neurotic, motivational as manipulative, meaning-making as meaning-obscuring.

It may be that it is in religion that the state of mind we are calling hope plays its most important role. This is especially true of religions that developed during and after the so-called Axial Age, the period of social ferment that produced the religions we now characterize as world religions.[19] Confucius, Lao-Tzu, Gautama Buddha, and, later, Jesus and Muhammad all taught a split between nature and supernature, the mundane and the sacred, between earth and heaven. Religious hope was living in one state—nature, mundane, earthly, samsara—and hoping for advancement to another—supernatural, sacred, heaven, Tao, nirvana. These religions are consistent in hoping for transformation to the transcendent realm, but they differ in what mechanism will bring about such transformation: Buddhist mindfulness, Confucian virtue, Taoistic balance and harmony, Christian faith in Christ, etc. Hope is certainly real and central, but it is realized in differing ways.

All of these understandings of hope—psychological, sociological, philosophical, religious—are valid ways of discussing hope. But it is important to keep them distinct. Hopefulness as an aid to physical and psychological health and hopefulness as a Christian fruit of the Spirit are both extremely important, but they are also very different. To reduce one to the other is to minimize the value of both. Which is why if one's concern, like ours, is with a religious understanding of hope, we need to ask a third question, one that follows naturally from the questions of the nature and object of hope: Hope for/in what, according to a religious tradition?

Hope in What, according to the Christian Tradition?

An excellent example of what can happen to our understanding of hope, when the categories we discussed in the last section are blurred, can be seen in some of the current expressions of hope in common Christian

18. Lewis, *Solon the Thinker*, 85.
19. See Bellah and Joas, *Axial Age*.

understandings. One of the definitions of Christian hope that I read in an online blog began this way: "Biblical hope is not a hope-so but it is a know-so. . . . Hope is not a feeling or an emotion. Hope is the knowledge of the facts."[20] This statement on hope turns hope—which, as we have seen, *is* at least partly an emotion—into knowledge. Instead of a theological definition of hope, this definition is a philosophical one—and a mistaken one at that. According to Hebrews 11, Christian hope is all about what is unseen, not what is seen.[21] It is about our human reaction to the promises of God, not about whether those promises are true. Put another way, one can believe God's promises are true without having hope in them—that is, without believing they will be a positive reality for me.

In addition to the Hebrews 11 passage on hope, 2 Corinthians 4:16–18 tells us to "not lose heart. Though our outer self is wasting away, our inner self is being renewed day by day. For this light momentary affliction is preparing for us an eternal weight of glory beyond all comparison, as we look not to the things that are seen but to the things that are unseen. For the things that are seen are transient, but the things that are unseen are eternal" (ESV). We all know for sure many transient things that, far from producing a reaction of hope in our hearts, produce profound despair. There are many things I know that I wish I had never heard of, like the statistics on child abuse in our country. Just knowing such things is not enough. What I hope for I don't know for sure, at least in the same way that I know the statistics for child abuse. What I hope for is that child abuse is reduced, if not eliminated. I may not know how that will work out in the case of child abuse; in fact, I may be skeptical. But I can have a realistic hope that God through Christ will work things out sometime in the future.

Hope is not about present knowledge but about the realization of future desires. In an article on Christian hope by the editors of *Encyclopaedia Britannica*, hope in Christian thought is acknowledged as "one of the three theological virtues, the others being faith and charity (love)."[22] But hope is distinct "because it is directed exclusively toward the future, as fervent desire and confident expectation. When hope has attained its object, it ceases to be hope and becomes possession."[23]

More recently, Christian understandings of hope have taken a decidedly hopeful turn toward what some call "hope theology" or the "theology

---

20. Wellman, "Christian Definition of Hope?"
21. "Faith is the reality of what we hope for, the proof of what we don't see" (Heb 11:1, CEB).
22. "Hope, Christian."
23. "Hope, Christian."

of hope." The theology of hope is theology that has as its central feature an emphasis on eschatology, the Christian doctrine of last things. That is, the theology of hope focuses on what is going to happen at the consummation of all things. This emphasis means that the way theological thinking is done changes from the classical methodology (i.e., what happens to us today is understood through the lens of what happened two thousand years ago, through the life and teachings of Jesus Christ), from missiological methodology (i.e., what happens to us today is understood by asking the question of all current events: What is God doing through each of these day-to-day events?), to a methodology that interprets the present—what is happening to us today—in terms of the future—what God promises will happen to us at the end of time. Theological thinking is not done in relation to past events or present events, but future events.

One can see this thinking most clearly in the writings of German theologian Jürgen Moltmann, who in 1964 wrote a book called *Theologie der Hoffnung* (later published in English as *The Theology of Hope*). The classical Christian theology of hope was first articulated by Thomas Aquinas in a series of questions and answers in his *Summa Theologiae*.[24] But making hope the center of theology came primarily from Moltmann. The theology of hope methodology has since been picked up and elaborated upon by numerous theologians, such as Lutheran theologian Wolfhart Pannenberg and Roman Catholic theologians Johannes Metz and Karl Rahner.[25]

If one can identify a biblical locus classicus for the theology of hope, it might be 1 Peter 1:3: "Praise be to the God and Father of our Lord Jesus Christ! In his great mercy he has given us new birth into a living hope through the resurrection of Jesus Christ from the dead" (NIV). Hope in the life, death, and resurrection of Jesus Christ means that the theology of hope is an ongoing, living thing that will never be settled until the eschaton actually takes place. Until then, we live with the unseen realities of our human hopes and dreams as influenced by our readings of scriptural promises.

Hope as a metaphor cluster can be used for a shorthand summary of Christianity, both positively and negatively. Negatively, hope is sometimes characterized as a pie in the sky, as foolish wishing, as withered leaves, ocean foam, or youthful good looks that will fade with time. On the positive side, the hopeful metaphor cluster includes wings, feathers, birds (falcons), sunbeams, light, candles in the dark, and our soul where hope can safely perch/reside.[26]

24. Aquinas, *Summa Theologiae* II.II.17, "Hope, considered in itself."
25. See Rahner, *Writings of 1965–67*, 256.
26. See Lakoff and Johnson, *Metaphors We Live By*.

With all this as background, let's move on to the core topic: what is *multireligious* hope?

What Is Multireligious Hope?

It is surely too simple to say, in response to the question of multireligious hope, that it is generic hope held by religious people in a religious context. But perhaps it is not too simple to begin our answer there.[27] Multireligious hope is hope in the context of more than one religious person and more than one religion. That is, the generic features of human hope still apply. Hope is a complex state of mind, both affective and cognitive; it is morally complex in that it can be either good hope or bad hope; and it is universal to all human beings, thus to all religions.

But we want to say more. Much more. We want to also say that because one can identify hope that has religious feelings and religious content associated with it, hope, religious hope, can be the occasion of engagement among people of different religious persuasions. When people belonging to different religious traditions engage one another, whether in formal dialogue or public ceremonies or over the backyard fence, hope can be a helpful way of stimulating the engagement in positive directions. Here are three ways:

First of all, hope itself can be a topic of discussion. As we shall see in more detail in the next section, hope is a universal human feeling, and all the major religions add content to hope that makes those feelings of hope communicable. People of different religions can get together and talk about hope, how it makes them feel, what they believe about it, and what it means in multireligious contexts.

Second, hope can be an attitude of engagement, an attitude that enables people of different religions to relate to and understand one another. People who have hope ("the feeling that what one wants will happen")—that is, who are hopeful—communicate with one another better than people who are depressed and are in despair.[28]

Third, hope—more specifically, hopeful feelings—can be a worthy goal of such engagements. As we shall see in one of the sections below, being hopeful that in some sense the type of interreligious interactions we are having today may lead to more peaceful coexistence among the religious in the future is a worthy goal of any interaction.

And why is this important? Because it may be the case that what has changed the most about interreligious interactions in the past fifty years is

---

27. See Halperin, *Emotions in Conflict*, esp. 84–100.
28. Petersen and Wilkinson, "Editorial Introduction," 113–18.

the increased frequency of first-person contacts with people of other religious traditions—or no religious traditions. Whereas some of us who are older may have grown up in relatively mono-religious cultures, with very little or no contact with the people and ideas of other religious traditions, that is rarely the case today. We meet the religious other in our neighborhoods and are exposed to new religious ideas on television, in the movies, and in the books we read. And so when we encounter a religious feature such as hope, which allows us to carry out these engagements positively, it is worth examining why it makes such a good multireligious vehicle.

Why Is Hope an Effective Multifaith Topic/Tool?

Hope is a human feeling. The first reason why hope is such a good multireligious engagement tool is because hope is first of all a human feeling, not a transcendent one. God (or whatever transcendent idea, principle, or person considered) does not hope, does not "feel that what one wants will happen." God knows what is going to happen; to say "God wants" is an unprovable anthropomorphism. We are dealing with a human state of mind, and the fact that we are dealing with a human state of mind means we are on a level playing field as we begin the game of engagement with religious others.

A corollary of this first reason is that all people have a capacity for hope, at least from a Christian perspective. Numerous biblical references point to this as a conclusion. For example, Ecclesiastes 9:4 reads, "Anyone who is among the living has hope—even a live dog is better off than a dead lion" (NIV). In Alexander Pope's *Essay on Man*, we find the famous quotation "Hope springs eternal from the human breast."[29] The implication of this for multireligious engagements is that anyone we engage will have the capacity for hope about something. An engagement that begins with the question of what one hopes for should get close to 100-percent participation.

In order to insure that the level playing field is maintained, however, it may be necessary to engage in something we might call "dialogical regression" as to the nature of hope.[30] The reason is this: for any religious person, the temptation when asked to talk about hopes is to immediately put them in their own religious context. This may be okay if it is clearly understood that that is what the Christian is talking about (the same applies to others in the conversation—their instinct to talk about Buddhist

---

29. Pope, *Essay on Man*, 48.

30. What I mean by dialogical regression has much in common with what Hans Joas calls "values generalization," by which he means attempts by specific values traditions "to come to terms with one another by developing more abstract understandings of what they have in common" (Joas, *Do We Need Religion?*, 32).

hope or Confucian hope or Muslim hope, etc.). A conscious ratcheting back of the definition of hope to the most basic universal definition—"a feeling that what one wants will happen"—may be necessary to get the conversation going in a productive direction.

When involved in a multifaith conversation, especially with relative strangers, it is usually best to start with the answer to the generic question of the nature of hope, then move to the more specific category of religious hope, before then opening the floor to expressions related to Christian hope, Buddhist hope, Confucian hope, Muslim hope, Mormon hope, New Age hope, and on and on. But don't be too quick to jump to these more specific definitions. So much is to be gained by staying at the generic level where the complex state of mind, the affective and the cognitive elements in hope, can be discussed, and where the morally complex nature of hope, teetering on the cusp between good hope and evil hope can be productive.[31]

Hope in some form is present in other religions. Since, as we have seen, hope is a universal human state of mind, then it goes without saying that hope in some form will be present in the teachings of non-Christian religions. This is easy to say, not so easy to prove. Perhaps better to leave it as a high probability. There may indeed be a religion or two that manage to completely eliminate hope from their teachings. Easier to do that than to entertain the parallel notion that only some human beings have hope and others are hopeless. Anyway, in averring that hope is as present in non-Christian religions as it is in Christianity, we need to be especially careful about two things:

First, make doubly sure it is religious hope you are talking about, not psychological hope or sociological hope or philosophical hope. Remember the distinctions we made above among these different kinds of hope. In another context, with more space for the argument, I would enjoy trying to make the case that it is religious hope that is the "real McCoy," the most essentially hopeful of all the hopes since it has to do so centrally with the eternal, the future, and the out-of-time-and-space. These hopes are the most hopeful of all the hopes. But for now, enough said for this time and place.

Second, assume a lot about the similarities among religious people when it comes to the affective dimension of hope, and assume as little as possible when it comes to considering the cognitive elements of hope across religious traditions. That human beings are all hopeful translates easily into the contention that religious human beings are all hopeful. But

---

31. In his novel *Remains of the Day*, Kazuo Ishiguro sees in hope (or its cousin, anticipation) an emotion that brings us together: "It is possible these particular persons are simply united by the anticipation of the evening ahead" (Ishiguro, *Remains of the Day*, 245).

there are real, essential differences regarding the content of what we hope for among the religions.

Take Buddhist hope as an example.[32] It would seem at first glance that hope should be nonexistent in orthodox Theravada Buddhism. The whole point of the *dhamma*, Gautama Buddha's teaching, is that everything we see and embrace is actually suffering, and the only way to avoid suffering is to not embrace (or reject) anything—that is to say, we should not hope for anything. As a so-called "orthodox" take on the Buddha's teaching, this may very well be true. But dig a little deeper. Even though it may be that to not hope for anything is enlightenment itself, almost all of us are not enlightened, and Gautama taught that in this in-between state we all find ourselves in, hope can be a useful tool we can use to develop a practice that will lead toward enlightenment. That the tool may be abandoned at a certain point does not gainsay its usefulness to us now, as we are in the process of "getting there." As a non-Buddhist, aren't you intrigued by this thinking? Wouldn't it make a great multifaith topic of conversation? Buddhists do have hope, but not, in the end at least, for the same things that Christians hope for.

Hope is about the future—not the past, nor even the present. Let's focus for a moment on the future aspect of hope. Generally speaking, hope is about the future, not the past—or even the present. And let's put that focus together with the future of multifaith engagements—a future that promises more and more everyday interchanges with people of other religious traditions.

As we said above, it may be that what has changed the most about interreligious interactions in the past fifty years is the increased frequency of first-person contacts with people of other religious traditions—or no religious traditions. It was once safe to say that since almost all of us grow up in religious cultures, where all of the people and ideas that surround us are Christian (or Muslim or Buddhist or whatever), we by default became part of that religious tradition. That is still true in many places, but in many more places it is not. We find ourselves surrounded by religious alternatives, and less and less are we pressured to maintain membership in the family religious tradition.[33]

The increased frequency of interreligious interchanges in the past fifty years has resulted in some positive interactions, but on balance we probably wouldn't be far off base to say that in the main it has resulted in increased conflict.[34] This includes fundamentalist religions subverting the political

---

32. See Bhikkhu, *Purity of Heart*, 34–40.
33. See Joas, "Age of Contingency," 63–77.
34. See Juergensmeyer, *Terror*.

process in their scrabble for advantage over other fundamentalist religions. Terrorists who use religious language and passions to incite their followers. Competing mission movements that too often degenerate into very unethical manipulation and coercion.

Good religious relationships with each other would be a pleasant change from these past conflicts. Those relationships will happen in the future; we can't change the past. In fact, if we take the three dimensions of hope that contribute to multifaith interactions—hope as a topic, as an attitude, as a goal—all three of them are most useful when seen as aspects of our collective futures, not the results of our collective pasts.

As we have seen, the aspect of Christianity that has to do with the future, Christian eschatology, may well need to be our theological focus as we move further in the twenty-first century. Jürgen Moltmann's theology of hope may very well need to be our model for a twenty-first-century theological approach that truly addresses the needs we are facing with religious pluralism around the world. Actually, Wolfhart Pannenberg has developed Moltmann's ideas the most in the direction of the religions of the world. The future of Christian theology is eschatology—this is not a canard; it is a multilayered truth.[35]

Hope allows for certitude and *ambiguity and for sophistication* and *naivety.* Multireligious conversations thrive on ambiguity and naivety. And ambiguity and naivety run throughout hope, both as a feeling and in the nature of its content.[36] The traits that characterize hope just happen to also be the mother's milk of interreligious interchanges. To say that interreligious dialogue thrives on these traits is also to suggest, I suppose, that it withers in the presence of their opposites: self-righteousness, superiority, and triumphalism. Successful interreligious interchanges intuitively discern the shifting line between commitment to one's religious ideals (a good thing) and insistence that *my* commitments be the framework and benchmark of all conversations. Religious hope eschews uninformed bravery as much as it does weak-minded obsequiousness.

What companion states of mind does it endorse? At the top of the list has to be humility or its cousin, a sense of fallibility. Know-it-alls do not do well with multifaith engagements. Know-it-wells do all right, but

---

35. See Pannenberg, *Basic Questions in Theology*, 234–49.

36. Consider an example of this hope's relationship to the other two heavenly graces, faith and love. Faith, when supported by hope, enables us to have trust and/or confidence in God's creation; love, when paired with hope, rises above mere human attainments to become a portal to God and the eternal. Hope only becomes real and attainable when it sees the object of its desire in both time and eternity, here and now, and then and there.

so do know-very-littles. The important frame of mind is a willingness to listen and a desire to understand.[37] Whether hope is considered in its most generic sense, as a feature of a specific discipline, and/or in a religious and theological sense, all of its traits seem amenable to being understood in either an ambiguous or naive sense:

1. Hope is a complex state of mind: both affective and cognitive.
2. Hope is a morally complex idea: it can be both good and evil.
3. The two root questions philosophers have always asked about hope are:
   a. Is hope a good thing or a bad thing?
   b. Is hope available or not?
4. When it comes to content, there are many "hopes": psychological, sociological, philosophical, religious.
5. Christian hope focuses on the unseen—that is, the doctrine of eschatology.
6. Hope is a human affect (therefore fallible); only enticements to be hopeful are divine.

Conclusion

It may be that what we have said above raises more questions than it answers. So be it. Hope, after all, is not an answering of all questions, but an enticement to want to see the future unfolding of the answers to those questions. Still, if I were to write a piece on hope as an element of multifaith engagement for a popular audience or, better, for an audience of practitioners either involved in multifaith engagements on a regular basis or, better still, in need of being inspired to seek out multifaith engagements on a regular basis, what would it be like? Would I simply tell the story of Pandora's box? Or Jesus's parable of the good Samaritan? Or relate stories of successful multifaith engagements that centered on hope? Or is there another way? How would I go about it?

Perhaps I would tell a story. One of my favorites is "The Valley of Dry Bones" in Ezekiel 37. The story begins with the author's spirit being taken by the Spirit of the Lord to a valley full of bones—dry, dead bones. The Spirit of the Lord asks the author whether or not he thinks the bones can live. The author replies, in effect, that he does not know—"Lord, you

---

37. See Muck, "Interreligious Dialogue," 187–92.

alone know," he replies. The Spirit of the Lord says he can make them live by connecting them together, covering them with skin, and breathing the breath of life into them. Then the Spirit of the Lord does this, and sure enough, the bones came to life.

Why is this a story about hope, religious hope, Christian hope, multifaith hope? It is a story of hope (specifically about a loss of hope) because the storyteller, in his interpretation of the story in verses 11–14, says that the dead bones represent the whole house of Israel, which has lost hope. It is a story of religious hope because of the nature of the author's answer to the Spirit of the Lord's question, "Can these bones live?" The proper answer is neither "yes" or "no": the "yes" answer would assume a wisdom about eternity that humans do not possess; the "no" answer would turn the Lord's subsequent enlivening of the dry bones into a cheap carnival trick. The "you alone know" answer locates the exchange in our submission to a superior power. It is a story of Christian hope because Israel's hope is our human response to a promise of God. When God says that he is going to open the Israelites' graves and give them life, we hope, we expect, that that promise will come true. Christian hope is a human response of positive expectation to a promise of God.

Finally, it is a story of multifaith hope, useful in our multifaith engagements, because it speaks of universals that members of almost any religious tradition can relate to: the universality of dry, dead bones (that is, death), the universality of human yearnings for the restoration of life (that is, life after death), the universality of a means by which we hope we can achieve life after death (the acting of a transcendent power on our behalf), and the universality of these three hopes among human beings everywhere.

I cannot imagine a multifaith partner not showing interest in hearing and responding to such a story. How might a Muslim friend respond to the story of the valley of dry bones in Ezekiel? Perhaps by relating to the submission inherent in the author's answer to the Spirit of the Lord's question: "You alone know," *Allahu akbar*, the hope of total submission. How might a Buddhist or Hindu friend respond? Perhaps by relating it to a similar story told by Gautama Buddha about the pieces of a disassembled chariot (the chariot's "bones"), showing the lack of a permanent "soul" in human beings, the hope of change, of karma-based rewards for our future rebirths. These and many other responses have the potential to both lead to a positive engagement with people of other religious traditions and create a setting where we can witness to the saving power of what God has done through Jesus Christ for all humanity. Why not try it?

7

Emotion, Valuation, Compassion, and Empathy

Engaging Cognitive Science and Theology on Willing Rightly on Account of the Other

MICHAEL L. SPEZIO

Introduction and Overview

SEVERAL CHALLENGES ARISE WHEN developing an interdisciplinary study intended to relate orthopathy to the concepts of empathy and compassion. First among these is how to approach the engagement of theology by cognitive science and vice versa. Is cognitive science at all concerned with theological claims about orthopathy? In its work on orthopathy, is theology concerned to understand how cognitive science construes the varieties of affective experience? A second challenge is how to understand the meanings of *pathos* in relation to orthopathy so that the concepts facilitate interdisciplinary work rather than impede it. To which aspects of the human person does the term *pathos* refer? Is human pathos distinct or separate from human reason? Is it grounded in human will? Does it refer to affective experiences, to emotions, to moods, to passions, to feelings? Is it fully passive or does it possess activity along with reactivity? Third, what are the ways in which right or proper pathos might be taken up in considering orthopathy?[1] Is orthopathy first and

---

1. By "right or proper," I intend to mean pathos that is proper to full human flourishing, allowing virtuous autonomy in interactive relationship that is grounded in humility, love, compassion, forgiveness, and mutual care.

foremost about proper pathos regarding God, or does orthopathy primarily have to do with proper pathos regarding and engaging moral principles or other creatures in interaction? For example, should orthopathy emphasize proper pathos for justice, which Anselm of Canterbury argued inclined humans toward that which is intrinsically good and which John Duns argued engendered an innate freedom that defines human rationality?[2] Or is it really the proper pathos of the full recognition and valuation of others in interactive relation,[3] out of which virtuous freedom and perception of justice emerge? As an overall challenge, can perspectives from the cognitive science of empathy and compassion help theologians of orthopathy reground accounts of human pathos in interactive relation while avoiding dichotomies between reason and emotion, cognition and affect, belief and feeling? This chapter takes up these questions and suggests directions that could be helpful in future interdisciplinary scholarship around concepts of orthopathy.

Empathy and Compassion in Multifaith Perspective

Why reflect on and seek deeper understanding of empathy and compassion specifically for developing orthopathy in multifaith perspective? While many good answers to this good question could be offered, one can begin by looking at two interreligious encounters between practicing contemplatives drawn from an array of religious traditions. The first encounter has its origins in 1984, in a gathering at St. Benedict's Monastery in Snowmass, Colorado, and lasted for more than twenty years in the form of the Snowmass Dialogues. The first invitations were sent by Father Thomas Keating to contemplatives from Buddhist, Hindu, Native American, Islamic, Jewish, and Christian traditions, "to meditate together in silence, and to share our personal spiritual journeys, especially those elements in our respective traditions that have proved most helpful to us along the way."[4] Over twenty years of annual gatherings convened with this intention, the group identified several critical "points of agreement" among all faith traditions. Included among these are the senses that "faith is opening, accepting, and responding to Ultimate Reality"; that "faith in this sense precedes every belief system"; and that the "practice of compassion" is "common to us all."[5] Concluding his discussion of these agreements, Father Thomas notes that "each tradition has developed teachings and practices designed to foster the full development of

2. Wolter, "Introduction," 11–14.
3. Spezio et al., "Humility as Openness"; Spezio, "Forming Identities in Grace."
4. Keating, "Introduction," xvii.
5. Keating, "Introduction," xvii, xviii.

the human person. Common elements need to be identified, affirmed and made more available to the world community as powerful means of promoting understanding, compassion and harmony."[6]

A second interfaith gathering of contemplatives occurred about twelve years after the first Snowmass Dialogue, in 1996, this time between Buddhist and Christian monastics and lay contemplatives, gathered at Gethsemani Abbey in Trappist, Kentucky, which was once home to Thomas Merton.[7] Among the recorded dialogues was a conversation between Bernardo Olivera and several Buddhist teachers. Olivera was at the time the Abbot General of the Order of the Cistercians of the Strict Observance (OCSO), a Benedictine monastic order of women and men also known as the Trappists. Olivera had participated in the Gethsemani Encounter shortly after a difficult trip to Algeria. He needed to be in Algeria to receive the remains of Trappist monks who had been killed in the sectarian violence that raged at the time, monks who had remained among the people and kept open their clinic at the Abbey of Our Lady of Atlas in Tibhirine well after they endured death threats and armed invasions by various factions.[8] Learning of this, one of Olivera's interlocutors raised a concern about the action of the monks because "from a Buddhist point of view . . . compassion seems to be missing."[9] The monks' decision to remain with the people they promised to serve was seen as selfish, because by this act, they should have known, presumably, that had their aggressors actually killed them, "the aggressors . . . [would] reap the karma for lifetimes for murdering them."[10] Olivera responded to this concern by pointing to the testament of Father Christian, the elected Titular Prior of Atlas. Father Christian had written his testament about two years prior to his eventual murder. In it, he envisioned his killing and wrote about the one who would carry out the act, "I would like, when the time comes, to have a moment of spiritual clarity which would allow me to beg the forgiveness of God and of my fellow human beings, and at the same time forgive with all my heart the one who will strike me down."[11] Father Christian concluded his testament by anticipating his reconciliation with the one who struck the fatal blow, saying, "And also you, my last-minute friend, who will not have known what you were doing: yes, I want this THANK YOU and this 'A-DIEU' to be for you, too, because in God's face I see yours. May we meet again as happy thieves in Paradise, if it please God,

6. Keating, "Afterword," 125.
7. Mitchell and Wiseman, *Gethsemani Encounter*.
8. Olivera, *How Far to Follow?*
9. Mitchell and Wiseman, *Gethsemani Encounter*, 231.
10. Mitchell and Wiseman, *Gethsemani Encounter*, 231.
11. Olivera, *How Far to Follow?*, 127.

the Father of us both."[12] Olivera emphasized forgiveness in response to the question he received about the perpetrators' guilt. In the subsequent dialogue, just four lines later, Chuen Phangcham, cofounder of the Midwest Buddhist Meditation Center and at the time copresident of the American Buddhist Congress, noted the compassion both at the heart of Father Christian's testament and at the heart of what the Buddha taught, as well as how such compassion is the only way to "defeat the suffering of human society today."[13]

These two historical multifaith encounters documented a deeply shared concern for and about developing compassion. By themselves, the dialogues and reported points of agreement do not fully explain or explore the reasons for the shared perspectives, nor do they unpack what may be a variety of conceptions of compassion and calls to empathy with them. The force of the dialogues is that they happened and that compassion's centrality was fixed at the center like a lodestar. As the Dalai Lama wrote in the foreword to the 1996 dialogues, "For Tibetans, the emphasis for many centuries has been on developing and upholding inner values such as compassion and wisdom."[14]

Theology and Science

On the challenge of how to relate theology and science, this chapter proceeds with an intentional respect for the broad claims and domain of theology in relation to other disciplines. At the same time, many difficulties in interdisciplinary work relating theological and scientific accounts of the human arise. Often this is because of hardened views within a discipline that interpret other disciplines away or engage in unceasing conflict with them.[15] This chapter focuses on engaging the cognitive science of affective dynamics, empathy, and compassion for the benefit of interdisciplinary work around orthopathy. In this effort, there can be no intention or thought of using cognitive science to substitute for theology or biblical hermeneutics, or in any other manner to push these disciplines aside. Nor can there be a view that allows either cognitive science or theology ultimate say and sway in creating proposals about human nature and how it might relate to orthopathy. Reductive physicalism, positivism, and eliminative materialism in philosophical interpretations of cognitive science[16] all have little to of-

12. Olivera, *How Far to Follow?*, 129.
13. Mitchell and Wiseman, *Gethsemani Encounter*, 234.
14. Dalai Lama, "Foreword," ix.
15. Spezio, "Moral Life."
16. Bickle, *Philosophy and Neuroscience*; Churchland, *Braintrust*; Singer, *Legacy of Positivism*; Dennett, *Consciousness Explained*; Boyer, *Religion Explained*.

fer broadly interdisciplinary scholarship of nearly any sort, including that seeking to engage theology focused on orthopathy. Their primary errors are both scientific and philosophical in that they deny or marginalize vast areas of critically important human experience—the actual phenomena they say they seek to understand—all while failing to see the central importance of hermeneutical bridge laws that make possible wider integrative inquiry.[17] Likewise unhelpful are theological accounts of the human person that adhere rigidly to substance or other dualisms that stubbornly ignore embodiment and biology or that refuse and refute all attempts to take them seriously.[18] Inattentiveness to and denial of human evolutionary biology and embodiment are errors clearly recognized by the Thomistic virtue theorist Alasdair MacIntyre in his later work.[19] Examples of authentic interdisciplinary theology are found in works by Celia Deane-Drummond and Stephen Pope.[20] The approach taken here will thus not be satisfying to those convinced that science and theology are nonoverlapping magisteria,[21] or that theology or science should each theorize about the other on the basis of their own disciplinary standards alone. However, it is likely that those pursuing open, exploratory, and interdisciplinary theological inquiry will find helpful resources in this chapter.

Pathos in the Context of the Current Inquiry

Our second challenge is how best to understand and select the variety of meanings pertaining to the concept of pathos in relation to orthopathy. What might *pathos* mean, and what are the most fruitful meanings in the context of the current inquiry? There is, unfortunately, no space for detailed exposition and argument in response to this question. Those who disagree with the semantic range of *pathos* engaged by this chapter will undoubtedly have good reasons to do so and will not find extended treatments here to convince them otherwise. Even so, the chapter seeks to engage *pathos* broadly, and the term is understood as experience or affect or emotion or passion or feeling, as *pathos* comes from the Greek verb *paschō*, meaning "to suffer," "to be affected," "to undergo," "to have a sensible experience."

---

17. Nathan and Del Pinal, "Mapping the Mind."
18. Farris, *Soul of Theological Anthropology*; McInerny, *Aquinas on Human Action*.
19. MacIntyre, *Dependent Rational Animals*, ii.
20. Pope, "Agape and Human Nature"; *Human Evolution*; Deane-Drummond, *Christ and Evolution*; *Wisdom of the Liminal*.
21. Gould, "Nonoverlapping Magisteria."

Cognitive Science and Affective Dynamics

Valuation and Entropy Minimization

Cognitive science has its own accounts of affective processing[22] that relate to the "affective tagging" or the affective features of much, if not all, of cognition.[23] The affective dynamics of mind in cognitive science are largely framed either as *valuational dynamics* or as *entropy-minimization dynamics*. In the case of valuational dynamics, often understood and formally modeled as valuational representations, what is modeled is both the agent's primary hierarchical-valuational systems—the organization of expected positive and negative values—and the temporally bound valuational congruences and incongruences between, on the one hand, an agent's valuational assessment of current states of affairs and, on the other, the anticipated valuational outcomes grounded in the primary valuational systems.[24] When seeking to understand valuation as represented in affective dynamics, think of the values that people place on relationships they have and hope to deepen, or the plans that they have that they hope to pursue, or the goals that they have that they plan to achieve. In each case, valuation signals a future-oriented, intentional plan of some kind. The amount of attention, intention, and memory that involves the person in the valued relationship, the event in the valued set of plans, or the goal in the valued set of aspirations for one's own self and community all signal a cognitive orientation emerging from value. Values can be updated through experience and learning as well. Perhaps one's predicted enjoyment of an event did not match the actual experience, and so one's value about that event and similar ones changes, perhaps decreases. One might learn something about another person that one never suspected, such as how creatively or kindly or compassionately or thoughtfully a person acted, completely out of the blue. Such experiences were not expected because the valuational model of the person did not include associating the high values of those actions with that person. Yet in the moment that we witness an unexpected kindness or experience an outpouring of authentic compassion, everything changes. We have learned, and what we have learned affects the valuational structures we have in our mind regarding that person.

---

22. Cognitive science generally views mental processes as forms of information processing that can be partially modeled using computational methods. For a comprehensive overview, see Thagard, *Mind*. See also Spezio, "Cognitive Sciences."

23. Abelson, "Simulation of 'Hot' Cognition"; Thagard et al., *Hot Thought*; Thagard and Stewart, "AHA! Experience"; Schröder et al., "Intention, Emotion, and Action."

24. Montague et al., "Imaging Valuation Models"; Cunningham and Zelazo, "Attitudes and Evaluations"; Dayan and Berridge, "Pavlovian Reward Learning"; Chien et al., "Inherent and Acquired Values."

It is precisely in attending to how interaction and experiential learning are critical to valuation and valuational learning that we see the need for understanding value beyond passive looking. We cannot think of humans as spectators, but as participants, in valuational dynamics. Valuational systems and dynamics, thus, must be understood in terms that go well beyond a spectatorial portrayal of the valuing agent. Valuation connects agents to others whom they value and entangles agents in the anticipated states of affairs involving those others and the agents themselves.[25] Valuation among agents is interactive, and emerging accounts of valuation emphasize its dynamical, recurrent interactivity.[26]

The other primary perspective that cognitive science uses to understand affective dynamics does not focus on valuation, but on the mind's and the brain's and the organism's tendency toward minimizing uncertainty by minimizing disorder. If, in anticipating an upcoming meeting with another person, I have a sense of calm or ease or joy, it means that my predictions about that meeting are that it will reinforce the stability and strength and depth of my relationship with that person. The meeting is anticipated to minimize the disorder in my life and in how I understand myself in relation to and my being welcome by others. If, instead of calm or joy, I have a sense of anxiety or fear, this means that my anticipation is for greater uncertainty as to the place I hold in relation to that person and perhaps by extension as to my welcome by others. So within the perspective of entropy minimization, instead of framing emotion as centered on value, affective dynamics are thought to reflect a person's hierarchical representation of expected states of affairs, sometimes conceptualized as ending in and ordered to terminal states. *Entropy*, or *uncertainty*, is defined as the disconnect between, on the one hand, experiential evidence and imagined/anticipated states of affairs and, on the other, the qualities of those experiences and imagined/anticipated states of affairs that bring me greater certainty and minimize the uncertainty about self, community, and the world around me.[27] This reduction in uncertainty, in disorder, is called entropy minimization.

There is no present evidence that clearly favors either the valuational representation or the entropy-minimization account of affective dynamics. It is likely that *bounded rationality*[28]—the goal-directed reflexivity

25. Vacek, "Orthodoxy Requires Orthopathy," 225–27.

26. Spezio, "Brains, Minds, Persons."

27. Friston, "What Is Value?"; Friston and Ao, "Free Energy, Value"; Friston et al., "Anatomy of Choice"; Seth and Friston, "Active Interoceptive Inference"; Clark et al., "What Is Mood?"

28. Simon, "Behavioral Model"; Tversky and Kahneman, "Framing of Decisions"; Gigerenzer, "Moral Satisficing."

of a person in consideration of their temporal and capacitative limitations—requires development of alternatives or refinements of both the valuational and entropy accounts. This is because the valuational account lacks compelling formal models of a person's goal representations and valuational assessments, while the entropy account requires too much detail in the representation of terminal states and lacks compelling models of internal states that could account for when the apparent entropy values do not match the reported affect.

Primary Axes of Cognitive Dynamics

Cognitive-scientific accounts of affective dynamics also rely on three primary axes or spectra that apply to cognitive processes in general: the explicit/implicit, top-down/bottom-up, and distal/proximal axes. Explicit processes are those in conscious awareness, including meta-awareness, while implicit processes occur outside of awareness, though they support explicit processes. Top-down processes are those resulting from learning during development, while bottom-up processes are generally available to an organism or species through evolutionary processes. For example, I need to *learn* that another person is a friend, to share enjoyable, mutually supportive, and sorrowful experiences with them, to take joy in a friend's presence. By contrast, a sudden and unexpected, very loud noise, such as someone slamming their palm on a flat desk, causes me to jump even though I have not *learned* that such a sound indicates danger to me. That automatic, bottom-up orienting is a part of my evolutionary heritage, for without it, my ancestors in paleoanthropological time would have been less likely to survive when such sounds, so much fewer and farther between, were far more dangerous. Distally oriented processes have broad temporal scales having to do with long-term memory and anticipatory assessment and future planning, while proximal processes are those with a much narrower time window and serve perceived near-term goals.

Affective processes can be explicit (i.e., feelings) or implicit (i.e., emotional indicators outside of direct, conscious awareness that nonetheless influence learning and behavior); top-down (i.e., joy in a friend's presence) or bottom-up (i.e., sudden fear onset in response to a very loud noise); and distal (i.e., discomfort in thinking about one's advance healthcare directive or sadness in anticipating a friend's departure) or proximal (i.e., disgust or anger in witnessing an act of racism or other abuse).

These processes are dynamic and are in constant, metastable flux within recurrent networks of information flow. Even when experienced as constant and stable, this experience results from a stable, dynamic network of interacting information.[29] In recent years, cognitive science has advanced a view that all cognition is goal-directed; that much of it is predictive over a range of time scales,[30] though not all goals are necessarily consistent with one another; and that there are likely multiple interacting networks for multiple types of goals and the types of learning best suited to each of them. One way to think about this is a reunification of cognition and conation, with a focus on various endpoints that can be variously understood as *teloi* (goals, or the sustained relational presence of the ends) or *skopoi* (targets, ends merely in the sense of attainment).[31] To be sure, there are still influential cognitive-scientific theories of affectivity that pit cognition against emotion, such as so-called "dual system" models or accounts of "thinking fast and slow" that name the fast as emotional and the slow as cognitive/rational.[32] Yet these accounts generally fail to make use of recent insights and computational models from decisional-valuational, social-cognitive-affective neuroscience (DVSCAN), models that increasingly suggest modulatory effects of valuation in a wide range of cognitive modes.[33] Even introductory texts in psychology are not immune to propagating error along these lines.[34] Yet current formal models of affective dynamics no longer support such radical dichotomies. What this means for the future interdisciplinary study of human emotional life and experience is a question still requiring answers. At the very least, this means that references to "emotional regulation" are no longer best understood as cognition suppressing or otherwise denying emotion as a category, nor controlling emotion as something external to cognition. Rather, emotional regulation is better framed as emotional tuning that is internally valuationally dependent. Scholars in and outside of cognitive science generally would not suggest that the concept of "attentional regulation" pits cognition versus attention, or that the concept of "memory regulation" pits cognition versus memory, or that "language regulation" pits cognition versus language, or that "motor regulation" pits cognition versus voluntary movement, because it does not make sense to do so. In just this way, it does not make sense to view emotional regulation as an external control of emotion by some nonemotional cognitive systems, at least from the perspective of cognitive science. While at present no unifying theory

29. See Spezio, "Brains, Minds, Persons."
30. Williford et al., "Projective Consciousness Model"; Pessoa, "Cognitive-Motivational Interactions"; Clark et al., "What Is Mood?"; Pennartz, "Consciousness, Representation, Action"; Clark, "Whatever Next?"
31. Annas, *Morality of Happiness*, 34.
32. Kahneman, *Thinking, Fast and Slow*.
33. Phelps et al., "Emotion and Decision Making."
34. Griggs, "Phineas Gage Story."

of human action has emerged within cognitive science, the renewed focus in cognitive science on goals and goal-directedness of minds and persons suggests emerging areas of fruitful overlap with accounts of orthopathy and other theological and philosophical theories of action.

Pathos and Reason in Relation to Theological Accounts of Willing Action

If *pathos* is taken to mean affect, emotion, feeling, or experience, reflection on orthopathy—statements about right or proper pathos—requires assessing what connection, if any, it has to reason. In this context, as already mentioned in passing in the last section, *reason* can mean both, on the one hand, an agent's reflecting on which ultimate ends to adopt and orient toward, along with deliberating about which ends are ultimate, and on the other hand, an agent's deliberation about the practical ordering of ends and actions on the way to the adopted ultimate ends.[35] Are emotion and feeling—pathos—always and ever in conflict with reason, and is orthopathy, then, an account in which reason suppresses or coerces emotion and feeling into a static structure or form, keeping it bound or allowing it only restrained movement—reason "forced, so to speak, to put [*pathē*] in harness"?[36] Is that what is meant by *orthopathy*? Or is pathos actually included in the scope of reason in the human person, who is embodied, embedded, and emergent in relationships? Within Western perspectives strongly influenced by Platonic and Cartesian systems of thought, it seems natural to talk about reason being ever in conflict with emotion, whether reason is understood as only instrumental logic or as encompassing a rational or "intellectual" appetite oriented toward the good.[37] Yet, as explored above, if emotion is framed within the congruence or incongruence between, on the one hand, what a person holds dear and highly values and, on the other hand, that person's valuationally guided perception of current states of affairs, then emotion—and its cognitively explicit manifestation in feeling—is no more or less in conflict with reason than are attention, memory, imagery, linguistic capability, etc.

Another way of asking how pathos relates to reason is, what is the relation of orthopathy to orthodoxy? Do accounts of human agency demand first an adoption of proper belief or faith and then an ordering of pathos according to this faith, or is a more integrative view possible? Theological

---

35. Gallagher, "Aquinas on the Will."
36. Augustine, *City of God, Books VIII–XVI*, 393.
37. Jordan, "Account of the Passions."

accounts of human agency exhibit a healthy diversity of views on how to relate aspects of human decision generally categorized under reason and valuation. Influential arguments from Thomas Aquinas and John Duns diverge significantly, but they nevertheless generally followed Augustine in developing a view that passion (pathos) is a passive capacity in persons—that which is acted upon and driven or drawn, often by sense impressions, and which generally "craves for what seems pleasant to the senses."[38] Reason, on the other hand, is that active capacity that "can see the gradation of things in an objective hierarchy of values" and "seeks for what seems true in the light of the intellect."[39] Augustine and Aquinas identified the passions as powers of the corporeal person and reason as the powers of the incorporeal or immaterial person.[40] Augustine did this in large part because persons are able to hold in mind the immaterial likenesses of material objects, something that powers of the corporeal aspect of the person could not do. So reason is in the incorporeal aspect of the person: it is "that power of the mind which can perceive [that] this likeness is itself neither a body nor an image of a body"—"the essence of his rational soul, which is certainly not material, since the likeness of a body which is seen and judged in the mind of a thinking person is not material."[41] Aquinas also held that "a passion properly speaking exists when there is a bodily change (*ubi est transmutatio corporalis*)," linking pathos to the corporeal aspect of the person.[42] In arguing for the immateriality of reason, however, Aquinas did not stress its capabilities to hold the immaterial likenesses of things, but prioritized reason's grasp of universals and of singular objects under the aspects of a universal (i.e., this proximal goal under the aspect of the ultimate good or *summum bonum*). He held that these activities were impossible for materially instantiated powers or capabilities of the person.[43]

Neither Augustine nor Aquinas condemned passion or disallowed its harmonious alignment with reason. Augustine criticized the great majority of Stoics when they condemned the goodness of compassion, claiming that Cicero "sounds better . . . more like a Christian, when he says in praising Caesar: 'Of all your virtues, none is more admirable and pleasing than your

---

38. Augustine, *City of God, Books VIII–XVI*, 212.
39. Augustine, *City of God, Books VIII–XVI*, 212.
40. Augustine, *City of God, Books VIII–XVI*, 31; Gallagher, "Aquinas on the Will," 565n17.
41. Augustine, *City of God, Books VIII–XVI*, 31.
42. Aquinas, "Aquinas's *Summa Theologiae*," I.II.22.3.
43. Gallagher, "Aquinas on the Will," 577n41.

mercy.'"[44] Augustine identified this virtue of mercy with "a certain feeling of compassion in our hearts, evoked by the misery of another and compelling us to offer all possible aid."[45] At the same time, Augustine denied that God or the angels have "the infirmity of our [human] passions,"[46] and so he clearly framed passion as an impediment to understanding and willing rightly. Aquinas similarly subordinated passion to reason but argued that passion in accordance with reason is morally good and that such passion does not reduce the moral goodness of moral acts.[47]

At this point, it appears as if both Augustine and Aquinas subordinated pathos, understood as emotion, affectivity, and feeling, to the cold dictates of reason. However, this is a mistaken conclusion if emotion, affectivity, and feeling are understood to also include aspects that are active and that do the ordering as well as undergo it. In fact, both Augustine and Aquinas described a person's capability for affectively oriented willing in just this active way. Augustine held that the person's active capacity for willing is detected in affections such as desire, joy, fear, and sadness, depending on whether one's inclinations are "in harmony" or "in disagreement" with states of affairs that a person "seeks or shuns."[48] Augustine's framing is similar to the framing of congruence and incongruence that plays a central role in valuational and entropy-minimization accounts of affective dynamics. Will is not passive affectivity, nor does it have a direct (i.e., efficient) cause outside of its own active affectivity.[49] Similarly, Aquinas held that a person's will is a rational affectivity that actively enables a person's own reflective orientation toward or away from ultimate goods. Further, this same reflective affectivity, acting from orientation toward or away from ultimate goods, similarly directs a person's intellectual capacities to conduct inquiries and to gain knowledge and understanding by shaping that person's perception of and reflection on any aspect of the states of affairs in the ongoing inquiry.[50] Strictly speaking, both Augustine and Aquinas excluded pathos, or passive affectivity, from the immaterial capacity of reason. However, they both purposefully included and located active affectivity within human reason. If orthopathy's pathos expands to include a wider conception of human affectivity, emotionality, and feeling, beyond passive receptivity, then it is clear

---

44. Augustine, *City of God, Books VIII–XVI*, 85.
45. Augustine, *City of God, Books VIII–XVI*, 85.
46. Augustine, *City of God, Books VIII–XVI*, 86.
47. Aquinas, "Aquinas's *Summa Theologiae*," I.II.24.1–3.
48. Augustine, *City of God, Books VIII–XVI*, 358.
49. Augustine, *City of God, Books VIII–XVI*, 254.
50. Sherwin, *By Knowledge*, 49–53.

that the accounts from Augustine and Aquinas support orthopathy as an active and guiding concern, rather than one merely passively determined and constrained by an orthodoxy external to it. Such an expansion of active and reflective affectivity accords with prominent models of affective dynamics in cognitive science, thereby pointing toward fruitful interdisciplinary engagement on orthopathy.

Acts of Willing Understood as Self-Determining Acts in Consciousness

Of course, a central difficulty in the present interdisciplinary encounter remains that cognitive science generally cannot make use of or address claims about immaterial souls that subsist along with or without material bodies. The difficulties that capacitative and substance dualisms present to authentic interdisciplinary engagement of theology and science have been taken up by a number of careful thinkers, including Nancey Murphy, Philip Clayton, and Gregory Peterson.[51] *Substance dualism*—the separate subsistence of immaterial soul and material body—and *capacitative dualism*—the seating of the human mind and reflective, rational agency in the immaterial soul rather than in the body—still prove for many theologians to be compelling positions in need of defending.[52] Even so, these defenders rarely concern themselves with how to relate immaterial, rational affectivity to current DVSCAN approaches, either out of a conviction that empirically informed fields of inquiry and the models they generate have no importance for theology and philosophy or are subordinate to theology and philosophy. Moreover, it is unfortunately highly likely that they and similar defenders of immateriality will miss opportunities presented by both scientific advances and visionary theological explorations for genuine advancement of our understanding of human relational agency and conscious valuation of others.

Resolutions to the hard problems of human consciousness and clear winners in the debates among dualists, emergentists, physicalists, and materialists are some way off. Happily, authentic interdisciplinary inquiry engaging theology and cognitive science has several options for proceeding without full resolution of these issues, while of course still attending to them and participating in them. One promising way for interdisciplinary work of this kind to move forward is to draw on perspectives of some early phenomenologists

---

51. Murphy and Brown, *Neurons Make Me Do It?*; Clayton, *Mind and Emergence*; Peterson, *Minding God*.

52. Loose et al., *Companion to Substance Dualism*; Farris, *Soul of Theological Anthropology*.

from Munich and Göttingen, since these groups sought to bracket claims of metaphysical certainty in favor of attempting careful analyses of the phenomena available to human consciousness. Their work also influenced several threads of inquiry in psychology and psychiatry, leaving historical traces that could be of some help in current investigations.[53]

Alexander Pfänder was one of the first Munich phenomenologists. He advanced one of the clearest conceptions of phenomenology as a method and wrote the first phenomenological study of the human will, which unfortunately as yet is not available in English.[54] He held that phenomenology as a method attempted to bracket ("has to leave in abeyance") several areas of inquiry and knowledge when approaching phenomena of consciousness: settled conceptual frameworks of phenomenal experiences that are accounted as knowledge of them; questions as to their reality or irreality; and questions regarding their causal or cultural or developmental origins.[55] Pfänder's account of human willing is a helpful addition to inquiries into orthopathy in that it supplements the accounts of active affectivity available from theological traditions with detailed proposals of how acts of rational affectivity (i.e., willings) appear in conscious experience. In his proposals about acts of willing, Pfänder distinguishes active affectivity in the acts of willing from what he calls "strivings and counterstrivings" that always have their phenomenal source in some event outside of the valuationally centered person-in-relation. Similar to claims that Aquinas made for the rational appetite of willing, Pfänder's definition of acts of willing places their phenomenal sources in aspects of the conscious identity of the personal agent who wills. Similar to claims in the valuational and entropy-minimization accounts of affective dynamics, Pfänder states that all acts of willing affirm and/or negate states of affairs in a manner that has nothing to do with spectatorial distancing between agents and their intentional, affectively embedded expectations.[56] Having nothing in common with distanced judgments, acts of willing "are expressions of intents" in which embedded agents propose, out of their own sense of who they are as persons in relation, one or more series of anticipated outcomes, generating "a practical act of proposing filled with a certain intent of the will which issues from the ego-center and, penetrating to the ego itself, induces in it a certain future behavior. It is an act of self-determination in the sense that the ego is both the subject and

---

53. Spiegelberg, *Phenomenology in Psychology*.
54. Pfänder, *Phänomenologie des Wollens*.
55. Pfänder, *Phenomenology of Willing*, 73.
56. Pfänder, *Phenomenology of Willing*, 20–22.

the object of the act."[57] Authentic acts of willing exclude wishing or mere supposition, but commit the person seriously and rigorously, even if that commitment is proximal and near term, due to the uncertainty of features in the distal future. The personal self "charges itself with [a self-created] intent" that can and will persist until the anticipated outcomes are present to and experienced by the person.[58]

Pfänder's proposals regarding acts of willing stress the conscious experiences of actively affective persons and their relations in self-determining perceptions, reflections, deliberations, and decisions about present and future states of affairs. The salient features in mind and consciousness do not find the source of their salience in a theoretical or spectatorial logic that distances the person from the ends or objects of some orthodoxy, understood as some right belief or knowledge or faith. Instead, the salient features of present and future states of affairs involving persons and their relations have their source precisely in both the active affectivity of what persons intentionally and reflectively value or devalue and the affectively grounded, intentional, self-determining acts regarding future valuation. These proposals share broad themes with current cognitive-scientific accounts of affective dynamics and with Augustine's and Aquinas's theological insights about human willing as rational affectivity. Theological accounts of orthopathy seeking to inform and form proper affective dynamics of persons in relation can draw on these shared emphases without following Platonic or Cartesian systems that maintain a strict duality or dichotomy between rational reflection on the features of objects, concepts, and their relations, on the one hand, and rationally affective intentions and action, on the other. Orthopathy may be best understood as encompassing orthodoxy and orthopraxy—a primary and required organizer of both when persons engage in more theoretical, abstract, and spectatorial inquiry.

Orthopathy and Ends

Our third central challenge in this exploration is to select the ends of theological accounts of orthopathy that have good chances of successfully engaging cognitive science. To start, it needs saying that theological frames of orthopathy begin with proposals about proper, active affectivity regarding human relationality and interactivity with God in individual, communal, societal, and institutional dimensions. Cognitive-scientific inquiry, however, is not a good fit within these frames for two primary reasons. First,

57. Pfänder, *Phenomenology of Willing*, 23.
58. Pfänder, *Phenomenology of Willing*, 23.

theologically, it makes little sense to claim that one can directly study human relationality and interactivity with God using empirical approaches. How would one, from a theological perspective, begin to justify requiring God's action in discrete and well-defined temporal windows in controlled experiments so central to scientific inquiry? Abrahamic understandings of God would likely declare such requirements of the divine to be impossibly confused at best and idolatrous at worst. Second, scientifically, there are no reliable methods or tasks or quantitative models for the direct study of such phenomenal interaction between participants of religious communities and divine presence, which becomes clearer as more efforts attempt such direct study with dubious results.[59] While it is possible to measure brain signals and develop cognitive and neural models from data collected during prayer, meditation, and other interactive rituals pertaining to a tradition's orientation toward God, those signals and models can only be related reliably to established protocols of psychological and behavioral and neural assessment involving robust and empirically justifiable cognitive tasks. So it is possible to relate assessments of perception, attention, memory, imagery, language, attitudes, and other dimensions of mental activity to signals and models emerging directly from the periods of prayer/meditation/contemplation, but only if the measures of these mental activities are made *in proximity to* periods of prayer/meditation/contemplation, not directly *during* such periods. Since there is no way to empirically assess the nature of a participant's felt or sensed or perceived or reported divine presence, cognitive science offers little in the way of detailed accounts of such directly experienced interactivity. Cognitive science is better suited to exploring remembrances of conscious phenomena or intensity during such periods. These scientific limitations suggest that orthopathy directed toward and in interactivity with God is not a fruitful avenue for interdisciplinary exploration involving cognitive science.

On the other hand, both theological and scientific perspectives favor considering orthopathy in interactions between human persons and between human persons and the more-than-human world.[60] Cognitive science includes methods for the study of social cognition, moral cognition and action, valuation, decision, etc., especially within DVSCAN.[61] Affective orientations and intentions toward ingroups and outgroups, conceptions

59. Schjoedt et al., "Highly Religious Participants"; Newberg et al., "Measurement of Blood Flow"; Harris et al., "Neural Correlates."

60. Abram, *Spell of the Sensuous*.

61. Nair et al., "Self for Others"; Spezio, "Cognitive Sciences"; Cacioppo et al., "Analyses of Human Behavior"; Kuss et al., "Reward Prediction Error"; Tang and Posner, "Tools of the Trade."

of justice in relation to rewards and punishments, and assessing moral responsibility and contributors to moral perception and action are available areas of inquiry within cognitive science. The question remains, however, what types of affective interrelations or orientations are best pursued. One possibility that stems from long consideration of the centrality of justice and that informs contemporary accounts of contractarian theory[62] is what John Duns, drawing on Anselm, called the "affection for justice."[63] Could orthopathy be best explored and understood in relation to proper affectivity toward justice, which Duns held to be critical to human freedom and its full alignment with divine commands? This direction could be pursued within an interdisciplinary engagement between theology and cognitive science around orthopathy. However, the foregoing discussion makes clear that this is not, in fact, the best place to begin such work. Why is this? The short answer is that DVSCAN shows the importance of embodied interactivity and relationality in the study of a person's valuationally guided beliefs, attitudes, and actions.[64] Beginning with affectivity directed toward a principle or duty rather than toward connective engagement with another agent, then, would reverse the importance of these two concerns and would likely get the developmental and formational order wrong as well.

Two brief theological reflections on biblical texts also recommend beginning with explorations of orthopathy regarding and in interactive relation, over and against an orthopathy directed toward a principle or conception of divinely commanded duty. In one such example, the phenomenological theologian Knud Ejler Løgstrup highlighted an active affective orientation that he illustrated with the story of the good Samaritan and that he named "the ethical demand."[65] Løgstrup pointed out that affections for or adherence to duty, social norms and conventions, and moral laws and rules substitute for an *original orientation of interactive trust* between persons, the kind of trust that he associated with love and sympathy.[66] Developmentally and formationally, Løgstrup argued, open trust between persons is primary, and trusting stances only become guarded, constrained, or closed down after experiencing failures and abuses of trust.[67] Social norms arise in such cases as expedient constraints on social interactions, substituting relationships of

62. Rawls, *Justice as Fairness*.
63. Hare, "Scotus on Morality."
64. Spezio, "Brains, Minds, Persons."
65. Løgstrup, *Ethical Demand*; Andersen and van Kooten Niekerk, *Concern for the Other*.
66. Løgstrup, *Ethical Demand*, 13.
67. Løgstrup, *Ethical Demand*, 9–18.

roles in the place of relationships among persons. The resulting relations between roles are "smooth and effortless, not least because they protect us against psychic exposure," and they simultaneously result in reducing opportunities for renewing authentic, interactive trust between persons.[68] Løgstrup illustrated this difference by contrasting the active affectivity of the good Samaritan in the story of the neighbor (Luke 10:25–37) with that of a Kantian Samaritan. In the original story, Løgstrup claims that the Samaritan acted solely for the sake of the other, being moved by "the needs of the victim and how best to help him."[69] Løgstrup then envisages the internal deliberation of a Kantian Samaritan, who "pauses to consider mercy as a duty, which may result in his conveying the assault victim to the inn and tending his wounds not from mercy but from duty"—with Løgstrup concluding, "Duty enters when I [the person confronted by the ethical demand] am trying to wriggle out of the situation."[70] Paul Ricoeur presents a similar perspective on the neighbor story in an essay from 1955.[71] Ricoeur notes that the Samaritan's "compassion," rendered in the Greek by a verbal cognate of the noun *splanchnon* (and so referencing the deep interior of the gut or the womb), actively directs the Samaritan's new, self-determined identity: no longer is the Samaritan, in relation to the one lying wounded, a member of a despised and distrusted outgroup. Rather, the Samaritan is now the *plēsion*, or the "near one" or "neighbor," to the one lying wounded. This is such a radical shift in the active affectivity and interactivity of the Samaritan that the Samaritan's entire journey changes focus and now becomes one originating in the Samaritan's valuing of and securing the wounded's present and future welfare and healing: "and when I come back, I will repay you whatever more you spend" (Luke 10:35b, NRSV). Ricoeur notes that encountering another in willing to become a near one or neighbor to that person "is the personal way in which I meet someone else, outside of all social mediation."[72]

A second set of reflections that supports orthopathy regarding self and others in interactive encounter comes from a central biblical text naming the attributes of God's compassion, also known as the Thirteen Attributes of Mercy, in Exodus 34. In the preceding chapter, Exodus 33, God responds to Moses's request to see his "glory" (*kābôd*; v. 18) by agreeing to show Moses not glory but his "whole goodness" (*kol-ṭôb*; v. 19). The next morning, Moses ascends Mount Sinai and sees the goodness of God spoken in the thirteen

68. Løgstrup, *Ethical Demand*, 19–20.
69. Løgstrup, *Beyond the Ethical Demand*, 76.
70. Løgstrup, *Beyond the Ethical Demand*, 76–77.
71. Ricoeur, "'Associate' and Neighbour."
72. Ricoeur, "'Associate' and Neighbour," 152.

attributes. The first attribute of God—translated as "merciful" in Exodus 34:6 in the NRSV and ESV—is best translated instead as "compassionate," because the Hebrew term *raḥûm* is from the root *rḥm*, which relates directly to the word for "womb" (*reḥem*)—just as in the case of the Samaritan's compassion. After "compassionate," God is described as "gracious," "slow to anger," and "abounding in kindness," or "love" (*rab-ḥesed*). These attributes are important to note for understanding orthopathy in relation to interactivity, not only because they are tied to God's goodness (and so also to human goods and goals) but also because of the *imitatio* traditions in Judaism and in Christianity.[73] If, as Augustine said, "the very essence of religion is to imitate the one whom we worship,"[74] then orthopathy may best proceed by developing clear narratives and discourses on compassion, kindness, and patience in the face of others' limitations and challenges.

While theological options in exploring orthopathy surely include attending to proper, active affective orientation in relation to God and may include emotional, valuational orientations to principle, divine commands, and duty, there are good reasons in interdisciplinary engagement with cognitive science to prioritize orthopathy in interactive encounter and relation with and among persons and the more than human. In this regard, and as reviewed above, there are also good reasons to focus on the affective dynamics of compassion and, arguably, those of empathy as well.

Cognitive Science and Orthopathy of Compassion and Empathy

Cognitive science, largely via DVSCAN, actively researches compassion and empathy in the interests of several outstanding questions about human persons, social groups, and the more than human. *Empathy* in cognitive science means largely what it did when E. B. Titchener coined the English term from the German *Einfühlung*; it refers to a person's capacity to affectively intuit the experiences, intentions, values, and perhaps beliefs of another, while maintaining representational clarity on which set is self and which is other.[75] Empathy is, then, the primary interactive channel contributing to theory of mind.[76] *Compassion* in cognitive science is a positive value orientation toward a person or group in danger or pain or distress, accompanied

73. Kreisel, "*Imitatio Dei*"; Spezio, "Forming Identities in Grace."
74. Augustine, *City of God, Books VIII–XVI*, 53.
75. Titchener, *Lectures*.
76. Premack and Woodruff, "Theory of Mind?"; Saxe and Houlihan, "Formalizing Emotion Concepts"; Schneider et al., "Current Evidence."

by a set of intentional goals and expected outcomes for their sake and a set of volitional motor plans that will bring material and social benefit and that can and will be activated when opportunity allows.[77] Neither empathy nor compassion should be confused with mirror neuron systems, for which there is little evidence.[78] Research into the cognitive and neural systems that make empathy and compassion more or less possible is actively ongoing and is informed by the valuational and entropy-minimization accounts of affective dynamics that are presented in this chapter.

Cognitive-scientific pursuits in regard to empathy and compassion include the study of the evolution of human social affiliation and cooperation; of evolutionary comparisons with other social species; of how genetics and developmental contexts and relationships (i.e., nature/nurture) and their interactions influence the formation, stabilization, and loss of compassion and empathy in persons and communities; of the importance of compassion and empathy to ingroup/outgroup dynamics, either reinscribing or overcoming seemingly insurmountable differences; and of possible, future social technologies and artificial intelligence systems that look to the trans- and posthuman.

Evolutionary investigations typically stem from the social brain hypothesis, which states that social mammals, especially hominids and hominins, have the kinds of brains they do (i.e., large, requiring disproportionately large metabolic resources) because of evolutionary processes favoring social bonding and support in groups.[79] Frans de Waal and some others—but not most scholars working in comparative primatology and paleoanthropology—have gone so far as to claim that nonhuman primates, such as bonobos and chimpanzees, have nearly the same, if not identical, capacities for empathy and compassion as human persons.[80] In this fully formed empathy model, humans are born largely or wholly orthopathic already, and they lose their natural capabilities for open, trusting, empathic, and compassionate affectivity as they fall prey to institutional systems of value that favor ingroups and actively cultivate the marginalization of outgroups. Perspectives such as these are difficult to sustain, though it is important to note that de Waal and his colleagues have collected and presented much that should encourage human persons and society to treat the more than human with much greater compassion than is often the case. A recurring problem with

---

77. Singer and Klimecki, "Empathy and Compassion."
78. Spezio, "Brains, Minds, Persons"; Schleim, "Brain Function."
79. Dunbar, "Cognitive Constraints"; Dunbar, "Social Role of Touch"; "Social Brain"; Fuentes, "It's Not All Sex."
80. de Waal, "Morally Evolved"; Preston and de Waal, "Empathy."

viewing empathy as fully formed at birth or soon thereafter is that there is an abundance of historical evidence from wisdom traditions and narrative accounts that demonstrate the relation-dependent plasticity of these systems.[81] For example, Pumla Gobodo-Madikizela's powerful account of empathic transformation in post-apartheid South Africa shows evidence for the kind of orthopathic account advanced in this chapter and in several other chapters in this book.[82] Gobodo-Madikizela, a clinical psychologist and researcher, had conversations with Eugene de Kock, one of the leaders of the apartheid-era, state-sanctioned, white-Afrikaner death and torture squads. Her account of those meetings is profound, and the story she tells can only be her own, given her own status as victim and survivor in the wake of South Africa's terrorizing apartheid state. She met with de Kock over six months in sessions that amounted to nearly fifty total hours of intense, face-to-face encounter. Due to her actively affective intention to return again and again, Gobodo-Madikizela experienced a change in her own empathic orientations both toward de Kock and toward other perpetrators as well. Orthopathy may fit what Gobodo-Madikizela describes as helping perpetrators to once again begin "acting as human beings" by experiencing genuine remorse and expressing genuine contrition, and formation in orthopathy may fit her own experience of enlarging empathy. She connects her own atypical empathic expansion to the empathic orientations she had already formed by the time the conversations with de Kock began. As she theorizes, "The possibility of making an empathic connection with someone who has victimized us, as a response to the pain of his remorse, stems significantly from this underlying dynamic," one in which most people form "an empathic connection with another person in pain . . . regardless of who that person is."[83] The theory of empathy transformation that emerged from her own experience depends on a valuational representation in which the self and other are both connected and valued as self and as other. She writes, "We are induced to empathy because there is something in the self that is felt to be a part of the self, and something in the self that is felt to belong to the other. Empathy feels with the other in a reciprocal emotional process."[84]

Notions of values belonging with both self and other cohere with recent work using formal cognitive models of valuational representation

---

81. See the following interdisciplinary accounts that take up the plasticity and developmental aspects of empathy: Peterson, "Love the Distant Other?"; Herdt, "Empathy Beyond the In-Group."

82. Gobodo-Madikizela, *Human Being*.

83. Gobodo-Madikizela, *Human Being*, 127.

84. Gobodo-Madikizela, *Human Being*, 127.

during decisions to rescue strangers in no position to return the favor.[85] There is also mounting evidence that intentional communities of compassionate, mutual valuation overcome otherwise insurmountable differences through changes to active affective dynamics in empathy and compassion.[86] Gobodo-Madikizela's conclusion is that such active, intentional affectivity suggests that "just as the Truth Commission's records ... offer evidence that ordinary people, under certain circumstances, are capable of far greater evil than we could have imagined, so are we capable of far greater virtue than we might have thought."[87]

Empathy and compassion, then, are not fully formed at birth or in early childhood, as both recent work in DVSCAN and Gobodo-Madikizela's detailed and groundbreaking book make clear. They are not reflexes that are necessarily dulled by participating in intentional communities of virtuous formation.[88] Nor are empathy and compassion, when encouraged and intentionally invited to mature as active, rational affectivities, restricted to ingroup members or dedicated to further marginalizing and denigrating outgroups. Recently, however, a number of influential scholars and public intellectuals who work in the areas of philosophy,[89] developmental moral psychology,[90] and social neuroscience and mindfulness[91] have accused empathy of just these deficiencies. The attacks themselves are deficient because they largely stem from viewing empathy as a kind of reflexive system incapable of learning. They also make use of suboptimal approaches in scientific-experimental designs and assessments of empathy and compassion.[92]

Perhaps the primary reasons that these critiques of empathy and compassion miss the mark, however, are twofold. First, they consistently treat empathy and even compassion mostly as passive affective systems that are in need of some cognitive control, and they view those control systems as somehow themselves not embedded in affective-valuational processing. That is, they neglect the most interesting insights that DVSCAN has generated about active affectivity over the last five to eight years. Second, they either intentionally reject or unconsciously neglect insights

---

85. Nair et al., "Self for Others."
86. Reimer, *Living L'Arche*; Reimer et al., "Maturity Is Explicit."
87. Gobodo-Madikizela, *Human Being*, 133.
88. MacIntyre, *Versions of Moral Enquiry*.
89. Prinz, "Against Empathy"; Singer, "Against Empathy."
90. Bloom, *Against Empathy*.
91. Klimecki and Singer, "Empathic Distress Fatigue"; Singer and Klimecki, "Empathy and Compassion."
92. Spezio, "Embodied Cognition"; Peterson, "Love the Distant Other?"; Peterson et al., "Rationality of Ultimate Concern."

about interactive relationships among humans that emerge from philosophical, theological, and hermeneutical traditions connected to orthopathic outlooks. But they might benefit from recent perspectives favoring and calls to enhance greater interdisciplinary engagement between cognitive science and philosophical perspectives on human agency.[93] I hope that this chapter has helped move those aims forward.

---

93. Thagard, "Cognitive Science Needs Philosophy"; Laplane et al., "Opinion."

8

Loving Our Religious Neighbors

Reflections on Scripture and Twenty-Five Years of Mormon-Evangelical Dialogue

CRAIG L. BLOMBERG

WHEN TWO OR MORE individuals from very different religious perspectives come together to talk about their beliefs in today's world, one of two scenarios most likely plays out. On the one hand, if they articulate their disagreements, the conversation is unlikely to proceed in a direction that would typically be called "loving." A debate may ensue, deeply held views may be shared with great passion, the other side may be misrepresented or at least caricatured, misunderstandings can result, and hostility or at least ill will tends to follow. On the other hand, to avoid these unpleasantries, participants may agree not to discuss their disagreements but highlight only that which unites them. If the reason the individuals have come together is a joint effort in the social or political realm, this may be an important and healthy strategy, but if the goal is genuine, mutual understanding of religious convictions, then silence concerning disagreements proves counterproductive. The apostle Paul in Ephesians 4:15 identifies the proper balance when he writes about "speaking the truth in love,"[1] and love in this context must have certain affective or emotional dimensions to it, rather than referring merely to behaving courteously.[2]

---

1. All biblical quotations in this essay are from the NIV.
2. Arnold comments, "The truth of the gospel needs to be proclaimed and upheld within the community of believers. But it needs to be done with a heart that is tender

Interreligious Dialogue: Past Trends

The so-called ecumenical movement, championed by the World Council of Churches and implemented locally by numerous national and regional daughter organizations, has often, especially from the 1970s to the present, practiced the "lowest common denominator" approach to Christianity by stressing agreements much more than disagreements within worldwide Christendom. In interfaith dialogue with other world religions, it has likewise tended to stress primarily what different faith perspectives share in common, making possible today the tragic conviction among outsiders who observe the processes only superficially that at their cores all religions are basically the same. Of course, there have been plenty of exceptions to these trends, but these generalizations are not without their merit as overall descriptors.[3] Theological justification for this approach comes naturally from the central scriptural command of neighbor love (Lev 19:18; Matt 5:43–48; Mark 12:31–33; Rom 13:8–10; Gal 5:14; Jas 2:8), with the clarification by Jesus that even one's enemy is one's neighbor (Luke 10:25–37).

In the academy, the situation is more extreme. Participants in the American Academy of Religion and Society of Biblical Literature (SBL), whose joint annual gatherings often exceed ten thousand in attendance and who together constitute the single largest body of academics teaching and researching in the fields of religious studies anywhere in the world, know the ground rules their organizations have established. One does not in any way try to promote one's religion in any presentation or paper delivered. Even to hint at such is labeled "apologetics," and there is no more pejorative epithet that can be applied to one's talk than that! One may describe what an influential person believes (or believed), but the findings of one's research must always be delivered descriptively and never prescriptively. In this fashion, regular participants may build up great friendships and experience even warm, loving relationships with those whose religious views are quite different from their own because they simply agree not to talk about their disagreements very much, if at all.[4]

Evangelical Christianity has historically erred in the opposite direction. While the discipline of apologetics refers simply to giving evidences for one's

---

and concerned about the feelings, growth, and well-being of fellow believers" (Arnold, *Ephesians*, 269).

3. For an excellent example of just how much progress the ecumenical movement *has* made on the intra-Christian level, see WCC, *Church*.

4. For an account of the evolution of the SBL into what it has become over the past generation, see Saunders, *Searching the Scriptures*. The membership is sent an annual reminder about the ground rules before each national conference.

faith, high-profile, successful apologists have often been characterized by a combative tone in their ministry. Even when they have been more winsome, the focus has almost always centered on the theological (and sometimes moral) errors of the "other." Wariness and posturing have tended to characterize whatever dialogues (more likely debates) that have gone on between opposing positions, and audiences have been warned against adopting the beliefs or behaviors of the "errant" party.[5] Support for this approach is frequently alleged to come from those passages in Scripture where the writers call down God's curses on proponents of heterodox teaching and/or immoral living (esp. Matt 23:13–36; Gal 1:6–10; Phil 3:1–3, 18–19).

Loving versus Cursing?

Do these twin emphases of Scripture fundamentally contradict each other? Must we choose to obey one at the expense of the other? A detailed survey even just of the New Testament suggests that these two responses to other people emerge out of quite different situations. Consistently when Jesus and the apostles, especially Paul, appear to get the angriest, it is when religious "insiders" who know better—leaders within their own movements—have perverted what was intended to be a relationship with the living God into a list of dos and don'ts far beyond anything Scripture can justify.[6]

Thus, Jesus's harshest and most sustained invective comes against a group of scribes and Pharisees in the temple precincts in Jerusalem that he berates for being hypocrites because they do not practice what they preach (Matt 23:3) and their additional traditions (the so-called oral law) bind "heavy burdens" on the people with which they do not in any way attempt to help them (v. 4).[7] The most famous single action in Jesus's ministry reflecting his anger against certain leaders in the temple is what Ben Witherington has dubbed Jesus's "temple tantrum" (Mark 11:15–19).[8] Despite centuries of theological overlay in which it has most commonly been called a "temple cleansing," it really is (at least one corner of) a temple clearing—a prophetic

---

5. No clearer or more distressing an example exists over the past generation than the ministry of Norman L. Geisler. For a sampling of the tone and contents that have characterized his public-speaking ministry much more so than many of his other published books, see Geisler and Roach, *Defending Inerrancy*. For an earlier illustration, see Geisler, *Battle for the Resurrection*. There were so many factual errors and misrepresentations of Murray J. Harris in this book that Harris had to devote an entire, lengthy appendix to refuting them in Harris, *From Grave to Glory*, 337–446.

6. For details, see Blomberg, "Definition of Heresy."

7. For an excellent, detailed study of Matt 23, see Turner, *Israel's Last Prophet*.

8. Witherington, *Christology of Jesus*, 107.

object lesson portending the temple's coming destruction if its authorities do not mend their ways.[9]

The same is true of the apostle Paul. In Galatians 1:8–9, he twice calls down God's curses on those who would preach a false gospel to the Galatian Christians. Here, understanding the context of this letter proves crucial. These false teachers practice what Paul will label "Judaizing" (*ioudaizein*; Gal 2:14)—Jewish residents of Jerusalem within the church, professing faith in Jesus as Messiah but requiring obedience to the entire Law, including circumcision, for Gentiles wishing to follow Jesus (v. 3; Acts 15:1). They come from the apostles in Jerusalem, though not necessarily with their blessing or representing their teaching accurately (Gal 2:12). They have dogged Paul to Syrian Antioch (v. 11) and now are infiltrating the churches in Galatia, possibly winning some of the Galatian Christians to their point of view. If the Galatian believers follow the Judaizers' thinking in its entirety, their very salvation will be at stake, because such thinking is requiring obedience to all the works of Torah for salvation, something Paul recognizes is impossible (3:10).

At the same time, both Jesus and the apostles (and especially Paul) can prove remarkably solicitous and considerate toward the most notoriously heterodox or immoral outsiders, whom society had rejected, ostracized, marginalized, or otherwise deemed second-class citizens. Thus, Jesus arouses the ire of onlookers when he invites himself to the home of Zacchaeus, the chief of tax collectors and particularly wealthy (Luke 19:1–10). Jewish tax collectors were viewed as particularly treasonous because they had sold out their people to work for the occupying military forces, the Romans. In addition, many overcharged the people so that they could skim extra profits off the top of what they turned over to Rome. Some even served as pimps, supplying Roman troops with Jewish prostitutes.[10] Yet the personal concern Jesus showed to Zacchaeus led him to repent and make amends with those he cheated, as well as giving away half of all his possessions (v. 8).[11] Earlier, Jesus had even called one tax collector, Levi (also called Matthew), to be one of his twelve closest followers and accepted an invitation to banquet in his home with others from this "riff-raff" of society (Mark 2:13–17). Similar examples could be given of Jesus's relationships with women (including prostitutes), Samaritans, the diseased (including the notoriously unclean lepers), and the demon-possessed.

---

9. See esp. Sanders, *Jesus and Judaism*, 61–76. For important nuancing, see also Evans, "Jesus and the 'Cave,'" 93–110.

10. See Corley, *Private Women, Public Meals*, 89–93.

11. Pilgrim thinks this is the passage in Luke that offers the golden mean or best paradigm for Christian giving. See Pilgrim, *Good News*, 129–30.

In a particularly famous passage in 1 Corinthians 9:19–23, Paul delineates how he bends over backward to be "all things to all people," so that he might facilitate the salvation of as many as possible. He speaks about Jews and Gentiles alike, both those under the Law and those not under the Law. As long as a cultural practice is not inherently sinful, Paul is willing to participate in it or be seen with those who do for the sake of the gospel. He knows that the scandal of the cross—of a crucified Messiah, the oxymoron of all time—is a serious enough and unavoidable obstacle that prevents many people from coming to faith (1 Cor 1:23).[12] Paul does not want to put any avoidable stumbling blocks in their way. Thus, even as he calls down anathemas on those who would require circumcision for salvation, he is willing to circumcise the half-Jew, Timothy, so that *non-Christian* Jews are not unnecessarily offended as the two travel about the empire evangelizing Jews wherever they can (Acts 16:1–5).[13] What at first glance seem like directly contradictory actions actually complement each other because in each case Paul's biggest concern is people's salvation and avoiding what might prevent it, be that legalism, on the one hand, or a disregard for people's scruples, on the other hand.

Loving One's Neighbor

It has often rightly been noted that love is the heart of biblical ethics.[14] The two love commands appear in the Torah (Deut 6:5; Lev 19:18)—as the most important commandments, according to Jesus (Mark 12:29–31)—though only in Jesus are both love for God and love for neighbor enunciated together. James also speaks of the command to love one's neighbor as the "royal" or "kingdom" law (Jas 2:8), and Paul finds it as the fulfillment of all of Torah (Gal 5:14). The Hebrew and Greek words used for "love" have a broad enough semantic range to encompass most of the same cognitive, volitional, and affective dimensions that English speakers and writers mean

---

12. "To exalt Jesus-crucified is to violate not just decorum but sound reasoning: it combines insensitivity with insanity—akin to merging the argument that Hitler was virtuous and that the earth is flat" (Kern, "'Word of the Cross,'" 88).

13. Walker, "Timothy-Titus Problem Reconsidered," 231–35; cf. Schnabel, *Acts*, 665–66.

14. E.g., McQuilkin and Copan, *Introduction to Biblical Ethics*, 20. They rightly stress that "the primary characteristic of biblical love is commitment to act for the well-being of another" (33), while adding, "to say that acting lovingly takes precedence over the emotion of love does not mean that biblical love is exhausted by acting lovingly. Without the emotion, love can be authentic, but it is not complete. If we act in love, ordinarily the affection will follow" (34–35).

by "love" in a variety of settings,¹⁵ so each use of the biblical love commands has to be studied in its immediate contexts to see if there are specific nuances that are being highlighted.

In Leviticus 19, the command to neighbor love appears in a verse that reads in its entirety, "Do not seek revenge or bear a grudge against anyone among your people, but love your neighbor as yourself." The importance of the command is then highlighted by the emphatic addition, "I am the LORD" (v. 18). Given that the command to love one's neighbor appears in antithetical parallelism to seeking revenge or harboring a grudge, there most likely is an emotional aspect to it. Given that "neighbor" parallels "anyone among your people," it is clear that a fellow Israelite (along with the alien or stranger in the land) is in view. The immediately preceding verse insists that the assembly under Moses's leadership "not hate a fellow Israelite" in their hearts (v. 17a). So, again, even though love and hate elsewhere can mean simply to "choose" and "reject" (or "not choose") or to "prefer more" and "prefer less," as classically in Luke 14:26 where Jesus speaks of hating family members,¹⁶ an affective dimension here in Leviticus 19 seems hard to deny. The Israelites must not hate each other in their hearts, in the seat of their emotions.¹⁷

Love here, nevertheless, must not be confused with tolerance. Leviticus 19:17b goes on at once to add, "Rebuke your neighbor frankly so that you will not share in their guilt." The Old Testament will repeatedly articulate and illustrate the principle that we are our brothers' keepers (Gen 4:9), but in a later era it will stress a change in which people are not punished in the same way that they once were for not warning others about *their* sins (see esp. Ezek 18; cf. Jer 31:29–30). This move to individual accountability continues in the New Testament, but the principle of holding fellow believers accountable remains, especially in the famous passage on church discipline in Matthew 18:15–17. The rest of Leviticus 19 contains numerous commands that can be viewed as illustrations of neighborly love: not stealing, lying, deceiving, swearing falsely, defrauding, holding back the wages of a hired hand, cursing the deaf or putting a stumbling block before the blind, perverting justice and showing partiality, slandering, and endangering a

15. See esp. Spicq, *Agape*.
16. See Stein, *Luke*, 397.
17. "While the term is often taken as meaning something other than a human emotion, such as the will, the context of vv. 17–18 shows that it is an emotional term, thus it is a command that says 'Love your neighbor whom you hate'" (Kiuchi, *Leviticus*, 354). It is also important to stress that to love someone as I love myself does not presuppose some pathology in which I actually hate myself. Nor does "as" mean "to the extent" that I love myself or imply some command to self-love. Rather it means, "just as I already love myself, now I should also love my neighbor." See further Milgrom, *Leviticus*, 234–35, for a variety of interpretations of "as yourself."

neighbor's life. And these are just the examples that appear in verses 11–16. The frequent repetition of the word "neighbor" (vv. 13, 15–18) shows that Leviticus 19 is not generalizing the love command to all people in this context. Verse 33, however, repeats the command to love the foreigner or immigrant in the land "as yourself." So the mandate is not ethnically restricted, even if it may be geographically restricted at this juncture.[18]

The still broader context of all of Leviticus 19 forms what has often been labeled "the Holiness Code."[19] Verse 1 introduces this section with the words, "The LORD said to Moses, 'Speak to the entire assembly of Israel and say to them: "Be holy because I, the LORD your God, am holy."'" Thus, loving one's neighbor as oneself is part of what it means to be holy.[20] Love is not in opposition to holiness or vice versa. Thus, it is loving to rebuke an errant neighbor, though the form (manner, wording, and tone of voice or writing) that such a rebuke takes has to be carefully thought through so that it can be seen to come from care for the person rather than merely anger or frustration.

Jesus's discussion of neighbor love in the Sermon on the Mount (Matt 5:43–48) has fueled considerable debate. In the last of his six antitheses, Jesus declares, "You have heard that it was said, 'Love your neighbor and hate your enemy.' But I tell you, love your enemies and pray for those who persecute you" (vv. 43–44). All five previous antitheses have explicitly quoted one of the Law's injunctions, but there is no Old Testament passage that commands anyone to hate their enemy in so many words. Many commentators, therefore, have suspected that Jesus uses the language "You have heard that it was said" throughout this teaching to refer not to the written Hebrew Scriptures per se, but to their oral recitation and interpretation.[21] While in the first five instances what the Israelites had heard was the same as what was written, here it is not. On this line of interpretation, Jesus is not challenging the written Law of Moses at any point, only the oral interpretations, normally aligned with Pharisaic *halakah* or legal tradition. After all, we have just seen that Leviticus 19:17 explicitly forbids hating a fellow Israelite.

On the other hand, "enemy" for Jesus may not be referring to a fellow Jew at all. The enemies of Israelites throughout the Old Testament were regularly the enemies of Israel—members of foreign nations living outside the Promised Land, often hostile to the nation and sometimes trying even to

---

18. See Hartley, *Leviticus*, 317–18.

19. Alternately taken to refer to Lev 17–19 or 17–26. See esp. Joosten, *People and the Land*.

20. Ross, *Holiness to the Lord*, 257.

21. E.g., Betz, *Sermon on the Mount*, 215–18.

conquer it. When ancient empires succeeded in conquering Israel, they often treated its people with great cruelty and exiled large numbers of people in the country. And the calls for the Israelites to fight back suggests that when Jesus speaks of hearing it said that one was to hate one's "enemy," the referent may well have been the foreigner living outside the land. There may be no explicit Old Testament text that says "hate your enemy," but the command to exterminate significant numbers of Canaanites in the time of Joshua could certainly be understood as implying it![22]

In either event, Jesus's teaching sharply contrasts with what people "heard that it was said." After listing a significant number of partial parallels in the Old Testament and Second Temple Judaism, W. D. Davies and Dale Allison opine that "despite all the parallels just listed, the succinct, arresting imperative, 'Love your enemies,' is undoubtedly the invention of Jesus's own mind and it stands out as fresh and unforgettable."[23] Jesus's rationale was that restricting one's love to those who offer love puts his followers in no better position than the despised tax collectors (Matt 5:46–47). Bandits, ruffians, and other notoriously wicked people almost always have a few close companions that they treat well, at least as long as they need their help. But a Christian ethic should be lived out on a much higher plane.

Can one come to have loving feelings for one's enemy? They certainly don't come easily. It is hard enough even if they repent, apologize, and ask for forgiveness, but what if they don't? Whatever love might mean in such a situation does not preclude church discipline, disfellowshiping, or even punishment, as the series of Jesus's teachings in Matthew 18:15–35 shows.[24] Perhaps love can be thought of as doing what is ultimately in the best interest of the other person, which may include protecting society from them (and them from the almost inevitable retaliation of someone else if they are left unprotected). On this definition, though, it would be hard ever to justify capital punishment, especially of the non-Christian, although it wasn't that long ago in the history of several Western countries that every prisoner on death row had the gospel clearly explained to them by a chaplain so that they had a chance for salvation in the life to come.[25] The Stockholm Syndrome has shown, however, that people can develop sympathetic feelings for their captors;[26] perhaps there is a sense in which Jesus intended his followers at least to try to understand those who harmed them in some way in light of

---

22. Evans, *Matthew*, 133.
23. Davies and Allison, *Saint Matthew*, 552.
24. See further Blomberg, "Building and Breaking Barriers."
25. Scott, "Priests, Prophets, and Pastors."
26. See, e.g., Sanders, *Stockholm Syndrome*, and the literature there cited.

their contexts, circumstances, and life history so that every feeling about them might not be unrelentingly negative. It is interesting to read biographies of some of the great tyrants of world history; it seems there are almost always at least a few close friends who find it possible to have somewhat happy relationships with these figures.[27] If the image of God is never entirely effaced from any human being, it should be at least theoretically possible for every person in some context to receive affection from someone else and especially from a Christian.

Jesus's enunciation of the double love command in conversation with the lawyer in the temple precincts during the last week of his life does not illuminate the meaning of neighbor love much beyond what we have already seen. The lawyer's reply, especially in the fullest Gospel account of the interchange (Mark 12:28–34), affirms Jesus's words and adds that "to love your neighbor as yourself is more important than all burnt offerings and sacrifices" (v. 33b). The Hebrew Scriptures had already taught as much with their priority of mercy above sacrifice (Hos 6:6). An exchange between a lawyer and Jesus in an entirely different context in Luke's Gospel, however, leads to the parable of the good Samaritan (Luke 10:30–37), a parable not found in any other Gospel. Here the key to recognizing the full meaning and original shock value of the story is to recognize the enmity between Jews and Samaritans in the first century. While certainly offering a model of compassion for the seriously wounded and endangered people of our world and a rebuke to those who would allow religion to become an excuse for their lovelessness, the full force of the story is missed unless one concludes that Jesus is answering the lawyer's question by teaching that even an enemy is one's neighbor.[28] Now it becomes clear how Jesus can command enemy love without contradicting the Old Testament's command to love (only?) one's neighbor. In seeing a dying person helpless and alone, surely an affective dimension to one's concern should be present, especially since we have no reason to think any of the passersby had had previous contact with the victim.

The apostle Paul cites the commandment to love one's neighbor twice. In Romans 13:8–10, he enjoins Christians in Rome not to leave any outstanding debt except the debt of loving one another, because "whoever loves others has fulfilled the law" (v. 8). He then gives sample commandments from the Decalogue, followed by a reference to all other laws, and claims they are all "summed up in this one command, 'Love your neighbor as yourself'" (v. 9). By way of at least partial definition, he adds, "Love does no harm to a neighbor" (v. 10a). It is not at first glance obvious why this definition

---

27. See, e.g., the remarkable little book by Friedrich and Thomson, *Hitler We Loved*.
28. See Blomberg, *Interpreting the Parables*.

should then lead Paul to conclude that "love is the fulfillment of the law" (v. 10b). But perhaps his point is that "the Christian who loves, and who therefore does what the law requires (vv. 9–10a), has brought the law to its culmination, its eschatological fulfillment."[29]

In Galatians 5:14–15, Paul similarly contrasts the loving with the harmful. Again, he declares that loving one's neighbor as oneself fulfills the entire Law (v. 14). The alternative is to "bite and devour each other," which leads to mutual destruction (v. 15).[30] Whether intentional or not, Paul's two quotations of the command to neighbor love together set up mutually exclusive options. In societies where people have set up all kinds of safeguards to prevent them from even having to interact with those they wish not to, it seems as though loving others and hurting them are not the only two options, or even the only main ones. Ignoring one's neighbor appears far more common! But in Romans, Paul says that not to harm someone is actually to love them, while in Galatians not to love them is actually to harm them. Each statement fits its immediate context, but put together, apathy and ignorance are excluded altogether.

James 2:8, finally, contrasts the preeminent law of neighbor love with discriminating against others. Showing partiality or favoritism, as loving as it might seem to the one given special privileges, cannot qualify as true love because of the hurt it causes to the one treated unfairly.[31] In a world in which reverse discrimination seems to be the dominant approach to compensating for previous discrimination, this is a huge, contrary principle. Mistreating majority races, privileged genders, or dominant ethnic groups is not Christian justice; two wrongs do not make a right. Already in the Holiness Code we read, "do not show partiality to the poor or favoritism to the great" (Lev 19:15);[32] yet ours is an era in which both of these sins tend to dominate, often at the same time!

---

29. Moo, *Epistle to the Romans*, 817.

30. "Perhaps their fighting stemmed from differing attitudes toward the Judaizers' activities among them. More likely, however, it was an expression of their own indigenous and loveless libertine attitudes. So in a comment similar to that of 5.12 Paul here sarcastically denounces the libertine tendencies present among his Galatian converts just as he earlier castigated the Judaizers in their midst" (Longenecker, *Galatians*, 244).

31. Exactly as Lev 19:15 against partiality is part of the context of neighbor love (v. 18). See Johnson, *Letter of James*, 236.

32. "Even though those who are disadvantaged are to be treated properly, no special favors are to be given to the poor in judicial settings" (Rooker, *Leviticus*, 257).

Implications for Interreligious Dialogue

Reverse discrimination has infected religious circles since at least the late 1960s. For years, Christians in the West had a kind of "most favored nation" status at the expense of adherents to other religions or those who favored no religion. Universities and colleges had departments of Christianity but nothing comparable for other worldviews. In the US, Christian pastors were generally respected civic leaders, and in the Bible Belt, even students in public schools had disproportionate exposure to Christian influences compared with those of other perspectives. What began as attempts to rectify imbalances have now in many places become institutionally enshrined so that Christians, especially Evangelical Christians, are systematically excluded from the public sector as much as possible.[33] Even as one segment of Western society still caricatures all Muslims as real or would-be terrorists, another large swath treats them with kid gloves and gives them religious privileges that would never be afforded to conservative Christians.[34] Ecumenical Christian efforts to bridge internal divisions do not get as much attention as they once did, not because the press has a greater appreciation of Evangelical efforts, but because all things Christian get shunted to one side by many, unless they deal with one or two hot-button issues of the moment.[35]

The result is a "lose-lose" scenario in many settings. Liberal Christians watch their churches losing numbers and feel marginalized by the mostly Evangelical megachurch movement. The megachurches, on the other hand, wonder why the press does little to publicize even huge humanitarian undertakings that they are involved in. In the US, members of non-Christian religions and even Atheists still feel sidelined compared to the sheer numbers that call themselves Christian, while Evangelicals look with dismay at the disproportionate number of Atheists who fill the world of higher education with the express purpose of changing the religious demographics for a future generation. Little wonder that interreligious dialogue is often rare, and attempts at it aren't naturally characterized by love.[36]

---

33. See esp. Carson, *Intolerance of Tolerance*.

34. The creation of words has powerful effects. "Islamophobia" has become standard. Its etymology suggests it should mean "fear of Muslims" (just like "homophobia" should mean fear of homosexuals). But it has come to refer to even the slightest act of discrimination, whether fear has anything to do with it or not. But where are the reporters documenting all the cases of Christianophobia? See further Shortt, *Christianophobia*.

35. In recent years, gender roles—and now sexual orientation—overwhelm all other topics that the press covers when dealing with religious institutions.

36. For excellent guidelines, however, see Cornille, *im-Possibility of Interreligious Dialogue*.

Evangelicals on the whole tend not to have many close friends who are faithful, practicing Jews, Muslims, Hindus, or Buddhists, even when they live close to areas where those groups proliferate. Particularly guarded or even hostile attitudes surface when the potential interreligious dialogue partner is a member of one of the sects that is an offshoot of historic Christianity, such as the Watchtower Bible and Tract Society (known popularly as Jehovah's Witnesses), the Church of Jesus Christ of Latter-day Saints (popularly known as Mormonism), or the Church of Christ, Scientist (Christian Science). Galatians 1:8–9 is freely tossed about in such settings as justification for such hostility.[37]

Nevertheless, the more one is convinced that a person or group of people are not true Christians at all, the more a godly believer should want to make others' salvation their highest priority. All the good will and good feelings toward someone else in this world proves ultimately futile if that person remains separated from God for all eternity. Confrontational evangelism has never won masses of people to the Lord, but it has proved somewhat effective in select contexts throughout history.[38] In the twenty-first-century Western world, however, its success rate appears to be at an all-time low. Loving relationships with individuals that demonstrate care for others created in the image of God—whether or not they ever become Christians—is, perhaps paradoxically, one of the best ways of gently leading people on a trajectory to following Jesus.[39]

To the charge that texts like Galatians 1:8–9 nevertheless form a timeless model for how to speak with those of other religions, several points are in order. First, as we have already seen, the context involved warnings against the Judaizers, religious insiders who were willfully distorting the faith to such a degree that no one could be saved by following their message. Interreligious dialogue (as opposed to intrareligious dialogue), virtually by definition, involves conversation with people deemed to be religious outsiders to each other. Even the so-called sects or "cults" that are offshoots of a parent religion are entirely separate groups today. They may make claims to be the true representatives of the parent religion, but to the extent that the historic expression of the faith rejects those claims, they can scarcely be termed religious insiders in any legitimate sense. Second, even the Judaizers, who still were within many of the first-century churches when Paul wrote, are not the people he is directly addressing in Galatians. He is writing

---

37. For a classic example, see Martin, *Kingdom of the Cults*, 170.

38. One thinks, e.g., of the early Billy Graham and his particularly fiery style, before he toned down his approach somewhat as he got older.

39. E.g., Prince, *Winning through Caring*; Sjogren et al., *Irresistible Evangelism*.

to those whom the Judaizers are trying to win over, warning them against doing so.[40] It is always much more appropriate for Christians to speak strongly in-house against positions they find damning than to do so when talking to adherents of those positions directly.

Third, the religious rhetoric in Paul's world was much more customarily filled with strong invective. Those from Jewish backgrounds would recall the curses the Israelites called down on themselves should they disobey the Law, while those familiar with Qumran would know how this group of Essenes spoke of all the rest of Judaism as accursed. In the Greco-Roman world, the original form of the Hippocratic Oath had doctors similarly call on the gods to punish them if they willfully harmed their patients.[41] At this early stage in church history, passionate rhetoric of this kind had not yet led to violence against members of other religions. The only religious hostility with which Christians were involved in the first century (and with rare exceptions throughout their first three centuries) was the persecution and even martyrdom that others inflicted on them. Tragically, this did not remain the case throughout the history of Christianity, when passionate rhetoric at times incited actual violence against unbelievers. The most recent, widespread examples were the pogroms against Jews in Nazi Germany in the mid-twentieth century, even if the case can be made that such behavior did not stem from anything at all genuinely Christian. The church was nevertheless manipulated so that many actual Christians were complicit, even if often indirectly. In a post-Holocaust world, then, interreligious dialogue cannot simply imitate biblical models without understanding the dynamics that gave rise to them and the very opposite effects that are often produced today by the same behaviors.[42]

The most wholesome and God-honoring forms of interreligious dialogue today, therefore, proceed along the lines that Richard Mouw has championed and modeled throughout his lengthy and distinguished ministry, which he has termed "convicted civility."[43] Little is gained if anyone's most central or deeply held views are not allowed to be discussed. Partners in dialogue must be able to talk about their most significant agreements *and* their most deeply seated disagreements. But conversations must always proceed with as much civility as possible. Mutual understanding must precede any actual debate over people's positions or views. The danger of

---

40. See Moo, *Galatians*, 75.

41. For these and similar texts and references, see Betz, *Galatians*, 50–52.

42. For excellent suggestions for applying Gal 1:8–9 in a modern Sri Lankan context, which have implications for most cultures as well, see deSilva, *Global Readings*, 91–92.

43. The title of chapter 1 in Mouw, *Uncommon Decency*.

misrepresentation of the other's perspective, even if unintentional, remains extremely high in interreligious exchanges. A good ground rule is that one should not be allowed to criticize another person's position until one can articulate it accurately enough that the other person can agree that it has been stated fairly.[44]

Even then, discussion should proceed in ways that do not unnecessarily threaten others. Calm, courteous language and tone of voice prove crucial. Asking questions of others rather than pontificating goes a long way toward fostering good will. Using "I-language" helps here as much as it does in marital relationships. "When I hear x, it seems to me that it must entail y" (where x is someone else's view and y is an undesirable consequence). "Help me understand why it doesn't entail that for you." This kind of language raises a key issue, rather than ignoring or avoiding it, but at the same time feels worlds different from "When you say x, it must entail y." I may remain strongly convinced that x does entail y, and if it is clear that I find unsatisfactory the other person's explanation of why it doesn't, my views are still crystal clear. But I have not impugned their integrity or fostered unnecessary ill will.[45]

Can we go an important step further and speak about loving those with whom we have interreligious conversations? Can that love include an affective or emotional dimension? My personal experience tells me that it can. I have been involved in various forms of Evangelical-Mormon[46] dialogue for the past twenty-five years now. For almost twenty of those years, groups of participants from both religions have met at least once, but more often twice a year in various venues around the country. Many people have come and gone, some joining us only once, many participating for quite a few years, and a few who have been present the entire time.[47] I can honestly say that I have very warm feelings for a number of the members of our Mormon "contingent," and I count several as very dear friends. I now bristle whenever I hear their viewpoints misrepresented, as often happens in the Evangelical world. I try to correct people when they perpetuate these misunderstandings. It is not merely my desire as an educator that makes me want to tell the truth about others' viewpoints, but now I recognize that some of my good friends are

---

44. Cf. Mouw, *Talking with Mormons*, 22–24, on Donald Grey Barnhouse's cautions about killing bluebirds when you thought you shot grackles!

45. I did my best to model this in Blomberg and Robinson, *How Wide the Divide?*

46. The Church of Jesus Christ of Latter-day Saints has declared that references to the Church and its members should move away from the term *Mormon*. However, it is used here out of popular reference and not a preference for the use of inappropriate terminology.

47. See the product of these gatherings in Mouw and Millet, *Talking Doctrine*.

being personally maligned and, at times, their integrity impugned. I know that they have committed to respond the same way when Evangelicals are similarly treated in Mormon circles.

None of this means I agree with all of their viewpoints. In fact, we have some very fundamental disagreements on certain issues. But the paradox and power of convicted civility is that one can share all of one's religious convictions without bracketing any of them, so that one's conversation partners very clearly understand one's beliefs, including in those areas where one would passionately wish their friends would come to share those beliefs. Yet it is precisely by refraining from actual proselytizing and by avoiding confrontational approaches or tones as often as possible that one is able to have such meaningful and wide-ranging conversations.[48]

Participation in this kind of dialogue is regularly misunderstood by those who have never tried it, and it is severely criticized by a few. It has been written, for example, that "while Blomberg is irenic and embracing with Mormons, he has great hostility toward those who uphold the 'fundamentals' of Scripture."[49] I have tried to be irenic but have not embraced Mormonism, and I have spoken pointedly, though hardly showing "great hostility," about a handful of ultraconservatives who have been consistently combative and who have consistently misrepresented those who differ from them on key topics. I have done this because that's exactly what Jesus and the apostles (especially Paul) did as models for us! The approach of these critics is precisely the approach of the Pharisees and the Judaizers in the first-century world, which has sadly often characterized significant swaths of conservative Christianity. If neighbor love extends even to one's enemies, to say nothing of those who are just different from us, then faithful Christian

---

48. See the outstanding balance between the need for both commitment and the possibility of conversion, on the one hand, and for bracketing a measure of that for the purposes of mutual understanding and parity of dialogue, on the other, in Cornille, *im-Possibility of Interreligious Dialogue*, 59–94.

49. Geisler and Farnell, "Erosion of Inerrancy," under "Blomberg's Shift in Hermeneutics." This article is chock full of misrepresentations and factual errors. The twelve most egregious I have highlighted in Blomberg, *Still Believe the Bible?*, 262–63n213. The irony is that the work they point to as indicating a major shift in my career was an article written near the beginning of it in 1984 in the *Journal of the Evangelical Theological Society*, to which they never objected until twenty-eight years later, immediately after I called out Geisler in print for his vendetta against Michael Licona. Even then, they never engaged with my argument but merely censored me and, sadly, led a number of readers seriously astray as to my actual beliefs. Equally errant and harmful are Geisler and Farnell, *Jesus Quest*; Farnell, *Vital Issues*. And yet, based on my personal experience with someone like Geisler from years ago and an understanding of his passion to uphold what he understood to be the sine qua non of Evangelical Christianity, I can even acknowledge some affection for him.

discipleship demands nothing less than interfaith dialogue with convicted civility. Neighbor love applies here as powerfully as anywhere, and it is even more incumbent in settings that have traditionally been characterized by vilification. But love never excludes rebuke of those insiders who draw the parameters of the faith far too narrowly.

Part III

Avenues of Orthopathic Multifaith Engagement

9

The Love of Christ Compels Us

Orthopathy, Mission, and Evangelism in Multifaith Environments

KAREN L. H. SHAW

WITHOUT QUESTION, THE BIBLE's leading human expert on mission and evangelism in multifaith contexts is Paul, a most passionate apostle. He pleads (Rom 12:1), cries (Acts 20:31; Phil 3:18), rejoices (Rom 5:3; Col 1:24; Phlm 7), curses (Gal 1:8–9; 1 Cor 16:22), groans (Rom 8:23; 2 Cor 5:2), longs (Rom 1:11; Phil 1:8, 23; 2 Tim 1:4), worries (Gal 4:11; 2 Cor 11:3, 28; 12:10), despairs (2 Cor 1:8), feels humiliated (1 Cor 4:9; 2 Cor 11:33), gets angry (Acts 15:2, 36; 23:3), is determined (2 Cor 2:2), maintains contentment (Phil 4:11–12), expresses frustration and dismay (Acts 14:14; Gal 3:1; 5:12), burns (2 Cor 11:29), loves (1 Cor 16:23; Phil 4:1), fears (1 Cor 2:3), trusts (2 Tim 1:12), and hopes (Rom 15:24; Phil 1:20). In the middle of expounding complicated theology, or while giving mundane ethical instructions, he is likely to burst out into doxology (Rom 1:25; 9:5; 11:36; 16:25–27; Gal 1:4–5; Eph 3:20–21; Phil 4:20; 1 Tim 1:17; 6:14–16; 2 Tim 4:18). Thus, Paul will be our guide in this chapter on orthopathic mission and evangelism in multifaith contexts. Of the hundreds of teachings and examples of orthopathy available in the Pauline corpus and in the accounts of Paul in Acts,[1] I select six gener-

---

1. I found over seven hundred passages in these books that either spoke directly about emotional states and attitudes or were written in a strongly emotional manner.

ously overlapping affective qualities that pervade Paul's missional theology, instructions, and practice.² The first will surprise no one.

Grace

In his book *What's So Amazing about Grace?*, Philip Yancey tells the story of a British conference on comparative religions, where experts from around the globe debated what, if any, belief was unique to Christianity. As Yancey relays it:

> The debate went on for some time until C. S. Lewis wandered into the room. "What's the rumpus about?" he asked, and heard in reply that his colleagues were discussing Christianity's unique contribution among world religions. Lewis responded, "Oh, that's easy. It's grace."
>
> After some discussion, the conferees had to agree. The notion of God's love coming to us free of charge, no strings attached, seems to go against every instinct of humanity. The Buddhist eightfold path, the Hindu doctrine of karma, the Jewish covenant, and the Muslim code of law—each of these offers a way to earn approval. Only Christianity dares to make God's love unconditional.³

God offers grace to people of all religious backgrounds (Rom 5:15–21). Indeed, Pauline mission is steeped in grace, a word he used more than one hundred times in his epistles.⁴

What does *grace* mean? Coldly logical Western theology has sometimes robbed the term of its affective quality, treating grace merely as a solution to a judicial dilemma. It is true that we find forensic analogies for grace, particularly in Romans (for Paul is well acquainted with Roman law), but grace is much more. Paul the Jew sees grace as God's radiant smile, as in the Levitical blessing (Num 6:24–26).⁵ His letters, without exception, begin and end with blessings of grace (Rom 1:7; 16:20; 1 Cor 1:3; 16:23; 2 Cor 1:2; 13:14; Gal 1:3; 6:18; Eph 1:2; 6:24; Phil 1:2; 4:23; Col 1:2; 4:18;

---

2. There are, of course, many more. I chose to focus on those most evident in Paul's explanations and in the practice of his own ministry.

3. Yancey, *What's So Amazing*, 45.

4. This chapter assumes the Pauline authorship of all the letters that claim it. However, if some were written by other authors seeking to imitate Paul's content and tone, this would only confirm how thoroughly passionate an impression Paul made in his life and ministry.

5. Karl Barth said, "Laughter is the closest thing to the grace of God" (Fitzhenry, *Harper Book of Quotations*, 223).

1 Thess 1:1; 5:28; 2 Thess 1:2; 3:18; 1 Tim 1:2; 6:21; 2 Tim 1:2; 4:22; Titus 1:4; 3:15; Phlm 3; 25). Paul is the apostle to the Gentiles who graciously welcomes them into God's people (Eph 3:2–8). Greek-educated Paul experiences and advertises grace as the gifts, favors, and acts of undeserved kindness shown by a patron to a needy inferior.[6] Not surprisingly, Paul uses the word this way especially in highly stratified Greek cultural settings (for example, 2 Cor 8:9; 9:8, 14–15; Eph 1:4–6; 4:7–11). We impoverish our appreciation of the word when we limit it to one understanding aligned with our own cultural values. We also impoverish our witness when we do so in multifaith environments, which are often also multiethnic.

Paul is passionate about grace, because he has experienced it (1 Tim 1:13–16). A violent enemy of Jesus and Jesus's followers, Christ graciously stopped Paul, redeemed him, and called him into the ministry of grace. The empathy is exquisite in Jesus's saying "It is hard for you to kick against the goads" (Acts 26:14).[7] From then onward, Paul lives with a poignant sense of grateful indebtedness to the kindness of God (1 Cor 15:10; Eph 3:8). Paul's great sin, he came to see, had been participation in acts of violence motivated by religious zeal.[8] Nothing will so enhance our witness and ministry among people of other religious convictions as daily, intense awe and gratitude for the profound mercy we have been shown.

For Paul, mission *is* a grace (Rom 1:5; 15:15–16; 1 Cor 3:10; 7:25; 15:10; 2 Cor 4:1; Gal 1:15; 2:9; Eph 3:2, 7–8), an unmerited honor given to him by Christ. In particular, Paul takes delight in his calling as apostle to the Gentiles (Rom 11:13), his calling to witness among those of different religious and ethnic backgrounds. Having received this calling as an undeserved gift, the apostle to the Gentiles feels himself indebted to all humanity and accountable for investing this grace as God's steward (Rom 1:14). Paul is thrilled at the chance to introduce polytheists to the bounty of God's love, even if that means jail, beatings, stonings, and shipwreck (2 Cor 7:3; 12:10). Suffering in order to proclaim to others the gospel of grace is a gift from God—not only for Paul but also for ordinary believers who share in the ministry (Phil 1:1, 29–30). We know that we are engaged in a ministry of grace when, despite all the difficulties, our hearts are buoyed with a sense of the great privilege to which we are called.

Paul's delight in bringing grace to the Gentiles is astounding. At one time, the "Pharisee of Pharisees" would have refused to touch, eat with, or

---

6. Richards and O'Brien, *Misreading Scripture*, chapter 7; deSilva, *Honor, Patronage, Kinship*, 126.

7. Unless otherwise noted, all Scripture quotations in this essay come from the NIV.

8. Flood, "Way of Peace," 34.

enter the home of a Gentile. Yet Acts and the epistles show him standing up for their right to keep their identity and culture, vehemently defending their dignity and inclusion (Gal 2:11–16), taking pride in his connection with them (Rom 11:13), bragging when they show the evidences of grace (2 Cor 8:1–2; 9:2), and living to serve them (1 Cor 9:11–23; 2 Cor 1:24; Phil 2:17). Although Paul is fully aware of Gentile sinfulness, degradation, and hard-heartedness, he is also *for* them. He doesn't just talk grace; he makes them feel it.

I live in an Islamic context. In the varied testimonies of Muslims who have trusted in Jesus, I find a common thread: nearly all were won through an experience of Christ's grace at an affective level. Some, like Paul, have had visions of Jesus that filled them with awe and comfort. Some were drawn by Gospel portrayals of God as a tender Father or Jesus as the holy friend of sinners. And nearly all, at some point, experienced the grace of God in practical ways through the love shown by Jesus's contemporary disciples. Teaching a doctrine of grace is one thing; communicating grace at the heart level is another. The greatest value of our ministry is in achieving the latter.

Once, my husband and I loaned our Orthodox neighbor Josh McDowell's *More than a Carpenter*. When he returned the book, we asked him if he found it convincing. He admitted that he had found McDowell's arguments compelling, then added, "But if that's the way Evangelicals talk to other people, I want nothing to do with them." "Let your conversation be always full of grace," writes Paul, "seasoned with salt, so that you may know how to answer everyone" (Col 4:6). Paul, who loves a good argument, recognizes the need to win people, not debates. It is hard to receive in one's heart what a strident voice says. Standards of gracious speech vary between religions, peoples, and cultures. A basic principle of ministry is to communicate using the language and style of communication that best enable the other to receive God's grace.

People will believe the behavioral and emotional messages we send before they believe our words. They will know whether we are *for* them. It is not lost on the world that some Christians eagerly support both missions in other countries and the exclusion of immigrants and refugees from their own. The mission of the true gospel of grace is the warm embrace of the other, the smile, the assistance, the unreserved welcome of God. Anything else is just religious imperialism.

Grace is profound generosity. Although Paul recognizes the right of gospel workers to receive support through their work, he cannot bring himself to do so (1 Cor 9:3–18). His financial sacrifice is a nonverbal witness to Christ's grace. Missionary support based on "dollars per conversion" may sound efficient, but it can have a devastating effect on how we view people from other backgrounds. Like Gehazi, the servant of Elisha, we could come to see God's work of grace in others as a means of meeting our own financial needs (2 Kgs 5:20–27).[9] To do so would be to morph grace into greed.

Tim Tennent tells of an extraordinary opportunity he had to speak at a mosque in the Boston area. After both Tennent and the presiding Imam had finished, one of Tennent's students asked the Imam, "Do you believe in grace?" "Yes, Muslims believe in grace," the Imam strongly affirmed. But then he added, "the only difference is that we believe you have to earn it."[10] Because grace is such a counterintuitive doctrine, Paul devotes quite a lot of time to clarifying misconceptions about how salvation by grace works. The apostle is protecting God's investment of grace in the lives of those who come to trust that grace. The Galatians need reminders that it is not enough to start with grace: one must finish the same way. Grace is not an excuse for continuing in sin (Rom 6:1–2, 15), but rather a teacher of self-control and godly living (Titus 2:12). It is tempting, when discipling new believers, to try to change their behaviors through rules, guilt, social pressure, and habituation. All religions have some in-built means of behavior modification. Paul warns that these means, which so easily infiltrate the church, do not save or produce true righteousness (Gal 4:8–10; Col 2:20–23). Only receiving the grace of Christ does that.

Humility

A true appreciation of grace must produce humility. Like grace, humility is characterized by certain thoughts and behaviors, but it begins with valuing (Phil 2:3) and appreciating who God is, who we are, and what we have been given (Phil 2:12–15).

A devout, Pharisaic Jew, Paul is clearly disgusted with the lifestyles of the pagans he describes in Romans 1:18–32. When he turns to his fellow Jews in chapter 2, we almost expect him to say, "It's disgusting! We're so much better than that! I thank God that I was not born a Gentile!" That's almost certainly what some of his own Jewish people were thinking, and Paul cuts them down to size in a few quick strokes at the start of Romans 2. He contends that a superior attitude shows contempt for God's overflowing kindness (v. 4). Paul accuses Jews of being no better, of deserving God's wrath with their "stubborn and unrepentant hearts" (v. 5). The hubris and hypocrisy of religious superiority causes the Gentiles to blaspheme (vv. 23–34).

---

9. Shaw, "Four Encounters."

10. Recounted by Tennent during a doctoral lecture at Gordon-Conwell Theological Seminary, South Hamilton, MA, January 2007.

Paul teaches that there is no difference (Rom 3:9, 22–24; Gal 3:28).[11] All of humanity is united in sin, and God longs to show his saving grace to all (1 Tim 2:3–7; Titus 3:3–8).

Paul enjoins humility (Col 3:12) and frequently warns against boasting (Rom 3:27; 1 Cor 1:29; 3:21; 4:6; 5:6; Eph 2:9; 2 Tim 3:2). Boasting is clear evidence that a person hasn't received the grace of God as a gift, but feels he or she is somehow deserving, more deserving than others (Eph 2:8–9).

When my husband, Perry, and I are on home assignment, we are frequently asked questions about Arabs or Muslims designed to elicit from us answers that prove the superiority of Christians, Westerners, or Americans over the people we love and serve. "Isn't it true that they value their own children less than we do and use them as suicide bombers?"[12] "How can you live in a country where women are not respected?" If we find these thinly veiled attempts at self-congratulations repulsive, imagine how they sound to Middle Easterners! People will not praise God because of our sectarian, racial, or national arrogance, particularly when it is built upon a comparison of the best of ours with the worst of theirs.[13]

The fact that we evangelize and send missionaries can make us feel superior, as though we are the rescuers of poor, benighted souls. Unfortunately, colonial missionary memoirs and contemporary missionary newsletters too often sound this pompous tone. Three theological truths guard against this attitude. First, we ourselves have nothing that we did not receive by the grace of God. Second, all our skills, education, efficiency, money, and efforts combined can save no one apart from Christ. Third, when we have more of something than others do, God requires more of us.

Sometimes we talk about evangelizing people of other faiths in terms of "bringing Christ to them," as though we alone possess Christ and others have no spiritual resources. Although Paul often speaks disparagingly of the state of people apart from Christ, the apostle believes firmly that God always leaves himself a witness (Acts 14:17; Rom 2:14–15) and that all people have spiritual resources available to them.[14] His practice is to find the witness to Christ in their own lives, culture, and even religion, and to build his own witness on the foundation Christ had already laid. In Lystra, it is the evidence

---

11. Shaw, "Pauline Anthropology."

12. Ironically, the person who asked this question had just heard a presentation about the tens of thousands of abortions that had taken place in the same country during the previous five years. He did not make the connection.

13. Glaser, *Bible and Other Faiths*, 199.

14. In his classic, *Eternity in Their Hearts*, Richardson provides historical examples of God leaving himself a witness in a variety of cultures prior to their exposure to the gospel.

of abundant harvests (Acts 14:17); in Athens, truths about God found in philosophical and poetic writings (Acts 17:26–28). We show humility and respect for both the work of God and for people of other backgrounds when we find signs of God's truth and activity already present in their cultures, practices, values, and even their sacred texts.

Given how vehemently Paul rejects boasting, he claims to do a lot of it. His bragging takes four forms. First, Paul boasts in the Lord, particularly in the cross of Christ (Gal 6:14). Second, he crows about his own weakness, so that the grace and power of Christ may be seen more easily (2 Cor 11:30; 12:10). Third, although he can't boast of his gospel ministry since he feels compelled to do it, he is proud to proclaim Christ without financial remuneration (1 Cor 9:15–18). Finally, Paul takes extreme pride in the spiritual growth and accomplishments of the people among whom he has served (2 Cor 7:4, 14; 1 Thess 2:19–20; 2 Thess 1:4). The great apostle to the Gentiles believes in his heart that he has nothing to brag about. Perhaps we do not either.[15]

Anger

I am uncomfortable associating anger with evangelism and mission. Anger toward the religious other seems to be the very soul of the pride I have just denounced. Yet there is no escaping the wrath of God in Paul's letters. God is outraged by sin. In Romans 1, Paul explains why. Humanity has chosen to suppress the truth about God, ignoring all the evidence, and to demean the Creator by portraying him as something less worthy than he is. We have not listened to God's wisdom, but only our own, nor have we worshipped and served him as he deserves.

According to Paul, God expresses divine anger in two ways. In the past and the present, God restrains the violent expression of his anger and simply lets people suffer the degrading and deadly consequences of their rebellion (Rom 9:22). "God gave them over" is one of the saddest expressions of Scripture (Rom 1:24). In the future, on the "day of wrath," God will no longer restrain his fury, and those who refuse the grace and truth God offers will die. Although there is currently much debate about how and for how long God will pour out his final anger, the Scriptures are clear that the day of God's anger will come—and with severity (1 Thess 1:10; 2:16; 2 Thess 1:6–9).

It is right that Christians share with God in God's wrath. When my Muslim friend tells me that on judgment day Jesus will prostrate himself in prayer to God behind Muhammad, my blood boils. When an Atheist mocks me for having Jesus as my "imaginary friend," I resent it bitterly. When

---

15. Sudworth, "Missional Discipleship," 92; Shaw, "Pauline Anthropology."

minority Christians lose their lives, their freedom, or their children because they have spoken the truth about Jesus where the majority reject his lordship, I seethe with the injustice of it. But as James notes, human anger does not accomplish divine righteousness (Jas 1:20). On the contrary, prolonged anger or anger that results in unrighteous behavior gives the devil, rather than the gospel, a foothold (Eph 4:26–27).

God's call to mission and evangelism is a call to love despite anger. God is angered by sin precisely *because* he loves so deeply, just as we often get angriest with the bad choices of those dearest to us.[16] The New Testament does not command us to express our ire to people of other religions. On the contrary, we are to put to death all the anger, wrath, and malice within us (Col 3:8; 1 Tim 2:8). When we are stewing, we are tempted to take revenge; but Paul warns us that vengeance belongs to God alone (Rom 12:19–20; 1 Thess 5:15).[17] Calls to take arms for God or to avenge verbal and physical violence against Christians and churches are just plain wrong, biblically speaking, however justified they may seem.[18] That sort of anger is reserved for the day of Christ's appearing.

But what about the other expression of God's indignation? When I first came to the Middle East, I was disturbed by the apathy shown by many Middle Eastern Christians toward the evangelization of Muslims. I was told repeatedly that Muslims were a hopeless case—utterly unconvertable. More than once I heard dedicated Christian leaders apply Matthew 7:6 to Muslims: "Do not give dogs what is sacred; do not throw your pearls to pigs." Were not these Christians simply expressing anger as God does—by leaving Muslims to believe what they want to believe and suffer the consequences?

Paul would vehemently object. Our message of justification saves all who would believe from God's wrath (Rom 5:9). Despite his anger, God chose to go to extreme lengths to love those who have rejected or misrepresented him. While allowing people to go their own way may be an expression of God's anger, it also expresses the kindness, patience, and tolerance of God in giving people opportunity to repent (Rom 2:4).[19] We are ministers of reconciliation, not avenging angels.

16. Elliott, *Faithful Feelings*, 227–28.
17. Flood, "Way of Peace," 35.
18. Fraser, "Karl Barth Taught Us."
19. I write particularly in the context of multifaith relationships. However, Paul does have occasion to cut off members of the two religious communities to which he belongs. After giving his Jewish brothers the first opportunity to receive the gospel, Paul responds to their rejection by leaving them to their unbelief and going to the Gentiles (Acts 13:47; 28:25–28). He hopes that by doing so, he will cause them to become jealous and come to believe (Rom 11:13–14). Paul practices or urges the shunning of certain

Two examples from the life of Paul illustrate anger channeled into love. In Lystra, the locals respond to a healing miracle by trying to worship Paul and Barnabas as incarnations of two of their pagan gods (Acts 14:11–12). The apostles are terribly distressed and tear their clothes. Yet their correction is gentle, reminding the Lystrans of God's goodness (Acts 14:15–17). In Athens, Paul is filled with anger at the predominance of idolatry (Acts 17:16),[20] but he directs that anger into an evangelistic speech characterized by respect and affirmation of the best in Athenian religion and culture. The anger we feel when we are confronted with the lies and sin in the religions of others needs to be redirected into creative expressions of the persistent love of our angry, patient, tenderhearted Father.

Peace and Reconciliation

Westerners have a tendency to understand the affective largely in terms of the self. Yet relationships profoundly impact our hearts and collective emotions: devastation at a betrayal, mutual contentment after a holiday meal and pleasant conversation, national euphoria when our athletes win the gold, ennui in a mildly dysfunctional and visionless workplace, tension during a church split, or communal grief when a child is murdered.[21] Paul everywhere assumes that the affective happens in the context of relationships with God and others. After grace, peace is Paul's most common blessing (Rom 1:7; 15:14; 1 Cor 1:3; 2 Cor 1:2; 13:11; Gal 1:3; 6:16; Eph 1:2; 6:23; Phil 1:2; 1 Thess 1:1; 2 Thess 1:2; 3:16; 1 Tim 1:2; 2 Tim 1:2; Titus 1:4; Phlm 3), and this peace carries with it both the sense of peace of mind (Rom 8:6; Phil 4:7) and relational health (Rom 14:17–19; 1 Cor 7:15; Eph 2:14).

People long to be at peace, to find integrity with self, others, and God. Religion often gives shape to that longing, as people "seek him and perhaps reach out for him and find him" (Acts 17:27). God, too, is longing to be reconciled with his estranged children, and his initiative at healing the breach in Christ forms the basis for inner tranquility, intimate Christian fellowship, and our attitude toward people of other religions (or of no religion). God's ultimate goal is to unite and restore all things in Jesus (Eph 1:10; Col 1:17–20). He wants to save all people (1 Tim 2:3–4).

---

church members because of gross immorality and/or false teaching (1 Cor 5:11, 1 Tim 1:20; 2 Tim 3:5). Again, in each case, the person is rejected or "handed over to Satan" with the hope that he may have a change of heart (2 Cor 2:7–8).

20. Strange, "Ministry."

21. Dennis Kinlaw argues convincingly that biblical personhood is always person-in-relationship, reflecting the persons of the Trinity. See Kinlaw, *Let's Start with Jesus*, 71–106.

Therefore, like Christ, we preach peace to those who are far and those who are near (Eph 2:17), who do not know the way of peace (Rom 3:10–18). Our message is profoundly affective: in Christ you can be at peace with God (Rom 5:1), with yourself, with people of other backgrounds, and eventually, with the whole of creation.

We ground our evangelism and mission, then, in the longings of both God and humanity for rapprochement. If God yearns to be reconciled, then we persuade and even implore people (2 Cor 5:11, 20). Christ's love compels us to do so (2 Cor 5:14). The intensity of our longing for the salvation of others reflects the ache of God. We are for others the face of God's longing. Whether or not they respond, we treat them as people of immense value, for God has treated them so.

Our lives must match our message, as we do everything in our power to live at peace with all people (Rom 12:18; Eph 4:2–4; 1 Thess 4:11–12). In everything from friendship evangelism to formal debate, our verbal and nonverbal communication should convey a readiness for peace consistent with the gospel (Eph 6:15; Titus 3:1–2). Christians should, in multifaith encounters, take the lead in modeling how the belief in an exclusive path to salvation can, after all, be compatible with humble, other-affirming relationships. We point to Jesus, rather than attacking people and religions. We voluntarily lay aside our culture, convenience, and preferences to demonstrate to others not like ourselves that God loves them and wants to win them as they are (1 Cor 9:19–22). We reject the extractionism that demands that people break completely with family, friends, culture, and nation in order to follow Christ.[22]

Peace and reconciliation are hard, slow work. Paul's letters show that learning to be at peace requires long-term discipleship. New believers need to learn how to honor and submit to non-Christian governments without compromising (Rom 13:1–7), to put the needs of others before their own (Phil 2:4), and to know the love and truth of Christ more profoundly, so that the fullness of Christ, whose goal is unity, will enable them to be built up together with others (Eph 3:16—4:16). The unity of the church is an essential witness to the God of peace. The heart cry of God to be reunited with his lost people becomes the basis for passionate evangelism, fervent prayer (Rom 10:1; 1 Tim 2:1–4), and patient, persistent, life-long discipleship.

---

22. Glaser, *Bible and Other Faiths*, 194.

Boldness and Zeal

It comes as a surprise to find Paul, of all people, asking his readers to pray for him that he will proclaim the gospel boldly (Eph 6:19–20). If *he* finds it difficult, it is small wonder that many of the rest of us are tempted to be overly cautious in sharing our faith with people of other religions. Paul is probably writing from a Roman prison, waiting to stand trial before the emperor. The sentence could be death. He has already suffered a long list of rejections, beatings, arrests, and attempted lynchings, not to mention the dangers of shipwreck and robbers on his travels. He keeps at it, for he is consumed by zeal to evangelize where Christ is not known (Rom 15:20; 2 Tim 2:10). But Paul is human, and the constant dangers and malicious rejections take their toll. So he urges his readers to arm themselves for spiritual warfare for the sake of the gospel, and to pray for courage and strength (Eph 6:10–11, 18–20).

Zeal has a bad reputation. Most people associate it with fanatic, arrogant, bigoted, self-righteous crusaders, people with a cause but without compassion, people with Taser tongues, stopped-up ears, engorged spleens, and granite hearts. This is exactly the sort of intense, hate-filled person Paul had become before he was blinded by the risen Christ (Acts 9:1–2).[23] His zeal and boldness do not die but, like the rest of Paul's personality, become transformed by that encounter into a zeal for blessing, rather than destroying, those of different religious persuasions.[24]

Paul sees his old self in the Jews who attack him and his ministry (Gal 1:13–14; Eph 3:4–6). He admits that they have zeal—a great quality in Paul's book (e.g., 2 Cor 8:17, 22)—but it is a faulty zeal, zeal "not based on knowledge" (Rom 10:2). The fundamental problem with their ardor is that they think that by their efforts in enforcing the Law they can bring about righteousness (Rom 10:3). Not true. Only Christ can produce that righteousness. There is a different flavor to the zeal of those who are filled with the Spirit of Christ, for they exude love, joy, peace, patience, kindness, goodness, faithfulness, gentleness, and self-control. Such evangelists are beautiful, for they bring good news (Rom 10:14–17), compelled by God's love (2 Cor 5:14).

Contrast the zealousness of Christians who assume that witness to Christ consists in telling others that their beliefs are wrong and criticizing them for not living up to biblical standards of holiness. Correcting and shaming people

---

23. Flood, "Way of Peace," 34.

24. Flood, "Way of Peace," 35. Flood notes how Paul, in quoting the Hebrew Scriptures regarding the Gentiles, omits all expressions of violence toward or superiority over them.

into conformity will not produce holiness. Zeal with theological and emotional intelligence is a wholehearted ardor (Rom 1:9; 6:17; 1 Cor 15:58) that attracts by its grace (1 Cor 1:3–5). It is this zeal that Paul enjoins.

What do godly zeal and boldness look like in us? For starters, we do not care what other people think of us, and we do not fear them (1 Cor 3; Gal 2:6; Col 2:16; 2 Tim 1:6–8). Boldness is having the courage to be disliked, disagreed with and rejected, and not taking these painful rebuffs to heart. Worrying about others' opinions of us will make us timid and tentative in our speaking and not convey confidence in our Lord Jesus Christ. In fact, Paul contends that we cease being servants of Christ and become servants of human opinion when we feel compelled to please them (Gal 1:10). Nor do we fear how people may harm us or our community (Phil 1:27–28; 1 Thess 2:2). Although most people are peaceable, fanatics exploit religions to foster violence. Even fanatics are not to be feared, for witnesses to the truth have often been martyrs, and we have a hope beyond the grave. Although Paul avoids persecution when he can do so with integrity, he will not run from his calling.

Paul cares nothing for what people think of him, but he cares a great deal for what people think of the gospel. He does everything in his power to present the gospel in ways that are winning and clear to his hearers (1 Cor 9:19–23; 2 Cor 14:23). He is distressed when believers give people outside the church unclear, incorrect, or embarrassing impressions of the faith (1 Cor 5:1; 6:1; 1 Tim 6:1; 2 Tim 2:9–10). Paul has died to his own reputation and even his own life, but he lives with fervor for the glory of Christ's name.[25] Zeal is "making the most of every opportunity," through wise and gracious responses to the questions of non-Christians (Col 4:5–6).

Christians fall into two equal and opposite errors regarding zeal. On the one hand, some confuse their own glory with Christ's and feel the need to "defend Christ," as though the one through whom the worlds were made needs human protection! We are Christ's witnesses, not his bodyguards.

On the other hand, some (and I am one of these) are so afraid of misrepresenting the gospel to people of other religions that we hesitate to say anything, missing one opportunity after another for fear of saying the wrong thing. This reluctance reminds me of a paramedic who had worked for sixteen years in an intensive care ambulance unit and who had urged untrained people to act in life-or-death situations, even when unsure of what to do. While admitting that it is possible to kill a person by administering the wrong treatment, he insisted he had never seen that happen. However,

---

25. For the application of the model of Pauline zeal to mission in India and Asia, see Vithayathil, "Paul, Model for Mission."

he had witnessed dozens of tragedies in which friends and family, paralyzed with the fear of doing the wrong thing, had stood helplessly by and watched their loved one die, as the ambulance came too late. I've learned over the years that even my mistakes can be used as a chance for reopening a spiritual conversation with Muslim friends.

Discussing faith with people of other religions can be difficult. Our faith matters intensely to us. The other person may raise doubts about the foundation of our lives. We also may say things that cause others distress as they wrestle with the possibility that they have been wrong all their life, or face the terrible choice of whether to trust Jesus or keep the love, security, and acceptance of everyone they cherish. It is rare for anyone to choose to follow Christ without first experiencing distressing internal conflict, and this tension is intensified in people raised in other religions, as they struggle with issues of loyalty, identity, and belonging. Faith is not too squeamish to walk empathetically with the other through this pain, having complete confidence that the knowledge of Christ is worth the profound loss and agonizing rejection that may follow.

Paul reminds Titus that God is raising up for himself a people "zealous for good works" (Titus 2:14; cf. 1 Thess 5:15, ESV). Devotion requires discipline. In his effort to win people from all backgrounds, the apostle is severe on himself: "I pummel my body and make it a slave" (1 Cor 9:24–27; 15:10; ESV). He does this not only by facing the hardships of travel and persecution but in the consistency and angst of his prayers for people (e.g., Rom 10:1; Eph 1:15–20; 3:14–21) and his willingness to carry the weight of daily concern for the people who had come to faith through his ministry (2 Cor 11:28).

Holy boldness is infectious. You would think that watching others suffer for the faith would discourage a person from being a courageous witness. Paul finds exactly the opposite (Phil 1:14). Our boldness in speaking of Christ to people of other backgrounds not only makes our witness more credible to them, not only builds our own devotion to our Lord Jesus, but also gives courage to others who are holding back.

Power and Weakness

Power in weakness is the hallmark of Christian witness in the world. Paul describes the psychological suffering he experienced in his ministry: fear and trembling (1 Cor 2:3), humiliation (1 Cor 4:8–13), feeling utterly crushed to the point of despair (2 Cor 1:3–11), anguish (2 Cor 2:4), confusion (2 Cor 4:7–12), daily pressure and anxiety, and indignation (2 Cor

6:3–10).²⁶ He writes to the Corinthians while being, "by his own admission, an emotional wreck" (1 Cor 2:3; 12:7; 2 Cor 1:8; 7:5).²⁷ Ask any sports coach about the relationship between passion and power, and you'll get an earful. Ultra-talented athletes relentlessly trained by premiere coaches can fail despite all their ability and strength, if they let discouragement, anger, or grief sap their energy, or if they become overconfident. A person's attitudes and emotions help create, as well as react to, the experience of physical, social, and moral strength.

The gospel is the power of salvation for every sort of person (Rom 1:16). Paul's confidence in the gospel's power protects his ministry (2 Tim 1:6–8, 12; 4:16–17). He has no need to be intellectually or emotionally manipulative in his efforts to win people (1 Cor 2:1–5; 2 Cor 1:12; 11:20–21; 1 Thess 2:5), for it is God who saves people in Christ.

Paul prays that the believers in the churches he has planted will know God's "incomparably great power for us who believe" (Eph 1:19–21). He urges them to "be strong in the Lord and in his mighty power," in order to stand against all sorts of temporal and spiritual forces (Eph 6:10–11; 1 Tim 2:1). Paul speaks from experience (1 Tim 1:12). He is able to maintain emotional equilibrium and contentment in the face of traumas and relentless hardships because of the power of Christ living in him (2 Cor 4:1, 16; 5:8). "I have learned to be content. . . . I can do all this through him who gives me strength" (Phil 4:11–13). Whether teaching, discipling, proclaiming, performing miracles, or simply persisting in ministry, Paul succeeds by the intense, quotidian experience of the energy of the risen Lord in him (Col 1:28–29). The experience of God's power brings hope, patience, joy, and godliness (Rom 15:13; Eph 1:18–19; Col 1:11, 27; 2 Thess 2:16–17).

This exhilarating, triumphant experience of power comes, ironically, through profound weakness. It is the power of the cross, the key theme of Paul's ministry. Instead of religious one-upmanship, Paul advocates the counterintuitive strategy of weakness and transparent vulnerability (1 Cor 2:1–5; 2 Cor 13:4). Only by allowing those of other religions to view our inadequacies can they witness firsthand the ability of Christ to make something out of nothing. Our weaknesses become a delight rather than a frustrating impediment to sharing our faith with others, others who may gloat over us at first but then be surprised to see something in us that could only come from God.²⁸ In fact, according to Jonathan Edwards, the only way we can be sure a person's conversion is genuine is by seeing in

---

26. Gorman, *Cruciformity*, 286–87.
27. Gorman, *Cruciformity*, 281.
28. Shaw, "Divine Heartbeats," 13.

him or her a change of affections, which could only have come about by the work of the Spirit.[29]

We do not offer a better religion, but the power of God in Christ. Therefore, we reject a competitive, triumphal attitude toward our Muslim, Buddhist, Hindu, Jewish, Animist, and Atheist neighbors. "Our struggle is not against flesh and blood," but for them, to introduce them to the life-giving vigor of the risen Christ. If we view others as the enemy, we will begin, like Cain, to draw on our own deadly force, or end up cowering as though Christ were not Lord over all the powers.

For people to see the power of Christ in us, two things must happen. First, we must cease relying on and showing off our own strength: our intellectual or speaking abilities, our more admirable morals, the superior benefits of our religion to society, or our ability to better manipulate the political apparatus and media for our religion's benefit. These will only serve as a distraction to the true gospel and confirm a worldly view of power that denies the necessity of the cross. Our role is to "always carry around in our body the death of Jesus, so that the life of Jesus may also be revealed in our body" (2 Cor 4:10). Therefore, we abstain from complaining or arguing as an essential part of our witness (Phil 2:14–16), welcoming the circumstances and people who will provide opportunities for God to show his strength in our weakness. We refuse to be despondent, regardless of the reactions of others, because we believe in God's power.

The second thing that must happen is beyond our control: God shows his strength in our lives and ministries in surprising ways. My Muslim neighbor Layla was touched by the compassion and healing power of Jesus when I prayed for her in his name and her test for cancer later came back negative. The Animist father of a Nigerian friend came to faith in Christ by observing that the prayers of Christians were more powerful in their effect than the practices of the local shaman. While we do not own the power or make the miracles happen, and we cannot force God's hand, we are confident of his ability and willingness to act.

One approach to mission seeks to influence the powerful of society to believe, hoping for a trickle-down effect. There is nothing wrong with this, and there are certainly biblical precedents. However, it may be that the power of God's salvation can be seen more clearly in the transformation of the poor and ignoble (1 Cor 1:26–29). They should not be dismissed, as though the success of our work depends on human wealth, position, and influence.

---

29. Edwards, *Treatise on Religious Affections*, 45. On the value of Edwards's "signs" for missionary practice, see Hiebert et al., *Understanding Folk Religion*, 374–84.

Recognizing that God alone is able to save takes the anxiety out of multifaith encounters. We stop looking at people as projects, as potential conversions needed to justify our budget and to prove that we are successful. We pray and serve, but we do not feel intense pressure to "fix" people and situations, or to win the argument for the sake of the Lord's reputation. God's reputation is God's problem. Our problem is our strength: only by dying to self and finding our vitality in God will we woo people from other religions to see the power of Christ as a source of hope.

Conclusion

I once met an Iranian who had come to faith in Christ through the ministry of Presbyterian missionary Bill Miller (1892–1993). Radin[30] was a schoolboy at the time, and he and his mates heckled, insulted, and threatened Miller as he evangelized. Miller responded with humility, patience, and grace. Denied the satisfaction of getting a reaction from the Christian, the boys resorted to calling out insulting things about Jesus. To their amazement and dismay, Miller began to weep. He told them, "Oh, if only you knew him!" The boys slunk away, ashamed. That evening, Radin slipped silently into Miller's house and gave his life to Christ. His gratitude and love were palpable as he talked about Jesus over half a century later.

Grace, humility, rechanneled anger, peace and reconciliation, zeal and boldness, power and weakness: in these, others see "not I, but Christ."

---

30. Not his real name.

10

Emotional Evangelism, Affective Apologetics

Adam C. Pelser

The Christian gospel is the incredibly good news that Jesus Christ has made a way for us to be saved from our enslavement to sin and spiritual death through his sacrificial death on a Roman cross and his death-defeating resurrection on the third day. By sinning against God and others, we have made ourselves enemies of God our Creator and heavenly Father. But all who place their faith in Christ for salvation are forgiven by God and live at peace with him forever (John 3:16; Rom 5:1). Jesus himself is the only true and living Way to this flourishing, eternal life (John 14:6; cf. 10:10).

Evangelism is the announcing of this wonderful news through preaching and personal witness. Apologetics is the practice of explaining the Christian faith in a way that helps people to see and understand the truth of the gospel more clearly. Dallas Willard defines apologetics as a "helping ministry of believers, relevant to both the evangelistic and the pastoral role, in which people with existential, concrete problems that hinder their trusting God in Christ are helped to a better view of the truths of God, of redemption and of life in the Kingdom."[1] Willard's definition highlights the two primary aims of apologetics: (1) increasing the confidence of the Christian and (2) helping the unbeliever overcome obstacles to believing in God and trusting God in Christ for salvation. Evangelism and apologetics thus go hand in hand. And as I will

---

1. Willard, "Apologetics Glossary."

argue here, proper appreciation for and cultivation of our emotions—indeed, orthopathy—is crucial to them both.

Seeing God with the Eyes of Our Hearts

On the day that Jesus rose from the dead, Cleopas and another follower of Jesus were walking from Jerusalem to the village of Emmaus. Luke tells us that their mood was solemn and their faces downcast as they reflected on Jesus's crucifixion. But they were also feeling a kind of puzzled amazement because they had heard reports that some of the women who followed Jesus had found his tomb empty and had seen a vision of an angel who proclaimed that Jesus was still alive (Luke 24:22–24). This was astonishing news, but Cleopas and his friend didn't know what to make of these miraculous reports.

A mysterious stranger approached them on their walk and asked what they were discussing. They were shocked by the stranger's apparent ignorance of the dramatic trial and crucifixion of Jesus. Where had this stranger been the past few days—under a rock?! But after listening to their explanation of the events that had taken place, the stranger surprised them even more by chastising them for their own ignorance of the prophecies that foretold the Messiah's suffering and resurrection glory (vv. 25–27). Over the course of their seven-mile walk to Emmaus, the stranger explained what the Scriptures prophesied about Jesus. When they arrived in Emmaus, the stranger acted like he was continuing on, but Cleopas and his traveling companion invited the wise stranger to stay and have dinner with them. Then Luke tells us that "when he was at table with them, he took the bread and blessed and broke it and gave it to them. And their eyes were opened, and they recognized him. And he vanished from their sight. They said to each other, 'Did not our hearts burn within us while he talked to us on the road, while he opened to us the Scriptures?'" (vv. 30–32).[2]

This fascinating account of Jesus's first post-resurrection supper points to a surprising truth about the way our emotions can function as evidence for God and the gospel. Cleopas and his companion seemed to recognize Jesus through their emotions—their hearts burning within them—before they even recognized him with their eyes. In fact, Luke suggests that in hindsight they realized that their emotions had been a kind of evidence that revealed the familiar identity of the resurrected Lord.

Of course, in our post-Enlightenment culture, it is widely believed that emotions cannot be evidence for anything. In a poignant scene in the recent

---

2. All Scripture quotations in this essay are from the ESV.

film *The Case for Christ*, Leslie Strobel expresses her newfound emotional confidence in the Christian faith to her still skeptical husband, Lee. In response, Lee's character gives voice to the view of many today: "Those are just feelings. Feelings aren't proof of anything!" Like the pre-Christian Lee, many critics of Christianity argue that religious and moral beliefs are ultimately based on emotions and, thus, that religious and moral beliefs are irredeemably irrational. We are told that if we want to be ideally rational in our judgments and decision-making, we have to check our emotions at the door of the classroom, the conference room, the courtroom, and even the church. After all, appeal to emotion is listed in many logic textbooks as one of the primary forms of informal logical fallacies. Many well-meaning Christian apologists have responded to such criticisms by arguing that belief in God and the gospel is supported by a great deal of historical, scientific, and philosophical evidence. Thus, they argue, Christian belief need not and, indeed, *should not* be based on emotions. But what if it isn't always irrational to believe on the basis of emotions? What if our emotions actually can be a kind of evidence for God and the gospel? I will argue here that they can.

In his classic apologetic work, *Pensées*, the French philosopher and mathematician Blaise Pascal wrote that "the heart has its reasons of which reason knows nothing. . . . It is the heart which perceives God and not the reason."[3] Pascal understood "the heart" to be the seat of all intuitive knowledge and not merely the seat of the emotions, but the emotions are the source of much of the heart's intuitive knowledge, especially intuitive-perceptual knowledge of God. One of the most direct and intimate ways that we can know God is through rational-emotional perception. And often the most compelling defense of the truth of Christianity is when Christians demonstrate gospel-shaped emotional lives of joy, hope, and peace, along with a humbly confident passion for the truth that is rooted in love for God and for our neighbors. Therefore, it is crucial for Christians not to neglect or ignore the emotions when they are helping others come to know God and see the truth of the gospel. All Christians engaged in evangelism and apologetics ought to learn how to cultivate accurate emotional perceptions in themselves and others so that, in the words of the apostle Paul, "the eyes of [our] hearts" might be "enlightened" (Eph 1:18).[4]

---

3. Pascal, *Pensées*, 127 (entries 423–24).

4. This paragraph and some material in the following section has been adapted, with permission, from Pelser, "Reasons of the Heart."

Emotional Value-Vision

In order to appreciate and make proper use of the emotional evidence for God, we must begin by correcting the misconception that emotions are inherently irrational. Contrary to this popular view, emotions can be important sources of information about the world. In fact, many philosophers and psychologists, going back at least as far as the ancient Greek philosopher Aristotle, have recognized that emotions are cognitive mental states that function as a kind of perception.[5] Like sense perceptions, emotions present specific features of their objects to our minds, making it seem to us as though the object really has the feature we are perceiving. Through our five senses we directly experience the physical features of material objects, such as their shape, temperature, color, flavor, aroma, and sound. Emotions, by contrast, enable us to experience—to "see"—nonphysical features of the world, such as beauty, wickedness, justice, and dignity. As C. S. Lewis puts it, emotions are "recognitions of objective value."[6] In short, *emotions are perceptions of value*. Emotions are a kind of *value-vision*. They are, to use the apostle Paul's phrase, "the eyes of [our] hearts" (Eph 1:18).

We see the shape and color of a snowcapped mountain range with the eyes in our heads, but we see and experience its *beauty* and *sublimity* with the eyes of our hearts. We see photographs of the physical imprisonment and killing of the Jews in the Nazi concentration camps with the eyes in our heads, but we see and experience the *horrific evil* of the Holocaust, or Shoah, with the eyes of our hearts. It is through visual perception that we see colors and shapes in all of their variety and particularity, but it is through emotions that we see goodness and badness, beauty and ugliness, in all of their variety and particularity. Specific emotion types help us to experience specific kinds of value or disvalue. In fear, for example, the object of fear really appears *dangerous*. In anger, the object really seems to be *morally culpable* for a serious *injustice*. In compassion, we perceive the object of our compassion as a *person of worth* whose well-being matters and whose suffering ought to be remedied if possible. In our emotional perceptions of awe, the object of our awe really appears *awesome* and *sublime*.

As perceptions of value, emotions can help us to "see" features of the world that point to God, and they can even help us to experience God

---

5. For some contemporary defenses of the kind of perceptual theory of emotions I will sketch here, see Roberts, *Spiritual Emotions*; *Emotions in the Moral Life*, 38–112; Zagzebski, *Divine Motivation Theory*, 51–95; Pelser, "Emotion, Evaluative Perception." For a helpful overview of perceptual theories of emotion and their competitors, see Deigh, "Concepts of Emotions."

6. Lewis, *Abolition of Man*, 19.

himself. Like Jesus's disciples on the road to Emmaus, people often recognize God with the eyes of their hearts even when they can't see him with the eyes in their heads. Of course, our emotions can serve as evidence for God and the gospel only when they are functioning properly—that is, only when our emotional vision has not been too blurred or blinded by sin or other sources of emotional malformation. As is the case with other kinds of evidence for God, the emotional evidence for God is easily missed by those who are not looking and by those who, on account of emotional malformation, do not have "eyes to see." Fortunately, just as sin has not completely deformed our physical senses or our ability to reason, neither has sin completely destroyed our ability to see the world rightly through our emotions.

The Emotional Evidence for God: Beyond a "Burning in the Bosom"

Readers who have engaged in much dialogue with Mormons might be wondering at this point how the emotional evidence for God is any different from the Mormon concept of a "burning in the bosom." According to a prophecy delivered by Joseph Smith, the way that he and his scribe, Oliver Cowdery, could know that their translation of a particular divine revelation was accurate was that they would feel a burning in their bosom. Here is the relevant passage from the Mormon scriptural book *Doctrine and Covenants*:

> But, behold, I say unto you, that you must study it out in your mind; then you must ask me if it be right, and if it is right I will cause that your bosom shall burn within you; therefore, you shall feel that it is right. But if it be not right you shall have no such feelings, but you shall have a stupor of thought that shall cause you to forget the thing which is wrong; therefore, you cannot write that which is sacred save it be given you from me. (9:8–9)

In popular Mormon thought, this concept of a "burning in the bosom" has been taken to be powerful spiritual evidence of the truth of the Book of Mormon and of divine revelation generally, at least for those who are fortunate enough to have experienced it.

The precise affective character of the burning in the bosom, however, is not entirely clear. Elder Dallin H. Oaks, first counselor in the First Presidency and president of the LDS governing body known as the Quorum of the Twelve Apostles, explains:

> What does a "burning in the bosom" mean? Does it need to be a feeling of caloric heat, like the burning produced by combustion?

> If that is the meaning, I have never had a burning in the bosom. Surely, the word "burning" in this scripture [*Doctrine and Covenants* 9:8] signifies a feeling of comfort and serenity. That is the witness many receive. That is the way revelation works.[7]

It sounds odd to my ear to characterize a "burning in the bosom" as "a feeling of comfort and serenity." The language of "burning" seems to indicate a kind of excitement or passion rather than serenity. Setting this interpretive question aside, the important thing to note here is that the kind of emotional evidence that can lend support to Christian belief has more specific perceptual content than the ambiguous "burning" feeling in Mormon theology.

In the absence of a carefully worked out view of the emotions, however, many Christian evangelists and apologists are not any better equipped to understand or describe the emotional evidence for God than are most Mormons who appeal to the inchoate concept of the burning in the bosom. Even Cleopas and his traveling companion could not do much better than to appeal to their "hearts burning within" in their attempt to describe their emotional evidence for Christ. If we don't understand how emotions work, we will not be equipped to explain how emotions can serve as evidence for God without unwittingly supporting the appeals of Mormons to a burning in the bosom (and other similarly inchoate appeals to emotion in support of non-Christian religious beliefs).

As explained above, particular emotion types are perceptions of specific kinds of value. For example, awe is a perception of sublimity and transcendent greatness. The related emotion of wonder is a perception of some object as exceedingly great beyond our ability fully to comprehend its greatness. The most effective presentations of traditional arguments for the existence of God, such as the cosmological argument, the teleological argument, and the design argument, evoke and appeal to the cosmic emotions of awe and wonder, helping us to see the beauty and sublimity of creation and then to see beyond it to our divine Creator. For it is precisely in and through such cosmic emotions that we see that "the heavens declare the glory of God, and the sky above proclaims his handiwork" (Ps 19:1).[8]

Likewise, the most effective presentations of the traditional moral argument for God's existence evoke and appeal to moral emotions such as admiration, anger, and guilt, which help us to see—and feel—the existence of an objective moral law, which then points to the existence of a divine Moral Lawgiver. As Paul explains:

---

7. Oaks, "Teaching and Learning," 13.

8. For an in-depth discussion and defense of the ideas in this paragraph, see West and Pelser, "Perceiving God."

> When Gentiles, who do not have the law, by nature do what the law requires, they are a law to themselves, even though they do not have the law. They show that the work of the law is written on their hearts, while their conscience also bears witness, and their conflicting thoughts accuse or even excuse them on that day when, according to my gospel, God judges the secrets of men by Christ Jesus. (Rom 2:14–16)

This passage is particularly relevant for multifaith engagement because it suggests that even those who do not believe in the gospel of Jesus Christ have God's law "written on their hearts" and will be judged by God according to how they acted and also how they felt ("their conscience . . . and their conflicting thoughts") in response to their emotional knowledge of God's moral law.

In light of the way that emotions can function as evidence for God, the best apologetic arguments do not appeal merely to cold, logical reasoning; they also appeal to our affect—that is, our feelings. In short, the most effective apologetics is *affective* apologetics. Yet the best apologetic arguments do not appeal to inchoate feelings like a "burning in the bosom," but rather to particular emotions that reveal particular kinds of value that point to the reality of God and the gospel. If the church is to present a compelling apologetic case for the Christian worldview, therefore, we don't just need careful logicians; we also need skilled painters, poets, photographers, filmmakers, storytellers, musicians, journalists, orators, and scientists who can shine emotion-evoking light on all of the various aspects of our world that reveal the existence of God and the truth of the gospel. We must help unbelievers turn their hearts toward God so that they might have spiritual eyes to see.

Of course, the kind of emotional arguments for God's existence that we have been considering in this section are primarily opposed to the worldviews of Atheists and Agnostics, who do not believe in the existence of God. Adherents of non-Christian theistic faiths, such as Islam and Judaism, might similarly appeal to such emotional evidence for the existence of God. In emotional evangelism and affective apologetics, therefore, we must go beyond presenting emotional evidence for the existence of God. We must help even those who belong to other theistic faiths to see—and *feel*—the unique truth of the gospel.

The Evidential Power of Gospel-Shaped Emotions

In his second letter to the Christians in Corinth, Paul exhorted them to live in such a way as to bear evidence to the authority of the apostles and to the truth of the gospel they preached. He writes:

> Are we beginning to commend ourselves again? Or do we need, as some do, letters of recommendation to you, or from you? You yourselves are our letter of recommendation, written on our hearts, to be known and read by all. And you show that you are a letter from Christ delivered by us, written not with ink but with the Spirit of the living God, not on tablets of stone but on tablets of human hearts. (2 Cor 3:1–3)

Often the most compelling evidence of the truth and power of the gospel is written on the hearts of those who follow Christ. As Christians, we are all called to demonstrate the reality of the gospel to those around us through our transformed emotions—indeed, through orthopathy. And while our actions and words are certainly important, it is often through right emotions that we can best reveal the power of Christ to save us from sin and death and the sanctifying power of the Holy Spirit that transforms us into the likeness of Christ. After all, the fruit of the Spirit—"love, joy, peace, patience, kindness, goodness, faithfulness, gentleness, self-control" (Gal 5:22–23)—is emotional through and through.[9] There are many ways in which our emotions can serve as evidence for the gospel, but here I will simply highlight some of the distinctive emotional evidence that flows from the three Christian virtues theologians have traditionally called the "theological virtues"—faith, hope, and love.

The Emotional Evidence of Christian Faith

In addition to belief and action, mature faith involves emotional trust. When we really trust people, we do not feel worried that they might not be trustworthy or that they might fail us when it really counts. I have great faith in my wife, Katie, that she will be faithful to me in our marriage. My faith in Katie's faithfulness is not simply a probabilistic belief or wager that she will honor her marriage vows (though I'd take that bet any day!); nor is it simply a matter of me acting in trusting ways toward her (say, by not searching through her emails or hiring a private investigator to follow her when she goes out). My faith in Katie certainly involves trusting beliefs and trusting actions, but it also involves emotional trust. I *feel* very confident that she will

---

9. See Roberts, *Spiritual Emotions*.

not be unfaithful. My feeling of confidence is itself an emotional perception of Katie's faithfulness, and it is a bulwark against the emotions of anxiety, fear, and doubt about our marriage.

The same is true of Christian faith in Jesus. Faith is not merely a matter of belief and action; it is also a matter of the heart. The Christian virtue of faith involves dispositions to believe and confess that Jesus is Lord, to actively trust him with our lives by taking up our cross and following him, and to trust him in our hearts. So, while Christians must strive to live in faithful obedience to Jesus even when we do not have the feelings of faith, we must also strive to cultivate the feelings of faith. A heart-based faith that is cut off from the head is likely to be "tossed to and fro by the waves and carried about by every wind of doctrine" (Eph 4:14), but a head-based faith cut off from the heart is likely to grow into prideful and unloving dogmatism. True faith in Jesus is not a loud, arrogant dogmatism, but a quiet, humble confidence in the risen Lord to save us from sin and death.

Just as my faith in Katie is a protection for me against emotions of anxiety, fear, and doubt about my marriage, so too faith in Jesus is a protection against the faithless emotions of anxiety, fear, and doubt about our ultimate flourishing. In fact, Jesus himself underscores the centrality of emotional vision in faith by contrasting it with these three emotions. Matthew records several instances of Jesus exhorting his followers with the phrase "O you of little faith." In three such passages, the primary evidence for the disciples' lack of faith was the presence of a negative emotional perception—namely, anxiety (Matt 6:25–34), fear (8:23–27), and a combination of fear and doubt (14:26–31).

Faith does not protect us from all of the trials and troubles of this life. But through the eyes of faith, we can learn to see our present troubles in light of our eternal life in loving communion with God. And when we do, we do not become anxious or fearful or doubtful about our present trials; rather, we take joy in them because we see them as mere momentary trials through which we can grow in moral and spiritual virtue (cf. Jas 1:2–4). As we mature in faith, our emotional vision of our present circumstances is informed more and more by our spiritual vision of eternity, overcoming anxiety with peace, fear with hope, and doubt with confidence. Through the emotional vision of faith, we can learn to see God's eternal kingdom breaking into our lives here and now. For our eternal, loving communion with God has already begun. "And this is eternal life, that they know you the only true God, and Jesus Christ whom you have sent" (John 17:3). For those with eyes to see, this brings great joy and comfort even as the storms of this life rage around us. And for those who do not yet believe, the evidence of mature emotional faith written on the hearts of Christians can be very compelling indeed.

The Emotional Evidence of Christian Hope[10]

In a passage that has become a kind of motto for Christian apologetics, Peter admonished Christians living in the first-century Roman Empire, "in your hearts honor Christ the Lord as holy, always being prepared to make a defense to anyone who asks you for a reason for the hope that is in you" (1 Pet 3:15). This verse is often quoted in support of the claim that Christians have an obligation to prepare themselves with well-reasoned arguments for the truth of Christianity, especially when its truth is called into question by non-Christian skeptics.

Notice, however, that Peter's admonition is not concerned primarily with responding to the doubts of skeptics; neither does he seem to be encouraging them to prepare themselves with the kind of arguments for the truth of Christianity that have become the common repertoire of today's Christian apologists. Rather, in response to the frightening prospect of persecution and oppression, Peter was encouraging his readers to see the world emotionally in light of the suffering, death, and especially the resurrection of Jesus Christ. As the context makes clear, he was admonishing them not to fear those who would slander them, mistreat them, and perhaps even kill them on account of their faith, but rather to internalize and live out the hope of the resurrection from the dead, which was theirs in Christ.

Peter assumed that their distinctive Christian hope, expressed in the face of persecution and even death, would cause some nonbelievers to ask for an explanation for their strange and seemingly inexplicable emotion. Hope is an emotion-perception of the likelihood of good prospects, so it does not make sense to have hope in the face of inevitably bad prospects. Yet the Christian is able to remain steadfast in her hope in the face of mistreatment and even death, for she knows that this life is not all there is and that death is not the end. Indeed, the good prospects for which the Christian hopes have been guaranteed by the risen Savior, who has conquered sin and death once and for all. As Paul explained to the Thessalonians, this is why Christians need "not grieve as others do who have no hope" (1 Thess 4:13).

For those who do not know Christ and the power and promise of his resurrection, hope in the face of death can seem very strange indeed. While some take the Christian's hope in the resurrection as evidence of

---

10. The material in this section on hope is adapted, with permission, from Pelser, "Reasons of the Heart."

the irrationality and absurdity of Christianity, others are intrigued by the despair-defeating hope of the Christian and take it as a sign of the truth of Christianity. After all, it is natural for humans to fear and even despair over death. So a faith that is powerful enough to give its adherents confident hope in the face of death and peace in the wake of the deaths of loved ones will often evoke sincere, not merely skeptical, questions. This is why Christian funerals are often excellent opportunities for evangelism.

The Emotional Evidence of Christian Love

In the final hours before his trial and crucifixion, Jesus left his disciples with this instruction: "A new commandment I give to you, that you love one another: just as I have loved you, you also are to love one another. By this all people will know that you are my disciples, if you have love for one another" (John 13:34–35). Here, Jesus points to the distinctiveness of Christian love as the primary evidence of Christian discipleship. Similarly, our love for one another in the church, together with our love for God and for our non-Christian neighbors, can be powerful evidence for the truth of the gospel.

Many Christians will agree that Christian love is an important—perhaps the most important—aspect of our Christian witness. But many will deny that Christian love essentially involves emotions or feelings. "Love is a commitment, not a feeling," they say. This common refrain is meant to communicate the truth that if you really love another person, you will be committed to treating that person in loving ways even when you do not feel any emotions of love toward him or her. Perhaps no one has communicated this truth about love more poignantly than C. S. Lewis. With reference to erotic or romantic love, Lewis explains:

> We must do the works of Eros when Eros isn't present. This all good lovers know, though those who are not reflective or articulate will be able to express it only in a few conventional phrases about "taking the rough along with the smooth," not "expecting too much," having "a little common sense," and the like. And all good Christian lovers know that this programme, modest as it sounds, will not be carried out except by humility, charity and divine grace; that it is indeed the whole Christian life seen from one particular angle.[11]

This is excellent advice. Lewis is right that we must not count on the fleeting feelings of erotic love, nor on the feelings of friendship and familial affection or any other "natural" love, to sustain our loving treatment of others. We

11. Lewis, *Four Loves*, 115.

must do the works of love even when the emotions of love are not present. Similarly, we Christians must obey God's commands and worship him alone even when we do not feel love for him.

Yet it would be a mistake to conclude that ideal Christian love—charity—does not involve loving emotions at all. Robert Roberts explains that "one aspect of the love of persons is therefore this: to love someone is to cherish him or her, to see (feel) the person as valuable, as good, as excellent, in some way that nears the heart of the person's being."[12] As we have seen, emotion is a kind of perception of value. It is one thing to judge that a person has value; it is another thing to directly experience or perceive the value of that person through one's emotions. A commitment to treat one's spouse, one's sibling, one's friend, and so on, with decency, respect, and kindness—absent any emotional perception or recognition of that person's preciousness and worth—is at best an incomplete and imperfect love.

After all, most of us do not just want our families, friends, and neighbors to *treat* us in loving and respectful ways (though we do want that!). We also want them to love us in their hearts, to care about what is good for us, and to see us as precious and valuable through emotions of love.

John affirms the connection between Christian love and emotions when he writes, "If anyone says, 'I love God,' and hates his brother, he is a liar" (1 John 4:20). Likewise, "There is no fear in love, but perfect love casts out fear. For fear has to do with punishment, and whoever fears has not been perfected in love" (1 John 4:18). Here, John argues that the emotions of hatred and fear are inconsistent with perfect love. This implies that perfect love has an emotional component. This is also revealed in the apostle Paul's teaching that "love is *patient* and *kind*; love does not *envy* or boast; it is not *arrogant* or rude. It does not insist on its own way; it is not *irritable* or *resentful*; it does not *rejoice* at wrongdoing, but *rejoices* with the truth" (1 Cor 13:4–6).[13] While many of the marks of love Paul identifies are dispositions to behave in characteristically loving ways, almost all of them, especially the italicized ones, are dispositions either to have or not to have certain emotions. So, while it is important to treat others lovingly even when we do not feel the emotions of love for them, emotions are nevertheless at the heart of mature Christian love.

Loving our neighbors involves treating them with loving kindness, but it also involves rejoicing with them when they flourish, mourning with them when they suffer loss, hoping for their redemption and salvation, feeling compassion for them when they suffer, and even occasionally feeling righteous

---

12. Roberts, "Unconditional Love," 159.
13. Italics added.

anger toward those who wrong them (though even when a serious wrong has been committed, we must be slow to anger and quick to forgive, since even the wrongdoer is our neighbor). And this is just as true of our Muslim, Jewish, Buddhist, Hindu, Baha'i, and Mormon neighbors as it is of our brothers and sisters in Christ. Jesus's commandment to love one's neighbor as oneself calls us not only to treat our neighbors with respect, but also to cherish our neighbors—including our enemies—learning to see them as valuable and precious children of God through the emotional vision of love. As we learn to do this, we will not only see the emotional evidence for God and the gospel more clearly; we also will become part of that evidence ourselves.

Zeal for the Truth versus Love of Winning Arguments

So far, we have seen how a correct understanding of emotions challenges the popular view that emotions are inherently irrational. We have also seen how orthopathy—the cultivation of proper Christian emotions—can enhance our evangelistic and apologetic efforts by providing emotional evidence for God and the gospel. Let me conclude with some brief reflections on the place of zeal in Christian apologetics.

Sadly, many aspiring apologists seem to be more concerned with winning arguments than with winning disciples for Christ. Orthopathy in apologetics offers a corrective to this trend. Although Christian apologetics involves articulating *arguments* in *defense* of the truth of the gospel and the Christian worldview, that does not mean that Christian apologists should be *argumentative* or *defensive* toward Atheists or members of other faiths.

Here, again, we can learn from Paul. Prior to his Damascus Road encounter with the risen Jesus, Paul was a zealous persecutor of Christians. After his conversion to Christianity, he was equally zealous to proclaim and defend the gospel, but his zeal was no longer manifest in violence. Rather, Paul's zeal for preaching the gospel motivated him to passionately and tirelessly preach the gospel everywhere he went. Paul humbly and creatively sought to present arguments for the truth of the gospel that would appeal to his hearers. His emotional evangelism and affective apologetics are beautifully illustrated in Acts 17.

Luke tells us that when Paul visited the city of Athens, his "spirit was provoked within him as he saw that the city was full of idols" (Acts 17:16). We then read that Paul was invited by some Athenian philosophers to share his views at the Areopagus, where he compassionately and persistently presented the gospel—not by condemning them for their idolatry, but by appealing to their own heartfelt awareness of the "unknown god" (v. 23). As

Paul exemplifies, our passion in evangelism should be like that of a medical doctor whose patients are suffering but can't see their need for treatment. Just as a doctor must have a good bedside manner if she is to build a relationship of trust and clear lines of communication with her patients, Christian apologists must have a good coffee-shop manner, sidewalk manner, and social-media manner if they are going to build the kind of trust and communication that will help their family, friends, and acquaintances see the truth of the gospel. And just as a patient is not very likely to trust a doctor who clearly is not taking her own medical advice, so too Christian apologists must reveal the evidence for the truth and power of the gospel in their own hearts if they hope to direct the hearts of others toward Christ.

Yet another important lesson we can learn from Paul's affective apologetics with the Athenians is that no matter how well we present the evidence for God and the gospel, many will continue in their unbelief—"Now when they heard of the resurrection of the dead, some mocked . . . but some men joined him and believed" (vv. 32, 34). Some Christians approach evangelism and apologetics with a kind of unbounded optimism. If we are just clever enough, well-read enough, and persuasive enough, every rational person will be able to see the force of our arguments and, eventually, repent and believe. Paul's example reveals that this optimism is misplaced. Rather than feeling discouraged and despairing when our efforts to preach and defend the gospel fail to draw our hearers closer to Christ, we must rest our hearts in the knowledge that God loves each one of our neighbors more than we ever will. And we must continue to pray with zeal that our resurrected Lord Jesus Christ would open the eyes of their hearts, revealing himself to them along their spiritual journey just as he revealed himself to Cleopas and Paul on their journeys to Emmaus and Damascus two thousand years ago.[14]

---

14. Disclaimer: The views expressed in this essay are my own and do not necessarily reflect the official policy or position of the US Air Force, the US Department of Defense, or the US government.

11

Hospitality and Religious Others

An Orthopathic Perspective

AMOS YONG

IN PREVIOUS WORK, I have presented a hospitality model for multifaith encounters and relations, one that urges Christians to be both hosts and guests of religious others, emulating and being empowered by the Holy Spirit.[1] In this chapter, I want to further explore both the promise and the challenge of such an approach. On the one hand, it seems eminently reasonable: Why not engage others with hospitable mutuality rather than antagonistic hostility? On the other hand, hospitality involves not just ideas but practices and, perhaps more importantly, interpersonal aptitudes and dispositions—all of which engage not just the cerebral aspects of our intellect (orthodoxy) but also the affective domains of our hearts, souls, and lives (orthopathy). In short, hospitality involves feeling and thus includes vulnerability on all fronts, and this in turn highlights both its potency and its perilousness for the Christian encounter with other faiths.

I will argue here, however, that a triune God in whom the Father sends his Son in the incarnation and pours out the Holy Spirit on all flesh demands nothing less than that Jesus's followers, who have been filled with his Spirit, also embrace this radically orthopathic *missio hospitalitatis*—the mission of hospitality. The four sections that follow explicate a basic missiology of hospitality in relationship to this exploration in theology of affections and feelings (orthopathy); examine applications of

1. See Yong, *Hospitality and the Other*.

such an orthopathic perspective to multifaith encounter and interreligious dialogue; and conclude by reconsidering the theological—explicitly, pneumatological and Trinitarian—warrants for such an approach to religious others. Our goal is to clarify what is at stake in a theology and missiology of hospitality and perhaps also to inspire (note: an affective notion) ventures along this less often trodden path.

Hospitality and the Other: Opportunities for and Challenges from "the Heart"

I began my work in theology of religions and came upon hospitality a bit belatedly. Much of my earliest work had been devoted to finding a way to understand and engage religious others on their own terms.[2] The existing methods, theological and otherwise, inherited from those in the Pentecostal and Evangelical churches and traditions in which I had been reared did not seem to help much in large part because of their non-dialogical approach: listening to those in other faiths was tolerated (rather than encouraged), so long as it was the first step toward the more important objective of gaining a hearing for the evangelistic proclamation of the Christian gospel. Alternatively, for those more academically trained, studying other religions and learning from those of other traditions was welcomed in order to hone one's apologetic responses. On the other side, as I had also come to realize, pluralist theologies of religions held, loosely speaking, that "all roads led to Rome," such that there were many religious pathways up the metaphorical mountain toward transcendent and ineffable truth and, hence, each faith tradition was complementary to, without ever ultimately contradicting, any of the others. If the latter, pluralist perspective appeared not to be able to recognize other faiths as really different from our own, then the former, Evangelical posture seemed unable to engage others in their otherness in the first place. I had proposed a pneumatological approach to other faiths, one that emerged from my intuition that the many tongues of the day of Pentecost not only portended the divine redemption of many cultures but also intimated the possibility that other faiths, in their radical dissonance, might yet, despite much bewilderment and perplexity, bear witness to "God's deeds of power" (Acts 2:11b).[3] If the former notion of cultural redemption was not too controversial, the latter suggestion regarding the possibility of other faiths having something to teach us (I did not go so far as to confidently affirm their salvific potential) was a bit more threatening,

---

2. Two of my first three books were in theology of religions. See Yong, *Discerning the Spirit(s)*; *Beyond the Impasse*.

3. Unless otherwise noted, all scriptural quotations in this essay are from the NRSV.

especially to those in my tribe that insisted on the centrality of mission and evangelism for Christian faith.[4]

It was through participation in the World Council of Churches (WCC) consultation process on religious plurality and Christian self-understanding, facilitated by their Faith and Order, Conference on World Mission and Evangelism, and Office on Interreligious Relations and Dialogue networks from about 2003–2004, that I came to see how a theology of hospitality could be helpful for thinking both theologically and missiologically about other faiths.[5] In particular, as I began to reflect in this vein, I realized that it is overseas missionaries who have much to teach us in this regard, since they have come to appreciate that hospitality runs both ways: it is not just about hosting people of other faiths, but it is also about learning how to be guests in cultural and even religious conditions much different from our own. And although most missionaries who come home on furlough give congregational reports about how many decisions for Christ have been made and how many baptisms have been conducted since their last visit—as representative of missionary "success," which translates into mission funding—when speaking more personally, they inevitably also bear witness to the fact that they have begun to make friends with those in their host cultures, who often identify with other religious traditions, and have begun to experience transformation in their attitudes toward them—if not also in their beliefs about themselves and their own faith. In other words, if we listen closely to our missionaries, we learn what they are learning: that those in other faiths have beliefs and practices that can challenge or enrich—sometimes both—our way of thinking and living.

If theology is shaped by and derives from practice, then a theology of hospitality emerges in part from Christian mission practices.[6] More precisely, a missiology of hospitality vis-à-vis those in other faiths is nourished by and through Christian hospitable practices in relationship to religious others. Hospitality becomes a powerful theological idea or set of ideas (orthodoxy) because it is rooted historically and concretely in the Christian encounter with other faiths (orthopraxy). A synergist is involved wherein a theology and missiology of hospitality both bubbles

---

4. Evangelicals in particular were less than impressed with my proposals. See, e.g., the criticisms of McDermott and Netland, *Trinitarian Theology of Religions*, plus my response, "Trinitarian Theology of Religions." The critical reaction, though, has been particularly among theologians rather than missiologists; we shall see clues for this difference of opinion among the two groups in what follows.

5. See the extensive use and discussion of the notion of hospitality in WCC et al., "Religious Plurality."

6. Besides my book *Hospitality and the Other*, I have also written elsewhere about this. See Yong, "Spirit of Hospitality"; "Guests, Hosts."

up out of and then returns to inform Christian mission (and ministry) practices. Hospitality thus potentially provides a framework for a theologically orthodox understanding of missiological orthopraxis vis-à-vis the Christian relationship to other religions.

Yet anecdotally, at least, missionaries are less public about how they are being transformed through the multifaith relationship and more apt to present themselves as agents of change, impacting and influencing the conversion of others. While the latter may indeed be true, that the former is not more pronounced may have something to do with how our understanding of hospitality may yet remain one-sided. We are fine with hosting others, for instance, including even those from other faiths, since hosts get to establish the ground rules for the encounter and thus retain some measure of control over what happens and how it happens. Being guests of others, however, particularly those of other faiths, may concede too much, leaving the Christian (missionary or evangelist) at the mercy of the religious other's protocols and parameters.

More particularly, I suggest, hospitality is a good idea but dangerous practice, or at least that is how we feel instinctively when considering those of other faiths. While the former, at the level of ideas, allows one to retain some measure of objectivity and distance, the latter, involving practical performance, involves some investment of ourselves and maybe also our family members and loved ones. This participatory dimension thus means that, in order for the practice to be authentically engaging, one has to be subjected to the circumstantial possibilities opened up in the hospitable relationship. As such, hospitable praxis includes not just embodied activity but also affective commitment. Put alternatively, hospitality works safely at the abstract level of theological orthodoxy but is subjected to the unpredictable give-and-take involving other religious persons within the historical sphere of missiological orthopraxy. And because the deeds of our hands are or ought to be for optimal results, accompanied by the presence of our hearts (orthopathos) in any hospitable exchange,[7] the stakes are exponentially higher as well. Along these lines, the next two sections explicate further both the promise and challenge of hospitality for Christian missiological practice and theological dialogue with those of other faiths.

Hospitality and Multifaith Encounters: From Agenda to Relationship

Hospitality as inter- and transcultural practice is primed to foster multifaith relationships. This is in part because the call to hospitality resounds across

---

7. For more on the interconnectedness between orthopraxis and orthopathos, see the collection of essays in Coulter and Yong, *Spirit, the Affections*.

the world's religious traditions, both transnational and indigenous.[8] Hence, people of all faiths and spiritualities are shaped by hospitable beliefs and practices. It is not surprising, then, that the encounter between religions across the millennia has been mediated, at least in part, by hospitality.[9]

Our goal here, however, is to explore more intently the hospitality of multifaith encounter via an orthopathic lens. From this perspective, we can view the practices of hosting and being guests of religious others in terms of the affections and feelings brought to and generated in such interactions. To put the matter this way, however, begs the prior question: Why not comprehend hospitality as practice rather than feeling? Isn't the meeting of others, religious others included, better understood as orthopraxis rather than orthopathy?

Surely this is possible. We might perceive hospitality merely as a means of serving others who are on their way. Take, for instance, a hotel owner or manager and his or her employees. We have all stayed a night or longer in such environments and have been the recipients of hospitality offered—in that sense, also guests of hotel hosts. In such contexts, there is a need: we as travelers need rest for the night, and there is a service being offered by the hotel—i.e., accommodations for our journey. From this perspective, little affectivity is involved or required. Rather, the hospitality relationship is contracted: we check in after a certain time, pay our bill, and check out by a certain time the next day, being careful to abide by the hotel policies and rules. (Failure to do so may incur other charges.) The hotel and its staff host us and we behave as appropriate guests. The practice of hosting and guesting unfolds according to accepted conventions. Everyone gets what they want and goes their own way—little to no feelings are involved or jeopardized.

Might multifaith encounters proceed according to this practice paradigm? Surely yes: we might come together, one side as host and another as guest, to explore common cause, for instance; to stand in solidarity for religious freedom against encroaching governmental regulations; or to work together for ecological and environmental justice.[10] In such a scenario, there is an important, agreed-upon practical agenda that brings people of more than one faith tradition together, perhaps one designated to play the host role and another to play the guest role. Again, religious and cultural conventions here guide the hospitality relationship, but the point of the encounter is less to deepen multifaith understanding and more to achieve (the former being in

---

8. See, e.g., Bazzano, *Spectre of the Stranger* (on Buddhist traditions); Siddiqui, *Hospitality and Islam*; Goshen-Gottstein, *Religious Other*; Reeves, *Safeguarding the Stranger*.

9. See Reiterer et al., *Hospitality*.

10. See, e.g., Ingram, *You Have Been Told*, for an exploration in the latter direction.

service of) certain agreed-upon outcomes. Hospitality can remain, thus, at the level of orthopraxis without ever shifting to the orthopathic register.

But in other situations and circumstances, the orthopathic dimension might well be more crucial in the giving and receiving of hospitality, such that the latter is undermined when the former is ignored. Let's say we have next-door neighbors who are of other faiths that we wish to invite over to our home in order to share a meal, and the gospel with that. How we host our guests of other faiths, however, might well lead to various forms of "sharing." Some classically organized rescue missions or food kitchens—in bygone eras, to be sure—may have fed the hungry, but only in the context of their listening to an evangelistic homily. In such cases, again, there is an understood tit-for-tat arrangement that remains at the level of praxis: "we" serve a hot meal and a gospel message, while "you" receive both.[11] This can easily be transposed into how we host our neighbors of other faiths as well, with the expectation not quite so blatant but nevertheless clearly communicated over the course of the meal or throughout our interactions. In other words, we signal in so many words that we wish to maintain the relationship so long as our neighbor retains a discernible interest in our religious way of life. Little emotional energy is expended in such cases, or only as much as is needed to solicit and sustain the interest of the religious other in our commitments. Once we sense that the other is no longer a viable candidate for religious conversion, then we shift our attention elsewhere.

On the other hand, perhaps our goal in inviting our neighbors of other faiths for a meal is not first to evangelize them but to get to know them, to welcome them to the community (if they are the ones who are new), and to just be neighborly. In that case, we host others not only in a house but in a home.[12] This means that we welcome them into our lives and even into our hearts. Along the way, of course, we share who we are, religiously committed and all, and find out that they also are religiously inclined or convicted, and the relationship goes where it may. But interactions do not wax or wane depending on how we assess their potential as proselytes; rather, we continue to be hospitable for no other reason than that they are our neighbors and perhaps even have become our friends. Along the way, our neighbors will surely size up our intentions and respond according to their own affective inclinations: if they feel welcome and safe in our presence, they might be willing to pursue a deeper relationship with us; if they feel threatened or offended in any way, we

---

11. This would be the modern Evangelical version of hospitality codes prominent in indigenous societies: gifts are given so that they can be reciprocated, even if in other respects or forms. See, e.g., Mauss, *Gift*, esp. chapter 1.

12. Bence, *Room at My Table*.

might exchange pleasantries in cordiality but will less likely pursue neighborhood initiatives in mutuality and reciprocity.

Similarly, if we were on the receiving end of the invitation from our neighbors of other faiths, we do not approach this occasion with evangelistic priorities. Instead, we are appropriately deferential to our hosts, following their cues. Perhaps religion comes up in the course of the conversation and we attempt to be sensitive to how the discussion unfolds. Even if not, we have to decide at the level of our gut—affectively, that is—about how much we will open up our own lives to our new hosts: Can we become friends, despite the religious differences,[13] or are we predetermined to remain acquaintances unless they become open to join us on our faith journey? How far are we willing to proceed at the level of common humanity—constituted as we all are by embodied desires and affective needs for empathy and solidarity[14]—even when such unity does not include religious commonality? Is it possible for our relationship to proceed on parallel tracks even if conversions occur in neither direction? This begs the question, surely, of what conversion entails.

Hospitality and Interreligious Dialogue: From Debate to Empathy

Intellectual conversion, while short of full religious conversion from one faith to another, is no less important when considering the orthopathic aspects of interreligious dialogue and discussion. There are various modalities of discursive interreligious engagements, some of which are much more cerebrally navigated and less affectively charged. Studying other faith doctrines, theologies, and ideas for the purpose of developing apologetic responses, both negative (to ward off the criticisms of others) and positive (to press critical questions upon others), is an intellectual undertaking requiring rigorous analytical efforts.[15] These are predominantly cognitive endeavors assuming a kind of objectivist stance over against the teachings of other faiths. In some cases, a good apologist is capable of anticipating counterresponses from the other perspective, at least theoretically imbibed, although in the end, even these are shown to be inadequate. For such apologetic purposes, required at some level

---

13. For more on interreligious friendship, see Fredericks and Tiemeier, *Interreligious Friendship*.

14. See Pell, *Hospitality*, which contends that compassion is intrinsic to the practice of hospitality.

15. Griffiths, *Apology for Apologetics*.

in all interreligious considerations, the less emotionally or affectively motivated, the more effective and convincing.

Interreligious dialogue might also be merely for the sake of curiosity, because one wants to understand others, their beliefs, and their practices better. This is part and parcel of the intellectual life, and one might come away from studying other faiths being more informed—and that might be the end of that. On the other hand, sometimes curiosity turns into wonder, even amazement. In these cases, one is touched not just in one's mind or intellect; but the wellsprings of intrigue that connect our heads and hearts are tinged as well. From such moments onward, an affective dimension begins to take shape. We have shifted from asking *what* to asking *why*, driven not just by the quest for intellectual comprehension but by having to better grasp the inner aspects of other religious lives and ways.[16]

We eventually begin to realize that religious understanding usually cannot remain at a merely cognitive level. Intellectual knowledge derived from reading or (bare) listening operates at an abstract and general level. One can read about riding a bike, but one only "knows" how to do so by practice. Similarly, doctrines are mere abstractions unless related to practices.[17] Trinitarian notions about the deity of Christ or the Holy Spirit are rooted as much, if not more, in the liturgical practices of the church's worship—baptism in the name of the Father, Son, and Holy Spirit, for example—as in Greek philosophical categories and arguments. From this perspective, one could wax eloquently about the doctrine of the Trinity to interested religious others, but at some point growth in their understanding will be inhibited apart from their taking a step (of faith!) performatively: to participate in the Christian cult—liturgical, devotional, or otherwise. In other words, theoretical knowledge *about* the Trinity can deepen personal experience *of* and interactions *with* the triune God.

Interreligiously, of course, understanding other faiths invites some measure of experiential participation. One might not be able to enter devotionally into the liturgical and cultic practices at the heart of other traditions, but to what degree might one be able to step into such spaces as observers rather than as participants? The line here is a fine one: to be present in a Buddhist meditational hall or in a Jewish synagogue or in an Islamic mosque when others are practicing their faith is to be able to *feel* what is happening to some degree. Hence, in theory one's presence in these environments could still be less than participatory in the full sense, although personal and experiential

---

16. On the openness of the interreligious path, see Moyaert, *Fragile Identities*. See also chapter 6 in Moyaert, *In Response*.

17. See chapter 2 of my *Hospitality and the Other* for further analysis of the relationship between doctrinal theory and performative practices.

exposure to these practices, even as they are being performed religiously by others, has affective impact. One cannot listen to others chanting from their holy scriptures without feeling the force of these chants to some degree, even if one is not engaging verbally in the practice oneself.[18]

So the point is this: to be present "in the flesh"—incarnationally and personally—amid the performance of other religious practices is to begin to engage with that reality in an affective manner quite different from, say, the ways in which we watch a YouTube rendition of the same. The kind of hospitality demanded in this "live" venue is but an extension of the openness that is part and parcel of the intellectual and academic life, which welcomes, inquires about, and pursues other perspectives and ideas.[19] But this begs an important set of questions: Does Christian orthodoxy obligate us to embark on trajectories of inquiry that open up to orthopraxic and especially orthopathic domains? Isn't scholarship, even that which is *about* other religions, "objective," rather than driven by a practical agenda (orthopraxis)? More importantly for our purposes, to what degree should interreligious dialogue as an academic enterprise be pursued if it invites, as possible next steps, increasingly more embodied practice and affective engagement? The risks involved in the latter, which are absent at the formal dialogical level centered around organized exchanges of ideas, exceed that of just biasing the results of inquiry (what academicians and scholars are trained to avoid) and threaten to captivate our souls (thus assaulting the very essence of our religious—Christian—identity). In short and put another way, isn't interreligious dialogue supposed to remain only an intellectual undertaking, and are we not confusing its purposes and hazarding our allegiances when we then set it on a performative and experiential course?

Obviously, one can draw one's lines wherever one feels comfortable, even as one can define one's parameters as needed or desired, and give good reasons for such. My point is that introducing orthopathic concerns presses the question of how to understand the dialogical encounter between faiths to begin with: Why limit such dialogical interaction to the discursive interchange of ideas? There may be good reasons in formal contexts, when scholarly and academic papers are presented, to understand interreligious dialogue in that way. But from an orthopathic standpoint, this is only one arena for interreligious dialogical interaction, or it may be only one aspect of the dialogue even when limited to this more discursive

---

18. I explicate these matters further in my analysis of the comparative theological project of Francis Clooney—in particular, his invitation to read other religious texts, including those intended for chanting, for theological purposes. See my "Clooney's 'Dual Religious Belonging,'" reprinted as chapter 10 in Yong, *Dialogical Spirit*, 225–50.

19. See Bennett, *Academic Life*.

and formally structured genre.[20] Other, more performative spheres can also be included under this rubric, and in such contexts it is not just what can be ratiocinated but also what can be experienced and felt that matters as part of the dialogue. More pointedly, in our postmodern context we realize that all cognition is emotionally laden, such that there is no avoiding the affective dimension, even if sublimated or subordinated to reasoned argumentation and negotiation.

Almost four decades ago, John Cobb intuited that multifaith encounters inevitably led beyond mere discussion, since a change of understanding, even intellectually, involved a transformation of the self.[21] Orthopathically, my point is perhaps more deeply either troubling or liberative (depending on one's perspective): that if the other touches not just one's head but also moves one's body and even the depths of one's soul, then one is not just transformed intellectually but converted personally in some sense. Hence, one can cross over and return in terms of intellectual sojourning—i.e., learning about the doctrines of religious others like one might learn about physics or chemistry—but this does not affect how one feels about oneself in relationship to others and the world. Inevitably, however, understanding the ideas of religious others involves—potentially, if not actually—appreciating their perspective, experiencing their reality, and feeling their potency.[22] The more we open ourselves up to the latter, the more we begin to feel the world as they do. Intellectual conversion hence includes embodied and affective aspects that are not neatly cordoned off and protected. When this happens, one can respond on behalf of religious others not just theoretically but with a certain sense of owning that rejoinder.

Toward Hospitable Orthopathy: A Trinitarian Invitation

The course of our discussion so far has perhaps highlighted that there may be more to lose than to gain if we embrace the orthopathic dimension of interreligious exchange: we might not only change our minds but be changed in our heart of hearts about other faiths and their devotees. If this happens, even if we remained Christians—i.e., if our "conversion" is not from our faith to the

20. For more on the centrality of affectivity and emotionality in multifaith endeavors, including especially the import of developing emotional intelligence in interreligious dialogue and relationships, see Swidler, *Dialogue for Interreligious Study*.

21. Cobb, *Beyond Dialogue*.

22. For more on the aesthetic and affective dimensions of multifaith encounters, approached through comparative theological method, see Roberts, *Tastes of the Divine*; Hillgardner, *Longing and Letting Go*; Dyrness, *Senses of Devotion*.

other's fully and personally—the other has become in part who or what we are, and this is bound, so the concern goes, to effect our own commitments to mission and evangelization—especially, although maybe not only, to those of whatever faith tradition we might have been touched by.

Let me step back to consider this orthopathic approach to the multifaith interface from a more theologically grounded perspective in order to discern possible paths forward. Considering first the divine nature and character—What could be more robustly theological than this?—forefronts also the missions of Christ and his Spirit. The hospitality of the Father that makes space for others through creation—the world as a whole and its various "parts"—is then manifest as a guest to others in the Word, the Son made flesh. Thus, Jesus is the Son of God who goes on a journey into a far country, as Karl Barth put it,[23] and becomes the paradigmatic guest, first in Mary's womb and then among human creatures at large. The author of the letter to the Hebrews puts it this way: "Since, therefore, the children share flesh and blood, he himself likewise shared the same things, so that through death he might destroy the one who has the power of death, that is, the devil. . . . Therefore he had to become like his brothers and sisters in every respect, so that he might be a merciful and faithful high priest in the service of God, to make a sacrifice of atonement for the sins of the people" (Heb 2:14, 17). "In every respect," then, Jesus became a guest fully vulnerable to his hosts, so that he is able, as specified later in the same letter, "to sympathize with our weaknesses"; "we have one who in every respect has been tested as we are, yet without sin" (Heb 4:15). The incarnation of the Word is, therefore, no mere linguistic abstraction: rather, it involved taking on fully the human condition, body, culture, feelings, and all. The incarnation is not just a doctrine to be believed but a historical, material, and pathic reality to be encountered, experienced, and transformed by.

The incarnation, however, is not merely the work of the Son but also the work of the Spirit. The Word was conceived in the flesh through the power of the Spirit. In turn, the resurrected and ascended Christ poured out his Spirit upon creaturely bodies.[24] As Saint Luke recounts, the apostolic message drew from the ancient prophets to explicate the Pentecost phenomenon in this way: "In the last days it will be, God declares, that I will pour out my Spirit upon all flesh" (Acts 2:17a; cf. Joel 2:28a). Not for no reason, then, did Luke's preceding description of this event record: "suddenly from heaven there came a *sound like the rush of a violent wind*, and it *filled* the entire house where they were sitting. Divided tongues, as of fire, *appeared* among them,

---

23. See Barth, *Church Dogmatics*, 4/1:157–210 (§59.1).
24. See Yong, "Christological Constants."

and a tongue *rested on* each of them. All of them were *filled* with the Holy Spirit and began to speak in other languages, as the Spirit gave them ability" (Acts 2:2–4).[25] Hence, the breath and wind of God is seen, heard, felt—palpably, tactilely, and kinesthetically. The Spirit thus follows in the missional path of the Son into the "far country" of creation, not taking on flesh in the same way but coming upon and being guest of fleshly bodies no less really. Saint Paul thereby asks, "Do you not know that you are God's temple and that God's Spirit dwells in you?" (1 Cor 3:16), and re-inquires: "Or do you not know that your body is a temple of the Holy Spirit within you, which you have from God, and that you are not your own?" (1 Cor 6:19). The Spirit thus embraces being the guest of carnality, and this is how the passion of the Spirit is manifest: through the groans and "sighs too deep for words," exhaled by human bodies (Rom 8:23, 26).

In short, the Son is the archetypal and exemplary guest, and the Spirit is the ongoing divine guest hosted by creaturely bodies. The triune God in the incarnational and Pentecostal missions is thus giver and gift/given, not separately but together,[26] and this involves not just disembodied minds but concrete physicalities, perceptible feelings, and impassioned hearts. Christian witness, therefore, is spiritually empowered—by the Holy Spirit—but no less embodied and thereby affective as well. Divine redemption is intended ultimately to restore creation to creator, to bridge the gulf of alienation and estrangement between creatures and deity in ways that allow the world to enjoy the hospitality of God through the Son by the Spirit.[27] The eschatological re-creation—the new creation even—will enable the full flourishing of all creatures according to divine hospitality: in the presence of God and of each other, each giving and receiving of the gracious gifts endowed and bestowed.

From a missiological and multifaith perspective, then, Christian witness inexorably, if not initially, involves this orthopathic dimension. Verbal evangelism remains mere words—abstractions, no less—unless accompanied by affective presence, gestures, and passion. In the process, what emerges is authentic and transformative interpersonal relations: we bear witness to people of other faiths in a mutually reciprocal and intersubjective fashion so that we also receive their testimony in turn. Herein is involved the interchange not just of concepts and ideas but of lives. We share of ourselves, our desires and passions, no less, even as we receive the embodied yearnings of our neighbors and interlocutors—our friends, in effect.

---

25. Italics added.
26. See Yong, *Spirit of Love*.
27. Camp, *Hospitality of God*.

This could include but need not require religious conversion. Yes, Christians will become Jews, Buddhists, etc., even as adherents of other faiths will embrace the Christian Messiah and his way. On the other hand, many more perhaps will not convert religiously but nevertheless will experience a range of converting experiences, both intellectual and emotional/affective.[28] We cannot but be touched and moved by sustained relationships with others who are different, especially those with religious convictions. Within the context of these interactions, we may not take up new religious affiliations, but we will come to hold our own religious identities differently, the ideas we have, the things we do, and the feelings that carry us.

In the so-called parable of the sheep and the goats (Matt 25:31–46), the Gospel writer specifies that the "sheep" are saved in their feeding the hungry, quenching the thirsty, welcoming the stranger, clothing the naked, caring for the sick, and visiting prisoners precisely because they were serving, unconsciously as such, the Lord Jesus in these guises.[29] The "goats," on the other hand, are cast "into the eternal fire" (v. 41) because they had not done these things and hence had not served Jesus either. Our conventional approach to hospitality is that we might be hosts who introduce our guests to life everlasting in Christ. This parable suggests instead that whether we are guests or hosts, our being in the presence of others is what makes available to us the saving power of Jesus. In other words, while we think we are evangelists of redemption for others, these aliens and strangers are the conduits of salvation for us, less because they are aware of functioning as divine emissaries but because Jesus Christ has chosen to save us in this way. Hospitality, then, whether we are on the welcoming or visiting end, involves in the divine scheme of things our introduction, through others, into the redeeming work of God.[30] And as God wishes to save us as whole persons, so also does that salvation renew our minds, straighten our hands, touch our hearts, and transform our lives—with others—in the process.[31]

---

28. For more on these and other domains of conversion, see Gelpi, *Conversion Experience*.

29. I exposit this parable elsewhere vis-à-vis developing a theology and missiology of disability. See Yong, *Bible, Disability*, 136–42.

30. Jipp, *Saved by Faith*.

31. Thanks to Nok Kam, my graduate assistant, for his feedback on the first draft of this essay. I am grateful also to Bonnie Sue Lewis for the invitation to give an earlier version of the chapter as one of the plenary presentations at the 2018 annual meeting of the American Society of Missiology, and for all of the feedback I received—including difficult critical questions—that have improved its argument. Last but not least, I appreciate comments from the book editors that have helped shape this final version.

Afterword

What's Next?

Paul Louis Metzger

THIS VOLUME HAS MADE several significant contributions to the work of Christian witness in our increasingly pluralistic society. It also serves as inspiration for ongoing developments along similar lines and on a variety of levels. This afterword will sketch out what these contributions and developments are. There are four: multidimensional exercise, multidisciplinary endeavor, multifaith diplomatic engagement, and multilevel enterprise.

Multidimensional Exercise

One of the key contributions this volume makes to the field of Christian witness in our increasingly pluralistic society concerns the sustained consideration of orthopathy. Certainly, Evangelical Christianity's emphasis historically on doctrinal truth claims is vitally important. In no way does attention to orthopathy (right passion) require abandoning or lessening concern for biblical and theological orthodoxy (right teaching). Similarly, attention to orthopathy does not entail jettisoning or softening orthopraxy, namely, obedience to Jesus Christ (right living/action). Instead of orthodoxy-*light* and orthopraxy-*light*, this book emphasizes orthodoxy-*plus* and orthopraxy-*plus*. The *plus* factor refers to orthopathy, which involves attention to right passions, emotions, or intuitions. Orthopathy is a necessary counterpart to orthodoxy and orthopraxy and should be treated as an equal. "What's next" includes ongoing attention to orthopathy as a healthy and necessary complement to orthodoxy and orthopraxy in Christian witness in our multifaith world.

It is worth noting that consideration of "plus" in contrast to "light" involves, among other things, awareness of what Jonathan Haidt in *The Righteous Mind* and elsewhere would categorize as conservatives' concern for purity, authority, and loyalty. If one wishes to convince conservative Evangelicals of the importance of orthopathy, it cannot come at the expense of orthodoxy. How can it be when they are ultimately inseparable, contrary to the perceptions of many? Anyone who does not show appreciation for the "plus" factor in conservative Christian circles not only fails to account for right teaching but also right passion, since Protestant theology going back to the early Luther and Melanchthon viewed the affections as foundational to their understanding of right doctrine, including theological anthropology and soteriology.[1]

Similarly, those who favor orthopathy-*light* fail to account for right practice. While it is beyond the scope of this volume, historically, doctrine was not divorced from right living. Truth claims were never separate from right conduct: truth was understood to culminate in virtue. Whereas today we tend to separate out "religion" and "science" as projecting alternative and conflicting sets of ultimate truth claims, historian Peter Harrison has demonstrated that in the ancient and medieval world, they were perceived as two dimensions of one reality with virtue as its end.[2] And yet virtue itself is never a matter simply of action, but also of heart intent. So even here, proper attention to virtue entails a pure heart and pious affection, as Christian Scripture makes clear (2 Chr 16:9, Ps 51:10–13; Prov 4:13; 1 Cor 13). Virtue is the goal or destination, but proper affection is in the driver's seat while sound doctrine provides the road map.

Here we see that the three "orthos" are never truly separate from one another. We may distinguish and dissect them, but they do not really exist in

---

1. Note, for example, Philip Melanchthon's rejection of grace as a quality inhering in the soul in his 1521 edition (in contrast to the 1543 edition) of the *Loci communes theologici*. In the earlier edition, Melanchthon critiques a behavioral and volitional basis for soteriology, favoring in its place an affective framework, claiming that "affection is overcome by affection" (Melanchthon, *Loci communes*, 27). In "On the Bondage of the Will," Luther provides a parallel defense of the centrality of the affections in soteriology and exclaims to Erasmus that Melanchthon's work, *Loci communes*, "deserves not only to be immortalized but even canonized" (Luther, "Bondage of the Will," 102). Unfortunately, Melanchthon's *Loci communes* underwent a transformation, departing from the revolutionary insights involving an affective spirituality that was an essential feature of the 1521 edition.

2. Harrison, *Territories of Science*.

isolation. Likewise, anyone whose witness lacks appropriate attention to one or more of the "orthos" will not ultimately be found persuasive. Effective communication entails proper and parallel attention to logos, ethos, and pathos. Consider for a moment someone who is quite able intellectually, but who lacks emotional intelligence. It is very likely that those around him will be persuaded to discount his otherwise compelling arguments because they feel disparaged or ridiculed by his blunt maneuvers involving rational prowess. Here I am reminded of a statement Floyd McClung wrote and Joseph Aldrich quoted in his *Lifestyle Evangelism*: "People don't care how much we know until they know how much we care."[3] Quite a simple point, but how foolish we are if we discount emotional intelligence in our drive to win an argument.

The last point I wish to make here regarding the importance of this volume's focus on right passion or affection is that preoccupation with a compelling Christian worldview may at times serve as a cover for the will to power over other competing ideologies that present themselves as all-encompassing, compelling, and strong. Molly Worthen speaks of Evangelical Christianity inheriting this drive to provide a robust defense of the faith, or Christian worldview, from certain Dutch Reformed progenitors who, along with others, contended against the imposing ideologies of national socialism and Soviet socialism.[4] While Evangelical Christians must be prepared to give a reason for the hope that is within them, as the first epistle of Peter exhorts us (1 Pet 3:15), we must be on guard against trying to gain the upper hand by providing an even more imposing worldview than is found in other faith traditions. A spirit of charity and civility in the Spirit and confidence in God's providential care will lead Jesus's people to guard against approaching fearfully the religious other as a threat. The "other" that we so easily fear changes from era to era, from rightful concern over national socialism in the past to an unfortunate, hostile stance toward Islam and other "competing worldviews" today. We must remember that whereas an imperfect love is cast out by fear, a perfect love casts out fear (1 John 4:18). Besides, our battle is not with flesh and blood, but against the principalities and powers in the heavenly realm (Eph 6:12). Given the biblical truth that greater is he who is in us than he who is in the world (1 John 4:4), we need not react and seek to destroy the religious and ideological other whom we may perceive as a threat. Rather, we should engage them in a way that is fully grounded in Christian Scripture but also with an open posture of charity, humility, and hospitality. Such a posture makes possible a more constructive way of engaging one another—sensitively

---

3. Aldrich, *Lifestyle Evangelism*, 35.
4. Worthen, *Apostles of Reason*, 27–28.

and peacefully, in truthful and meaningful ways—while safeguarding against weaponizing the Bible in our witness.

The previous reflections draw attention to socio-psychological, historical, and biblical-theological-missional perspectives. As such, the prior paragraphs reflect another unique feature and contribution that this volume makes—specifically, what we referred to above as a multidisciplinary endeavor.

Multidisciplinary Endeavor

This book provides excellent treatments not only of Scripture and theology in addressing Christian witness in a pluralistic society, but also other important offerings in such spheres as social psychology and neuroscience. Similar to the point on right doctrine above, we are not calling for Bible or theology-*light*, but Bible and theology-*plus*. "What's next" includes further research along such multidisciplinary lines.

Over against the long-standing Draper-White "conflict thesis," which pits faith and science against one another and disparages faith,[5] and over against the long-standing trauma in Fundamentalist-Evangelical circles going back to the "Scopes Monkey Trial" in 1925, which disparages mainstream science,[6] here we find complementary ways of engaging diverse phenomena, including scientific findings' import for how we engage the religious other. Coming to terms with neurological and psychological drives will help inform us as to why Christians of various stripes approach the religious other the way they do. In particular, this information will shed light on our Evangelical preoccupation with such moral intuitions as purity, loyalty, and authority. We will be better able to discern when our wariness and fear of the religious other result from accurate readings of Christian Scripture and when they result from biological drives and psychological wiring triggered by preservation of tribal groupings at all cost in the face of perceived threats. It is hoped that Evangelicals will be far less frequently known for competitive tribal aims and strategies involving hostility, as the Pew Research studies mentioned in the introduction to this volume

---

5. Refer to the following two sources critiquing the long-dominant "conflict thesis" involving faith and science: AAAS DSER, "Science and Religion"; Numbers, *Galileo Goes to Jail*.

6. George Marsden wrote of the trauma experienced by Fundamentalist Christianity in the aftermath of the trial: "It would be difficult to overestimate the impact" of this trial "in transforming fundamentalism" (Marsden, *Fundamentalism and American Culture*, 184).

suggest.[7] Rather, it is hoped that we Evangelicals will be increasingly known for cooperative, altruistic aspirations and actions involving hospitality, in keeping with the Bible's consistent high regard for the alien in our midst, who is our neighbor (Luke 10:25–37).

Multifaith Diplomatic Engagement

The last point on hospitality naturally gives rise to the importance of multifaith diplomacy. "What's next" includes deliberation on the necessity and vitality of a faith that weds proclamation evangelism and religious diplomacy. Most Christians are not itinerant evangelists going from town to town, preaching the good news of Jesus Christ. Most of us are rooted in communities, where we rub shoulders daily with people of different faith perspectives in our places of employment, our neighborhoods, and our homes. While we are always to be prepared to give a reason for the hope within us with gentleness and respect (1 Pet 3:15), we must come to terms with the realization that we are not always asked to share. Nor are we generally, if ever, welcome to share the good news repeatedly with the same people. So until we share, and after we share, what should we do?

In addition to proclamation evangelism, we must cultivate a deep appreciation for multifaith diplomacy. In keeping with what was said under the first two sections, the aim here is not to settle for evangelism-*light* but to promote evangelism-*plus*. How will people find our faith tradition appealing if we do not sow seeds of neighborliness that lead them to ask us to share the reason for the hope within us? And how will those who have experienced trauma and transitioned out of our religious movement ever enter into meaningful conversations and relationships with us if we do not cultivate a diplomatic and hospitable disposition?

Unfortunately, such dispositional cultivation along these lines is easier said than done. For many conservative Christians, talk of diplomacy and hospitality can easily come across as signs of compromise. Bound up with our fears related to moral intuitions of purity, loyalty, and authority, Evangelicals tend to emphasize proclamation evangelism and look askance at interfaith dialogue and diplomacy. The former approach more readily safeguards distinctiveness and quite often fosters a sense of superiority. The latter approach more easily removes distinctions and tends to emphasize equality among faith traditions—a trajectory often celebrated by liberal elements of Christianity but criticized by conservative Christian groups.

---

7. Refer back to this volume's introductory discussion of the two Pew surveys: "How Americans Feel"; "Increasingly Warm Feelings."

This volume helps us discover the importance of developing a more comprehensive view of Christian witness. The editors cherish what I have often referred to as the biblical mandate to ground the Great Commission in the Great Commandment(s): love of God and neighbor—which (1) is the essence of what Jesus commands his disciples to teach their followers to obey, as recorded in Matthew 28:20; (2) provides the context for witness that affirms people's dignity as created in God's image; and (3) never reduces care or relationship with our neighbor as a mere means to proclaiming the good news. Such instrumentalism is disingenuous, as it conceals an evangelistic hook in the bait of friendship. Not only does it discount the dignity of people of other faiths or no faith, but quite often it diminishes their respect for the gospel as well. It turns a gospel that is inherently friendly and neighborly into a form of friendship evangelism that is friendly in name only.

Multilevel Enterprise

The preceding discussion signifies the practical import of this volume. While academically framed, this book's implications for witness in the public square and neighborhoods of our pluralistic society are immense. "What's next" for research that takes up the mantle of this volume includes sustained deliberation on the relation of the academy to the church assembly and neighborhood association, of the lecture hall and classroom to the sanctuary and living room. Otherwise, no matter how important the research, it will make very little difference for how people in our faith communities live and engage those of other faiths. Similarly, no matter how important people's experience in their concrete cultural contexts involving friendships with people of different religious and spiritual paths, it will make very little difference in how scholars go about their research if multilevel partnerships are not established. In general, academics may need to take the initial step in cultivating such multilevel partnerships to demonstrate the import of such hybrid work by making sure everything we research along the lines of orthopathy—including in disciplines like neuroscience and social psychology, along with scholarly reflection on religious diplomacy—has import for Christian witness in concrete, practical settings.

"What's next" will require academics and practitioners alike to become more ambidextrous and see the fundamentally important role both groups play for effective Christian witness in our multifaith society. In my own multifaith work—involving dialogue and potlucks with Zen and Tibetan Buddhists, support for Muslim hospitality initiatives, and town-hall panels bringing together Evangelicals and members of The Church of Jesus Christ of Latter-day Saints, as well as involvement with an evangelistic association's city-wide efforts in the Portland-Metro area—I have learned a great deal intellectually and experientially from the perspectives and passions of various practitioners of diverse faiths. In addition to encouraging fellow Evangelicals who are evangelists to see the need for diplomacy-*plus*, these zealous Christians with rich, practical wisdom for Christian witness, together with dialogue partners in diplomacy efforts from Evangelical Christian and other faith-tradition backgrounds, stretch me to think academic-*plus* while encouraging them to safeguard against academic-*light*.

Similarly, a recent Louisville Institute grant initiative led by John Morehead has served as a fitting template for effective multilevel partnerships that complements this volume. The grant (in two phases) has brought together academics and practitioners under the auspices of Multi-Faith Matters: "Multi-Faith Matters is a support hub for Christians and churches who are seeking to fulfill the Great Commission and the Great Commandments in a multi-faith world."[8] As one of the academic contributors, I have been enriched through exchanges with the other scholars, as well as by the pastoral practitioners who are engaged in multifaith practices in conjunction with their Christian communities. It reminds me of a similar endeavor years ago that the Association of Theological Schools (ATS) oversaw with financial support from the Henry Luce Foundation. Those of us from the Roman Catholic, Mainline Protestant, and Evangelical-Charismatic families that constitute ATS were inspired and challenged by the testimonies of prison, military, and hospital chaplains of various Christian persuasions who told us what Christian witness looks like on the front lines. It was our ambition as academics to take what we learned there to help foster a theological education in seminary contexts that helps prepare pastors for effective ministry in a multifaith society.[9]

This present work serves as a rich resource and essential complement to those grant initiatives for seminary educators like myself as we seek to support pastors and other practitioners in fostering truthful and meaningful Christian witness in our multifaith age. Will we build on this volume's vital missional endeavor by seeking to answer the question, What's next?—in multidimensional, multidisciplinary, multifaith diplomatic, and multilevel ways?

8. See the Multi-Faith Matters website (Morehead et al., "Who We Are"); Metzger, "How Multi-Faith Engagement Matters."

9. Refer to the ATS publication dedicated to this subject: Graham, "Christian Hospitality" (a special issue of the journal *Theological Education*). See in particular the following article dedicated to Evangelical Christian engagement included in this issue: Han et al., "Christian Hospitality," 11–31.

Appendix

Questions for Reflection and Discussion

Chapter 1

1. Surveying biblical attitudes to non-Jewish outsiders, Robinson claims that the "prevailing response in the Old Testament is negative in tone" due to concerns for human rebellion and idolatry. However, he also notes how God revealed himself to all peoples, including certain Gentile followers of God. Robinson likewise finds both dialogical approaches *and* "confrontation and critique" in the New Testament. How might a Christian theology of religions find balance between disagreement with non-Christian religions, on the one hand, and hospitable understandings and forms of interaction, on the other?

2. Jesus's encounters with Gentiles and Samaritans can provide us with examples for contemporary multifaith encounters. His interactions with Samaritans are particularly striking in this regard, given the cultural and religious enmity between them and the Jews. What attitudes and virtues did Christ exhibit in his encounter with the Samaritan woman of John 4? And how might these challenge Christians today as they engage members of religious groups with similar histories of conflict (e.g., Muslims or Mormons)?

3. As Robinson notes, Christian responses to "aggressive behavior from some Muslims and Hindus (for example) have not always followed the example of Christ when he encountered similar behavior." Based on Robinson's discussion of the Gospels' healing stories, how might

we follow Christ's model of compassionate engagement with others, even in the face of doctrines we find heretical and alleged wrongs and transgressions?

4. In his discussion of the "recognition of particularity," Robinson argues that religions have irreconcilable differences. How might we pursue conversations and relationships with adherents of other religions that maintain a balance between deep differences, on the one hand, and common ground, hospitality, and cooperation, on the other?

Chapter 2

1. Christians have tended to emphasize orthodoxy and orthopraxy, right doctrine and right practice, both in academia and in the church at large. Orthopathy, or right emotions, has not received as much attention. Yet Cochran claims that "orthopathy can and should be embraced as part of the Christian life." What are the two theological reasons she provides in support of this claim?

2. This chapter argues that orthodoxy and orthopathy should complement one another in the Christian life. Christianity in the West has tended to emphasize orthodoxy and a faith of the head rather than the heart. The concern may stem from fears that orthopathy might lead to anti-intellectualism and a marginalization of theology. But what are the risks of overemphasizing orthodoxy at the expense of orthopathy? How might a failure to connect orthodoxy to orthopathy, mind to heart, shortchange both the ethical and intellectual life of the Christian?

3. Cochran suggests that Jonathan Edwards can serve as a model for the integration of orthodoxy and orthopathy. In his view of the affections, Edwards looks to Christ as an example of moral perfection that includes the "affectionate heart." He also affirms, in Cochran's words, that "Christ's exemplary virtue is lived out in particular affections." What affections or emotions does Jesus express in the Gospel accounts, and how does he express them?

4. In light of Cochran's discussion of emotions and multifaith engagement, how do you react emotionally when conversing with adherents of other religions—or even when merely *thinking* about other religions? In addition, Cochran refers to emotions being grounded in specific religious traditions. How might multifaith conversations involve

a discussion of the differing ways religious traditions understand and draw upon the emotions?

Chapter 3

1. Every human being has a sense of individual and social identity. We think of ourselves as belonging to a variety of different groups, and these groups then relate to each other in various ways. Differing senses of social identity can have positive and negative aspects. What types of religious identities do you ascribe to (e.g., Christian, Evangelical, Baptist, Presbyterian, Pentecostal)? What kinds of positive experiences have you had as your religious group relates to those from a different religious group? Have you seen or experienced negative interactions between religious groups?

2. This chapter discusses moral foundations theory and suggests that conservative Christian beliefs align with concerns for loyalty/betrayal, authority/subversion, and purity/sanctity. Consider how your moral concerns might connect to your faith in these areas. How important is it to you, for example, that Evangelicals maintain loyalty to the gospel and the church? How do you think and feel about those who adhere to a scriptural authority other than the Bible, such as Mormons with the Book of Mormon or Muslims with the Qur'an? Do you feel the purity of your faith threatened when someone from another religion shares their doctrines and worldview with you?

3. Competition between religious groups can lead to conflict and prejudice. Christianity is still the religious majority in the US, but church membership is declining and other religious traditions are growing. These shifting religious dynamics can lead to increased competition for the hearts and minds of the American people. When you think of America as a religious marketplace rather than a Judeo-Christian nation, and when you consider that your loved ones will be exposed to a wide variety of religions in the coming decades, how does this make you feel? Do you feel a sense of conflict? Does it lead to negative feelings about other religions (e.g., anger, fear, disgust)?

4. The authors of this chapter suggest that a modification of group identity can reduce prejudice and help improve interactions with others. Other than your own specific religious identity, what group identities might give you a new perspective when relating to those of other religions? Also, in light of the fact that certain kinds of contact can reduce

prejudice and improve relationships, what kind of interaction (e.g., conversations with neighbors, hospitality dinners, community betterment projects) can you and your church consider as a way of engaging those of other religions?

Chapter 4

1. Human beings may very well have developed a disgust response as a means of protection from harm, including disease and socio-moral violations. In the social realm, disgust is also a means of responding to others perceived as a possible threat. This may help explain why many Evangelicals are very concerned about syncretism, the blending of Christian doctrine with those of other religions. Think about times when you've read about or spoken with a member of another religion, about their beliefs and practices. How did this make you feel? Were you concerned that listening to a religious teaching that conflicts with Christianity—one that might be thought of as sacrilegious—might contaminate or compromise the purity of your doctrinal beliefs?

2. We often think of other religious groups as threats when we see them as posing potential harm to us. This includes symbolic threats to our beliefs and worldviews. What religious groups do you feel most threaten Evangelicals in America (e.g., Mormonism, "New Age," Islam)? Do you see increasing religious diversity and syncretism as a significant threat to Christians? Why or why not?

3. Apologetics, or the defense of the faith, has been an important part of Christianity for centuries. It can be done positively or negatively. Many Evangelicals, for instance, use apologetic arguments to respond constructively to the truth claims of other religions and provide persuasive arguments for Christianity. But many others also engage in apologetic denunciation to tear down other religious worldviews while simultaneously affirming their own. Does an apologetic of annihilation build bridges or fences between Christians and those of other religions? Should a faith characterized by trust and humility draw upon positive or negative forms of apologetics?

4. This chapter concludes with a consideration of Jesus's approach to purity. In the Judaism of his time, this was an important aspect of religious and social life. It was also an area where Jesus got into conflict with the Pharisees. In Jesus's dispute with the Pharisees over ritual purity in Matthew 9, Jesus emphasizes mercy and embrace over purity

and separation. While Christians are called to live holy lives and to maintain doctrinal purity, when we shy away from or negatively respond to those in other religions out of fears of contamination, are we following the example of Jesus?

Chapter 5

1. This chapter discusses emotions as *construals*. How does the author define this term? What does it mean to think of a construal as "a value-colored perception"? The chapter also identifies emotions as based on concerns. What kinds of value-colored perceptions and concerns do you experience when thinking of or relating to a Christian? A Muslim? A Mormon? A Sikh?

2. Some might think of courage as a virtue undertaken *after* the elimination of fear. But this chapter argues that courage does *not* eliminate fear, even though daring can at times replace fear over the course of the courageous action. Can you think of a time when you or someone you know acted courageously while also being fearful? If you were to talk to a Muslim from Iraq or Syria (or any other country frequently associated with terrorism), would that involve a combination of courage and fear?

3. Various fictional examples of conversations are included in this chapter. Before one such exchange, the author asserts that "hope and despair concern the prospects of attaining something important." In our relationships with those of other religions, we hope to attain something important. What types of things do you hope you will attain in multifaith conversations and relationships? What do you hope your religious neighbor will attain?

4. Many Christians ask God for courage when sharing their faith with others. Understandably, we want boldness when sharing the good news. But do you also ask for other Christlike virtues and affections when evangelizing? How might you seek more compassion, more grace, etc., in multifaith relationships?

Chapter 6

1. Beginning his chapter by defining *hope*, Muck shares the story of Pandora's box as an early example of hope in the Western tradition. He also mentions that hope can be good or bad and that understanding

it goes beyond questions of definition. How would you define hope as you understand it within your Christian tradition? Can it include both positive and negative aspects, and if so, how? As hope is connected to religion, what do you hope for with respect to both your own faith and multifaith contexts?

2. In his discussion of hope in the Christian tradition, Muck references Hebrews 11:1 and 2 Corinthians 4:16–18. These passages describe a Christian hope that is based on things unseen, which involves trust and faith. Given the Evangelical emphasis on faith connected to evidence, how can hope be included in the mix so as to find a balance between evidentialism and naivete?

3. Muck then moves to a discussion of multireligious hope. In the first study question for this chapter, you were asked to think about what you hope for in multifaith contexts. Christians emphasize evangelism, so quite naturally you might hope that your multifaith conversation partner embraces the gospel and accepts Christ. How might you broaden your sense of multireligious hope beyond the desire for the other's salvation (as important as that is)? Additionally, Muck argues that hoping for a more peaceful coexistence among the religions is "a worthy goal of any interaction." Do you see this as a valid part of Christian hope, and can you embrace it as such, regardless of the response to evangelistic efforts?

4. This chapter concludes by stating that hope provides an effective "tool" in multifaith encounters. How might you use this tool with a multifaith contact in your life? Further, how might you relate a Christian understanding of hope to, say, Muslim, Buddhist, or Hindu understandings of hope? What do you think of Muck's idea about using the story of the valley of dry bones (Ezek 37:1–14) as a topic for multifaith conversation?

Chapter 7

1. In this chapter, Spezio notes that so-called "dual system" models and accounts of "thinking fast and slow"—cognitive-scientific theories of affectivity that pit cognition against emotion—are still influential today. Have you been influenced by these or other likeminded theories? If so, how? Moreover, why does Spezio suggest that such theories fail? Do you agree with his assessment? Why or why not?

2. According to Spezio, how are empathy and compassion similar to and different from each other? Are they fully formed at birth or in early childhood, or can they be formed and shaped throughout adulthood in "intentional communities of compassionate, mutual valuation"? Are compassion and empathy necessarily restricted to ingroup members, such as fellow Christians or Americans? Do they inevitably marginalize and denigrate outgroups, such as Muslims, Mormons, and Buddhists? Why or why not?

3. At some length, Spezio discusses Pumla Gobodo-Madikizela's potent, first-person account of empathic transformation in post-apartheid South Africa. Based on your reading of the chapter, how did Gobodo-Madikizela undergo such a transformation? What do you think it was, specifically, about her experience that facilitated this change? Have you experienced an empathic transformation in your own life, or have you heard/read of one in another person's life? If so, describe.

4. Imagine what it would be like to be a victim and survivor of extreme religious persecution and/or terrorism. Would you share Gobodo-Madikizela's intention to seek reconciliation with the perpetrator(s)? Both generally and specifically, how do you think you would go about such a transformation? Would any of the biblical texts and/or theological concepts that Spezio discusses in his chapter play a role in this process? Please describe.

Chapter 8

1. In the section of his chapter entitled "Loving versus Cursing?," Blomberg references various New Testament texts involving strong disagreements with false and hypocritical religious leaders (e.g., Matt 23:13–36; Gal 1:6–10; Phil 3:1–3, 18–19). Conservative Christians often cite these texts in support of their combative, confrontational approach to religious outgroups. But as Blomberg argues, Jesus and Paul appear to get the angriest toward religious "insiders." So do these texts even apply to religious outsiders?

2. Jesus commands his followers to love not only their neighbors, but also their enemies (Matt 5:43–48; cf. Luke 10:25–37). Do you think love characterizes Christian engagement of Muslims and Mormons today? Further, do you feel a tension between the call to live a holy life and the command to love those who may threaten the purity of that holiness?

3. Interreligious dialogue is usually frowned upon by conservative Christians. It is often associated with being liberal or compromising one's convictions. By contrast, Blomberg commends a form of dialogue in which religious differences are recognized and discussed in a respectful and civil way. How do you evaluate this approach to interreligious dialogue? Is it possible to share truth claims in winsome ways rather than by denouncing or combating another's beliefs?

4. Sharing from personal experience in Evangelical-Mormon dialogue, Blomberg notes how he has cultivated warm, loving friendships with a number of his dialogue partners over the years, all while maintaining serious disagreements with them. He refers to this as an example of "the paradox and power of convicted civility." What is so powerful and paradoxical about convicted civility? How does this approach differ from more common forms of evangelism and apologetic engagement?

Chapter 9

1. Shaw discusses several "overlapping affective qualities that pervade Paul's missional theology, instructions, and practice." The first of these is grace. Moving beyond the idea of grace as a forensic act of justice, Shaw reminds us that grace involves "gifts, favors, and acts of undeserved kindness shown . . . to a needy inferior." Grace was not only a doctrine for Paul related to justification by faith, but also a way of living in relation to others. Evangelicals talk a lot about grace in evangelism and theologies of evangelism, but do we live it out among those of other religious traditions as generously as we should?

2. Other qualities that Shaw discusses are humility and anger. Paul not only saw the risen Christ but was also the church's first major missionary and theologian. He surely had reason to boast, but he emphasized humility instead. Much of our evangelistic and especially apologetic approaches involves a sense of pride in the truth, which outsiders may very well view as arrogant and condescending. How might we balance the confidence of our religious convictions, on the one hand, and humility in our relationships, on the other? In terms of anger, moreover, Paul emphasized the importance of sound doctrine, but he did not adopt a God-like posture or presume divine indignation. Returning again to popular approaches to apologetics, how can humility help keep our anger in check, while also leaving judgment to God?

3. Peace and reconciliation are major themes in the New Testament, especially in the Pauline epistles. As Shaw writes, "We ground our evangelism and mission, then, in the longings of both God and humanity for rapprochement. If God yearns to be reconciled, then we persuade and even implore people (2 Cor 5:11, 20)." Yet "whether or not they respond, we treat them as people of immense value, for God has treated them so." Conservative Evangelicalism is not known for an emphasis on peacemaking or reconciliation. How can we overturn this reality, and how can we include peacemaking and reconciliation as major facets of our approaches to evangelism and mission? How can we live in peaceful and conciliatory ways even among those who reject the gospel?

4. The final affective quality that Shaw discusses is "power in weakness." Paul faced many challenges, pressures, and anxieties. He acknowledged his weaknesses and looked to God for strength to accomplish his mission. In fact, it was Christ's power working through him that empowered him for effective ministry. When people observe you in multifaith encounters, do you suspect they can see Christ's strength in your weaknesses? Our natural tendency is to want to present a compelling case for our faith, but how might a confident faith also embrace a weakness aided by Christ's strength as an essential part of our witness?

Chapter 10

1. Traditionally, the emphasis in apologetics has been on rational argumentation, and emotions have been seen as irrational and untrustworthy. Pelser, however, argues for the importance of both rationality *and* emotion in apologetics. Given Evangelicalism's emphasis on rational evidences for the faith, is the argument that emotions are equally important in apologetics a surprise? How might Evangelicals embrace emotional intelligence as part of the apologetic process?

2. Pelser describes emotions as "perceptions of value" and a kind of "value-vision." Thus, emotions provide greater depth in our understanding of and relationships with others. With our emphasis on rationality, Evangelicals might more naturally associate emotional value-vision with ideas and arguments. That certainly has its place. But is it possible to also associate such vision with persons? How can an emotional apologetic not only find value in a good argument, but also in seeing

others as persons of worth—regardless of their response to our apologetic efforts?

3. Contrasting a Christian emotional apologetic with the Mormon idea of a "burning in the bosom" and "testimony" about their truth claims, Pelser argues that a more appropriate approach involves an appeal "to particular emotions that reveal particular kinds of value that point to the reality of God and the gospel." He then lists painters, poets, storytellers, and others who might be able to "shine emotion-evoking light on all of the various aspects of our world that reveal the existence of God and the truth of the gospel." What would this look like in practice? How, for example, can a storyteller highlight certain emotions and their corresponding values for the sake of commending the gospel?

4. In one subsection, Pelser discusses "the evidential power of gospel-shaped emotions." He avers that "while our actions and words are certainly important, it is often through right emotions that we can best reveal the power of Christ." Some have said that Evangelical apologetics related to other religions, particularly "cults" or new religious movements, feels more like an attack or a harangue. If right emotions reveal the power of Christ, then how might the expression of negative emotions in our apologetics hamper the power of Christ and the credibility of our witness?

Chapter 11

1. It may be fair to generalize that Evangelicals do not practice much by way of hospitality with other religions. Our hospitality may be extended more frequently "in-house"—namely, to other Christians. Yong states that "hospitality works safely at the abstract level of theological orthodoxy but is subjected to the unpredictable give-and-take involving other religious persons within the historical sphere of missiological orthopraxy." Do you think this is accurate? Is it easy to affirm the validity of hospitality in the abstract—and yet more challenging when faced with the realities of living this out? What are the implications of this for Evangelicals practicing hospitality in American society?

2. Yong discusses the cognitive, intellectual aspect of learning about other religions. This can be used to sharpen an apologetic or to become more familiar with the beliefs and practices of a given religion. But we often miss the affective and emotional components. In order to address this deficiency, Yong suggests that we should shift "from asking

what to asking *why*," from mere "intellectual comprehension" to better grasping "the inner aspects of other religious lives and ways." How well do you balance these forms of understanding and inquiry? Do you spend more time trying to comprehend another religion (say, in order to make a more effective apologetic argument against it) or trying to grasp how people feel in their practice and embrace of their religion?

3. The author discusses a Trinitarian framework for orthopathy and multifaith interactions. He argues that the Father creates hospitable space in creation; Jesus the Son manifests this hospitality in the flesh; and the Holy Spirit "follows in the missional path of the Son into the 'far country' of creation." What do you think of this Trinitarian approach to divine hospitality? How might you more self-consciously seek to emulate the hospitable work of the Father, Son, and Spirit in multifaith contexts?

4. At the end of this chapter, Yong reminds us that evangelism includes an emotional dimension. However, questions remain as to what emotions we harbor toward our religious neighbors and how they are perceived by those we engage. When you think of the tone and approach of popular Christian books on multifaith engagement and apologetics, what emotions and attitudes might those of other religions think we bring to our relationships with them?

Bibliography

AAAS Dialogue on Science, Ethics, and Religion (DSER). "Science and Religion: The Draper-White Conflict Thesis." YouTube video, 4:59. February 4, 2019. https://youtu.be/ZLoZc5DIU9o.

Abelson, Robert. "Computer Simulation of 'Hot' Cognition." In *Computer Simulation of Personality*, edited by Silvan S. Tomkins and Samuel Messick, 277–98. New York: Wiley, 1963.

Abram, David. *The Spell of the Sensuous: Perception and Language in a More-Than-Human World*. New York: Vintage, 1997.

Aldrich, Joseph C. *Lifestyle Evangelism: Learning to Open Your Life to Those Around You*. Sisters, OR: Multnomah, 1993.

Allport, Gordon W. *The Nature of Prejudice*. Cambridge, MA: Perseus, 1954.

Altemeyer, Bob. *Right-Wing Authoritarianism*. Winnipeg: University of Manitoba Press, 1981.

Andersen, Svend, and Kees van Kooten Niekerk. *Concern for the Other: Perspectives on the Ethics of K. E. Løgstrup*. Notre Dame, IL: University of Notre Dame Press, 2007.

Anderson, Craig. "Truth, a Potential Foundation of Morality." Unpublished manuscript, April 24, 2008.

Annas, Julia. *The Morality of Happiness*. New York: Oxford University Press, 1993.

Aquinas, Thomas. "New English Translation of St. Thomas Aquinas's *Summa Theologiae* (*Summa Theologica*)." Translated by Alfred J. Freddoso. January 10, 2018. Online. https://www3.nd.edu/~afreddos/summa-translation/TOC.htm.

———. *Summa Theologiae*. Translated by the Fathers of the English Dominican Province. 2nd ed. 5 vols. New York: Benziger Brothers, 1920.

Arnold, Clinton E. *Ephesians*. Zondervan Exegetical Commentary on the New Testament. Grand Rapids: Zondervan, 2010.

Augustine. *The City of God*. Translated by Marcus Dods. Revised by Kevin Knight. 1887. Reprint, Denver: New Advent, 2017. Online. http://www.newadvent.org/fathers/1201.htm.

———. *The City of God, Books VIII–XVI*. Translated by Gerald G. Walsh and Grace Monahan. Fathers of the Church 14. Washington, DC: Catholic University of America Press, 1952.

Azumah, John. "Christian Responses to Islam: A Struggle for the Soul of Christianity." *Church and Society in Asia Today* 13.2 (2010) 83–94.

Baillie, Donald M. *Faith in God*. 2nd ed. London: Faber, 1964.

Barclay, John M. G. *Pauline Churches and Diaspora Jews*. Tübingen: Mohr/Siebeck, 2011.

Barth, Karl. *Church Dogmatics*. Vol. 4/1, *The Doctrine of Reconciliation*. Edited by G. W. Bromiley and T. F. Torrance. Translated by G. W. Bromiley. London: T & T Clark, 1956.

Bazzano, Manu. *Spectre of the Stranger: Towards a Phenomenology of Hospitality*. Eastbourne, UK: Sussex Academic, 2012.

Beall, E. F. "The Contents of Hesiod's Pandora Jar: *Erga* 94–98." *Hermes* 117.2 (1989) 227–30.

Bebbington, David W. *Evangelicalism in Modern Britain: A History from the 1730s to the 1980s*. London: Unwin Hyman, 1989.

Beinart, Peter. "When Conservatives Oppose 'Religious Freedom.'" *The Atlantic*, April 11, 2017. Online. https://www.theatlantic.com/politics/archive/2017/04/when-conservatives-oppose-religious-freedom/522567.

Bellah, Robert N., and Hans Joas, eds. *The Axial Age and Its Consequences*. Cambridge, MA: Belknap, 2012.

Bence, Evelyn. *Room at My Table: Preparing Heart and Home for Christian Hospitality*. Nashville: Upper Room, 2014.

Bennett, John B. *Academic Life: Hospitality, Ethics, and Spirituality*. Bolton, MA: Anker, 2003.

Bennett, Oliver. "The Manufacture of Hope: Religion, Eschatology and the Culture of Optimism." *International Journal of Cultural Polity* 17.2 (2011) 115–30.

Berreby, David. *Us and Them: Understanding Your Tribal Mind*. New York: Little, Brown, 2005.

Betz, Hans Dieter. *Galatians*. Hermeneia. Philadelphia: Fortress, 1979.

———. *The Sermon on the Mount*. Hermeneia. Minneapolis: Fortress, 1995.

Bhatia, Amit A. "American Evangelicals and Islam: Their Perspectives, Attitudes and Practices towards Muslims in the US." *Transformation* 34.1 (2017) 26–37.

Bhikkhu, Thanissaro. *Purity of Heart: Essays on the Buddhist Path*. Valley Center, CA: Metta Forest Monastery, 2006.

Bickle, John. *Philosophy and Neuroscience: A Ruthlessly Reductive Account*. Dordrecht: Kluwer Academic, 2003.

Bird, Michael F. *Jesus and the Origins of the Gentile Mission*. Library of New Testament Studies 331. London: T & T Clark International, 2007.

Blomberg, Craig L. *Can We Still Believe the Bible? An Evangelical Engagement with Contemporary Questions*. Grand Rapids: Brazos, 2014.

———. *Interpreting the Parables*. 2nd ed. Downers Grove, IL: InterVarsity, 2012.

———. "The New Testament Definition of Heresy (or When Do Jesus and the Apostles Really Get Mad?)." *Journal of the Evangelical Theological Society* 45.1 (2002) 59–72.

———. "On Building and Breaking Barriers: Forgiveness, Salvation and Christian Counseling with Special Reference to Matthew 18:15–35." *Journal of Psychology and Christianity* 25.2 (2006) 137–54.

Blomberg, Craig L., and Stephen E. Robinson. *How Wide the Divide? A Mormon and an Evangelical in Conversation.* Downers Grove, IL: InterVarsity, 1997.
Bloom, Paul. *Against Empathy: The Case for Rational Compassion.* New York: HarperCollins, 2016.
Boyer, Pascal. *Religion Explained: The Evolutionary Origins of Religious Thought.* New York: Basic, 2001.
Brewer, Marilynn B. "Intergroup Relations." In *Advanced Social Psychology: The State of the Science*, edited by Roy F. Baumeister and Eli J. Finkel, 535–71. New York: Oxford University Press, 2010.
Brewer, Marilynn B., and Kathleen P. Pierce. "Social Identity Complexity and Outgroup Tolerance." *Personality and Social Psychology Bulletin* 31.3 (2005) 428–37.
Buckner, Ed. "Atheism: Adherent Essay." In *Handbook of Religion: A Christian Engagement with Traditions, Teachings, and Practices*, edited by Terry C. Muck et al., 602–5. Grand Rapids: Baker Academic, 2014.
Burch-Brown, Joanna, and William Baker. "Religion and Reducing Prejudice." *Group Processes and Intergroup Relations* 19.6 (2016) 784–807.
Cacioppo, John T., et al. "Multilevel Integrative Analyses of Human Behavior: Social Neuroscience and the Complementing Nature of Social and Biological Approaches." *Psychological Bulletin* 126.6 (2000) 829–43.
Calvin, John. *Institutes of the Christian Religion.* Translated by Henry Beveridge. 1845. Reprint, Peabody, MA: Hendrickson, 2009.
Camp, Caleb. *The Hospitality of God: Discovering and Living Kingdom Hospitality.* Bloomington, IN: WestBow, 2017.
Carden, Paul, ed. *World Religions Made Easy.* Peabody, MA: Rose, 2018.
Carson, D. A. *The Intolerance of Tolerance.* Grand Rapids: Eerdmans, 2012.
Cary, Phillip. "*Sola Fide*: Luther and Calvin." *Concordia Theological Quarterly* 71 (2007) 265–81.
Cates, Diana Fritz. *Aquinas on the Emotions: A Religious-Ethical Inquiry.* Moral Traditions Series. Washington, DC: Georgetown University Press, 2009.
Cha, Jung-Sik. "Some Aspects of Theological Anthropology in Jesus' Emotions." *Korean Christian Theology Publications* 103 (2017) 373–98.
Chien, Samson, et al. "Congruence of Inherent and Acquired Values Facilitates Reward-Based Decision-Making." *Journal of Neuroscience* 36.18 (2016) 5003–12.
Churchland, Patricia S. *Braintrust: What Neuroscience Tells Us about Morality.* Princeton, NJ: Princeton University Press, 2011.
Cimino, Richard. "'No God in Common': American Evangelical Discourse on Islam after 9/11." *Review of Religious Research* 47.2 (2005) 162–74.
Clapper, Gregory S. "Affections." In *Dictionary of Scripture and Ethics*, edited by Joel B. Green et al., 44–45. Grand Rapids: Baker Academic, 2011.
Clark, Andy. "Whatever Next? Predictive Brains, Situated Agents, and the Future of Cognitive Science." *Behavioral and Brain Sciences* 36.3 (2013) 181–204.
Clark, James E., et al. "What Is Mood? A Computational Perspective." *Psychological Medicine* 48 (2018) 2277–84.
Clayton, Philip. *Mind and Emergence: From Quantum to Consciousness.* New York: Oxford University Press, 2004.
———. *Religion and Science: The Basics.* New York: Routledge, 2013.
Cleveland, W. Scott. "The Emotions of Courageous Activity." *Res Philosophica* 92.4 (2015) 855–82.

Cobb, John B., Jr. *Beyond Dialogue: Toward a Mutual Transformation of Christianity and Buddhism*. Minneapolis: Fortress, 1982.

Cochran, Elizabeth Agnew. "The Moral Significance of Religious Affections: A Reformed Perspective on Emotions and Moral Formation." *Studies in Christian Ethics* 28.2 (2015) 150–62.

———. *Receptive Human Virtues: A New Reading of Jonathan Edwards's Ethics*. University Park: Pennsylvania State University Press, 2011.

Coffey, John, ed. *Heart Religion: Evangelical Piety in England and Ireland, 1690–1850*. Oxford: Oxford University Press, 2016.

Cook, Corey L., et al. "No Good without God: Antiatheist Prejudice as a Function of Threats to Morals and Values." *Psychology of Religion and Spirituality* 7.3 (2015) 217–26.

Corley, Kathleen E. *Private Women, Public Meals: Social Conflict in the Synoptic Tradition*. Peabody, MA: Hendrickson, 1993.

Cornille, Catherine. *The im-Possibility of Interreligious Dialogue*. New York: Crossroad, 2008.

Corrigan, John. *The Oxford Handbook of Religion and Emotion*. Oxford: Oxford University Press, 2008.

Costa, Paul T., and Robert R. McCrae. "Influence of Extraversion and Neuroticism on Subjective Well-Being: Happy and Unhappy People." *Journal of Personality and Social Psychology* 38.4 (1980) 668–78.

Cotter, Wendy J. *The Christ of the Miracle Stories: Portrait through Encounter*. Grand Rapids: Baker Academic, 2010.

Cottrell, Catherine A., and Steven L. Neuberg. "Different Emotional Reactions to Different Groups: A Sociofunctional Threat-Based Approach to 'Prejudice.'" *Journal of Personality and Social Psychology* 88.5 (2005) 770–89.

Coulter, Dale M. "Introduction: The Language of Affectivity and the Christian Life." In *The Spirit, the Affections, and the Christian Tradition*, edited by Dale M. Coulter and Amos Yong, 1–28. Notre Dame, IL: University of Notre Dame Press, 2016.

Coulter, Dale M., and Amos Yong, eds. *The Spirit, the Affections, and the Christian Tradition*. Notre Dame, IL: University of Notre Dame Press, 2016.

Cowan, Douglas E. *Bearing False Witness? An Introduction to the Christian Countercult*. Westport, CT: Praeger, 2003.

Crisp, Richard J., and Miles Hewstone. "Multiple Social Categorization." In vol. 39 of *Advances in Experimental Social Psychology*, edited by Mark P. Zanna, 163–254. San Diego: Academic, 2007.

Cunningham, William A., and Phillip David Zelazo. "Attitudes and Evaluations: A Social Cognitive Neuroscience Perspective." *Trends in Cognitive Sciences* 11.3 (2007) 97–104.

Dalai Lama. "Foreword." In *The Gethsemani Encounter: A Dialogue on the Spiritual Life by Buddhist and Christian Monastics*, edited by Donald W. Mitchell and James A. Wiseman, ix–x. New York: Continuum, 1999.

Danaher, William J., Jr. *The Trinitarian Ethics of Jonathan Edwards*. Columbia Series in Reformed Theology. Louisville: Westminster John Knox, 2004.

Davies, Kristin, et al. "Cross-Group Friendships and Intergroup Attitudes: A Meta-Analytic Review." *Personality and Social Psychology Review* 15.4 (2011) 332–51.

Davies, W. D., and Dale C. Allison Jr. *A Critical and Exegetical Commentary on the Gospel according to Saint Matthew*. Vol. 1. International Critical Commentary. Edinburgh: T & T Clark, 1988.

Dayan, Peter, and Kent C. Berridge. "Model-Based and Model-Free Pavlovian Reward Learning: Revaluation, Revision, and Revelation." *Cognitive, Affective, and Behavioral Neuroscience* 14.2 (2014) 473–92.

de Waal, Frans. "Morally Evolved: Primate Social Instincts, Human Morality, and the Rise and Fall of 'Veneer Theory.'" In *Primates and Philosophers: How Morality Evolved*, edited by Stephen Macedo and Josiah Ober, 1–80. Princeton Science Library. Princeton, NJ: Princeton University Press, 2006.

Deane-Drummond, Celia. *Christ and Evolution: Wonder and Wisdom*. Theology and the Sciences. Minneapolis: Fortress, 2009.

———. *The Wisdom of the Liminal: Evolution and Other Animals in Human Becoming*. Grand Rapids: Eerdmans, 2014.

Deigh, John. "Concepts of Emotions in Modern Philosophy and Psychology." In *The Oxford Handbook of Philosophy of Emotion*, edited by Peter Goldie, 17–40. Oxford: Oxford University Press, 2010.

Dennett, Daniel C. *Consciousness Explained*. New York: Little, Brown, 1991.

deSilva, David A. *Global Readings: A Sri Lankan Commentary on Paul's Letter to the Galatians*. Eugene, OR: Cascade, 2011.

———. *Honor, Patronage, Kinship, and Purity: Unlocking New Testament Culture*. Downers Grove, IL: IVP Academic, 2000.

Didion, Joan. *The Year of Magical Thinking*. New York: Vintage International, 2006.

Dixon, Thomas. *From Passions to Emotions: The Creation of a Secular Psychological Category*. Cambridge: Cambridge University Press, 2003.

Dobolyi, David, et al. "Moral Foundations Theory." *Moral Foundations*, October 2019. Online. https://moralfoundations.org.

Dockery, D. S. "Fruit of the Spirit." In *Dictionary of Paul and His Letters*, edited by Gerald F. Hawthorne et al., 316–19. Downers Grove, IL: InterVarsity, 1993.

Duckitt, John, and Chris G. Sibley. "Right-Wing Authoritarianism and Social Dominance Orientation Differentially Moderate Intergroup Effects on Prejudice." *European Journal of Personality* 24.7 (2010) 7583–601.

Duke, Robert. "Peacemaking Left Behind: Can Orthopathy Help Evangelicals Promote Peace?" In *Doing Good, Departing from Evil: Research Findings in the Twenty-First Century*, edited by Carole J. Lambert, 177–95. American University Studies VII; Theology and Religion 279. New York: Peter Lang, 2009.

Dulles, Avery Cardinal. *A History of Apologetics*. 1971. Reprint, Eugene, OR: Wipf & Stock, 1999.

Dunbar, Robin I. M. "Cognitive Constraints on the Structure and Dynamics of Social Networks." *Group Dynamics: Theory, Research, and Practice* 12.1 (2008) 7–16.

———. "The Social Brain: Mind, Language, and Society in Evolutionary Perspective." *Annual Review of Anthropology* 32 (2003) 163–81.

———. "The Social Role of Touch in Humans and Primates: Behavioural Function and Neurobiological Mechanisms." *Neuroscience and Biobehavioral Reviews* 34.2 (2010) 260–68.

Dunn, James D. G. "Jesus and Purity: An Ongoing Debate." *New Testament Studies* 48 (2002) 449–67.

Dupuis, Jacques. *Christianity and the Religions: From Confrontation to Dialogue.* Maryknoll, NY: Orbis, 2002.

Durber, Susan. "Political Reading: Jesus and the Samaritans—Reading in Today's Context." *Practical Theology* 4 (2002) 67–79.

Dyrness, William A. *Senses of Devotion: Interfaith Aesthetics in Buddhist and Muslim Communities.* Art for Faith's Sake 7. Eugene, OR: Cascade, 2013.

Edwards, Jonathan. "Charity and Its Fruits." In *Ethical Writings*, edited by Paul Ramsey, 123–398. Vol. 8 of *The Works of Jonathan Edwards*. New Haven, CT: Yale University Press, 1989.

———. "Dissertation One: Concerning the End for Which God Created the World." In *Ethical Writings*, edited by Paul Ramsey, 403–536. Vol. 8 of *The Works of Jonathan Edwards*. New Haven, CT: Yale University Press, 1989.

———. *A History of the Work of Redemption.* Transcribed and edited by John F. Wilson. Vol. 9 of *The Works of Jonathan Edwards*. New Haven, CT: Yale University Press, 1989.

———. *Religious Affections.* Edited by John E. Smith. Vol. 2 of *The Works of Jonathan Edwards*. New Haven, CT: Yale University Press, 1959.

———. *A Treatise on Religious Affections.* 1746. Reprint, Grand Rapids: Baker, 1982.

Elliott, Matthew A. "The Emotional Core of Love: The Centrality of Emotion in Christian Psychology and Ethics." *Journal of Psychology and Christianity* 31.2 (2012) 105–17.

———. *Faithful Feelings: Rethinking Emotion in the New Testament.* Grand Rapids: Kregel Academic & Professional, 2006.

Erasmus, Desiderius. *The Adages of Erasmus.* Translated by William Barker. Toronto: University of Toronto Press, 2001.

Esler, Philip F. "Jesus and the Reduction of Intergroup Conflict: The Parable of the Good Samaritan in the Light of Social Identity Theory." *Biblical Interpretation* 8 (2000) 325–56.

Evans, Craig A. "Jesus and the 'Cave of Robbers': Toward a Jewish Context for the Temple Action." *Bulletin for Biblical Research* 3 (1993) 93–110.

———. *Matthew.* New Cambridge Bible Commentary. Cambridge: Cambridge University Press, 2012.

Farnell, F. David, ed. *Vital Issues in the Inerrancy Debate.* Eugene, OR: Wipf & Stock, 2016.

Farris, Joshua R. *The Soul of Theological Anthropology: A Cartesian Exploration.* Routledge New Critical Thinking in Religion, Theology, and Biblical Studies. New York: Routledge, 2017.

Firth, David G. "Models of Inclusion and Exclusion in Joshua." In *Interreligious Relations: Biblical Perspectives*, edited by Hallvard Hagelia and Markus Zehnder, 70–88. T & T Clark Biblical Studies. London: Bloomsbury T & T Clark, 2017.

Fitzhenry, Robert I., ed. *The Harper Book of Quotations.* 3rd ed. New York: HarperPerennial, 1993.

Flood, Derek. "The Way of Peace and Grace: How Paul Wrestled with Violent Passages in the Hebrew Bible." *Sojourners* 41 (2012) 34–37, 46.

Fraser, Giles. "Karl Barth Taught Us Not to Use Religion to Mask the Stench of War." *Guardian*, December 31, 2015. Online. https://www.theguardian.com/commentisfree/belief/2015/dec/31/karl-barth-religion-stench-war-germany-first-world-war.

Fredericks, James L., and Tracy Sayuki Tiemeier, eds. *Interreligious Friendship after Nostra Aetete.* New York: Palgrave Macmillan, 2015.
Friedrich, Christof, and Eric Thomson. *The Hitler We Loved and Why.* 1977. Reprint, York, SC: Liberty Bell, 2004.
Friend, Joseph H., and David B. Guralnik, eds. *Webster's New World Dictionary of the American Language.* Cleveland: World, 1966.
Friston, Karl, and Ping Ao. "Free Energy, Value, and Attractors." *Computational and Mathematical Methods in Medicine* 2012.5 (2012) 1–27.
Friston, Karl, et al. "The Anatomy of Choice: Active Inference and Agency." *Frontiers in Human Neuroscience* 7.598 (2013). Online. doi.org/10.3389/fnhum.2013.00598.
——— . "What Is Value—Accumulated Reward or Evidence?" *Frontiers in Neurorobotics* 6.11 (2012). Online. doi.org/10.3389/fnbot.2012.00011.
Fuentes, Agustin. "It's Not All Sex and Violence: Integrated Anthropology and the Role of Cooperation and Social Complexity in Human Evolution." *American Anthropologist* 106.4 (2004) 710–18.
Gaertner, Samuel L., and John F. Dovidio. *Reducing Intergroup Bias: The Common Ingroup Identity Model.* New York: Psychology, 2000.
Gallagher, David M. "Thomas Aquinas on the Will as Rational Appetite." *Journal of the History of Philosophy* 29.4 (1991) 559–84.
Garcia, Robert K., and Nathan L. King. "Getting Our Minds Out of the Gutter: Fallacies That Foul Our Discourse (and Virtues That Clean It Up)." In *Virtues in Action: New Essays in Applied Virtue Theory*, edited by Michael W. Austin, 190–206. New York: Palgrave Macmillan, 2013.
Garland, David E. *Reading Matthew: A Literary and Theological Commentary on the First Gospel.* Macon, GA: Smyth & Helwys, 2001.
Gaventa, Beverly Roberts, and Richard B. Hays. "Seeking the Identity of Jesus." In *Seeking the Identity of Jesus: A Pilgrimage*, edited by Beverly Roberts Gaventa and Richard B. Hays, 1–24. Grand Rapids: Eerdmans, 2008.
Geisler, Norman L. *The Battle for the Resurrection.* Nashville: Nelson, 1989.
Geisler, Norman L., and F. David Farnell. "The Erosion of Inerrancy among New Testament Scholars: A Primary Case in Point—Craig Blomberg." *Norman Geisler* (blog), 2012. Online. https://normangeisler.com/the-erosion-of-inerrancy-craig-blomberg.
———, eds. *The Jesus Quest: The Danger from Within.* Maitland, FL: Xulon, 2014.
Geisler, Norman L., and William C. Roach, eds. *Defending Inerrancy: Affirming the Accuracy of Scripture for a New Generation.* Grand Rapids: Baker, 2012.
Gelpi, Donald L. *The Conversion Experience: A Reflective Process for RCIA Participants and Others.* New York: Paulist, 1998.
George, Timothy, and John Woodbridge. *The Mark of Jesus: Loving in a Way the World Can See.* Chicago: Moody, 2005.
Gerstenberger, Erhard S. "Sensitivity towards Outsiders in Old Testament Theologies." In *Sensitivity towards Outsiders: Exploring the Dynamic Relationship between Mission and Ethics in the New Testament and Early Christianity*, edited by Jacobus Kok et al., 27–40. Wissenschaftliche Untersuchungen zum Neuen Testament 2.364. Tübingen: Mohr/Siebeck, 2014.
Gervais, Will M., et al. "Do You Believe in Atheists? Distrust Is Central to Anti-Atheist Prejudice." *Journal of Personality and Social Psychology* 101.6 (2011) 1189–1206.

Gibson, Richard J. "Whose Tears? The Emotional Life of Jesus." In *True Feelings: Perspectives on Emotions in Christian Life and Ministry*, edited by Michael P. Jensen, 113–40. Nottingham, UK: Apollos, 2012.

Gigerenzer, Gerd. "Moral Satisficing: Rethinking Moral Behavior as Bounded Rationality." *Topics in Cognitive Science* 2.3 (2010) 528–54.

Glaser, Ida. *The Bible and Other Faiths: Christian Responsibility in a World of Religions*. Downers Grove, IL: InterVarsity, 2005.

Gobodo-Madikizela, Pumla. *A Human Being Died That Night: A South American Woman Confronts the Legacy of Apartheid*. New York: Houghton Mifflin Harcourt, 2003.

Goplen, Joanna, and E. Ashby Plant. "A Religious Worldview: Protecting One's Meaning System Through Religious Prejudice." *Personality and Social Psychology Bulletin* 41.11 (2015) 1474–87.

Gorman, Michael J. *Cruciformity: Paul's Narrative Spirituality of the Cross*. Grand Rapids: Eerdmans, 2001.

Goshen-Gottstein, Alon, ed. *The Religious Other: Hostility, Hospitality, and the Hope of Human Flourishing*. Interreligious Reflections. Lanham, MD: Lexington, 2014.

Gould, Stephen Jay. "Nonoverlapping Magisteria." In *An Evolving Dialogue: Theological and Scientific Perspectives on Evolution*, edited by James B. Miller, 315–25. Harrisburg, PA: Trinity, 2001.

Graham, Jesse, et al. "Moral Foundations Theory: The Pragmatic Validity of Moral Pluralism." In vol. 47 of *Advances in Experimental Social Psychology*, edited by Patricia Devine and Ashby Plant, 55–130. San Diego: Academic, 2013.

Graham, Stephen R., ed. "Christian Hospitality and Pastoral Practices in a Multifaith Society." Special issue, *Theological Education* 47.1 (2012).

Green, Lisa Cannon. "New Study: Pastors Grow More Polarized on Islam." *LifeWay Newsroom* (blog), October 22, 2015. Online. https://blog.lifeway.com/newsroom/2015/10/22/new-study-pastors-grow-more-polarized-on-islam.

Greene, Joshua. *Moral Tribes: Emotion, Reason, and the Gap Between Us and Them*. New York: Penguin, 2014.

Griffith, Mark, ed. *Aeschylus: Prometheus Bound; Text and Commentary*. Cambridge Greek and Latin Classics. Cambridge: Cambridge University Press, 1983.

Griffiths, Paul J. *An Apology for Apologetics: A Study in the Logic of Interreligious Dialogue*. 1991. Reprint, Eugene, OR: Wipf & Stock, 2007.

Griggs, Richard A. "Coverage of the Phineas Gage Story in Introductory Psychology Textbooks: Was Gage No Longer Gage?" *Teaching of Psychology* 42.3 (2015) 195–202.

Gustafson, James M. *Can Ethics Be Christian?* Chicago: University of Chicago Press, 1977.

Hagelia, Hallvard, and Markus Zehnder, eds. *Interreligious Relations: Biblical Perspectives*. T & T Clark Biblical Studies. London: Bloomsbury T & T Clark, 2017.

Haidt, Jonathan. *The Righteous Mind: Why Good People Are Divided by Politics and Religion*. New York: Pantheon, 2012.

Haidt, Jonathan, and Jesse Graham. "When Morality Opposes Justice: Conservatives Have Moral Intuitions that Liberals May Not Recognize." *Social Justice Research* 20 (2007) 98–116.

Haidt, Jonathan, and Craig Joseph. "Intuitive Ethics: How Innately Prepared Intuitions Generate Cultural Variable Virtues." *Daedalus* 133.4 (2004) 55–66.

Halperin, Eran. *Emotions in Conflict: Inhibitors and Facilitators of Peace Making.* Routledge Studies in Political Psychology 2. New York: Routledge, 2016.
Han, Sang-Ehil, et al. "Christian Hospitality and Pastoral Practices from an Evangelical Perspective." *Theological Education* 47.1 (2012) 11–31.
Harak, G. Simon. *Virtuous Passions: The Formation of Christian Character.* 1993. Reprint, Eugene, OR: Wipf & Stock, 2001.
Hare, John E. "Scotus on Morality and Nature." *Medieval Philosophy and Theology* 9.1 (2000) 15–38.
Harris, Murray J. *From Grave to Glory: Resurrection in the New Testament.* Grand Rapids: Zondervan, 1990.
Harris, Sam, et al. "The Neural Correlates of Religious and Nonreligious Belief." *PLoS ONE* 4.10 (2009). Online. doi.org/10.1371/journal.pone.0007272.
Harrison, Peter. *The Territories of Science and Religion.* Chicago: University of Chicago Press, 2015.
Hartley, John E. *Leviticus.* Word Biblical Commentary 4. Dallas: Word, 1992.
Heim, S. Mark. "The Pilgrim Christ: Some Reflections on 'Theocentric Christology' and Enculturation." In *Christian Faith and Multiform Culture in India*, edited by Somen Das, 107–27. Bangalore: United Theological College, 1987.
———. "Scriptural Paths for Interfaith Relations." *Review and Expositor* 114.1 (2017) 63–70.
Herdt, Jennifer A. "Empathy Beyond the In-Group: Stoic Universalism and Augustinian Neighbor-Love." *Philosophy, Theology, and the Sciences* 2.1 (2015) 63–88.
———. *Putting on Virtue: The Legacy of the Splendid Vices.* Chicago: University of Chicago Press, 2008.
Hesiod. *"Theogony" and "Works and Days."* Translated by M. L. West. Oxford World's Classics. Oxford: Oxford University Press, 1988.
Hewstone, Miles, et al. "Models of Crossed Categorization and Intergroup Relations." *Journal of Personality and Social Psychology* 64.5 (1993) 779–93.
Hiebert, Paul G., et al. *Understanding Folk Religion: A Christian Response to Popular Beliefs and Practices.* Grand Rapids: Baker, 1999.
Hillgardner, Holly. *Longing and Letting Go: Christian and Hindu Practices of Passionate Non-Attachment.* Oxford: Oxford University Press, 2017.
Hodson, Gordon, and Kimberly Costello. "Interpersonal Disgust, Ideological Orientations, and Dehumanization as Predictors of Intergroup Attitudes." *Psychological Science* 18.8 (2007) 691–98.
Holmén, Tom. "A Contagious Purity: Jesus' Inverse Strategy for Eschatological Cleanliness." In *Jesus Research: An International Perspective*, edited by James H. Charlesworth and Petr Pokorný, 199–229. Grand Rapids: Eerdmans, 2009.
"Hope, Christian." *Encyclopaedia Britannica*, February 22, 2012. Online. www.britannica.com/topic/hope-Christianity.
Hornsey, Matthew J. "Social Identity Theory and Self-Categorization Theory: A Historical Review." *Social and Personality Psychology Compass* 2.1 (2008) 204–22.
Ingram, Paul O. *You Have Been Told What Is Good: Interreligious Dialogue and Climate Change.* Eugene, OR: Cascade, 2016.
Ishiguro, Kazuo. *The Remains of the Day.* New York: Vintage International, 1988.
Jensen, Michael P., ed. *True Feelings: Perspectives on Emotions in Christian Life and Ministry.* Nottingham, UK: Apollos, 2012.

Jeremias, Joachim. *Jesus' Promise to the Nations*. Translated by S. H. Hooke. London: SCM, 1958.

Jipp, Joshua W. *Saved by Faith and Hospitality*. Grand Rapids: Eerdmans, 2017.

Joas, Hans. "The Age of Contingency." In *Faith as an Option: Possible Futures for Christianity*, 63–77. Translated by Alex Skinner. Stanford, CA: Stanford University Press, 2014.

———. *Do We Need Religion? On the Experience of Self-Transcendence*. Yale Cultural Sociology Series. Boulder, CO: Paradigm, 2008.

Johnson, Kathryn A., et al. "Moral Foundation Priorities Reflect US Christians' Individual Differences in Religiosity." *Personality and Individual Differences* 100 (2016) 56–61.

Johnson, Luke Timothy. *The Letter of James: A New Translation with Introduction and Commentary*. Anchor Bible 37A. New York: Doubleday, 1995.

Johnson, Philip. "The Aquarian Age and Apologetics." *Lutheran Theological Journal* 34.2 (2000) 51–60.

Joosten, Jan. *People and the Land in the Holiness Code: An Exegetical Study of the Ideational Framework of the Law in Leviticus 17–26*. Supplements to Vetus Testamentum 67. Leiden: Brill, 1996.

Jordan, Mark D. "Aquinas's Construction of a Moral Account of the Passions." *Freiburger Zeitschrift für Philosophie und Theologie* 33.1–2 (1986) 71–97.

Juergensmeyer, Mark. *Terror in the Mind of God: The Global Rise of Religious Violence*. Comparative Studies in Religion and Society. 3rd ed. Berkeley: University of California Press, 2003.

Jung, Carl G. *Memories, Dreams, Reflections*. Recorded and edited by Aniela Jaffé. Translated by Richard Winston and Clara Winston. Vintage Books ed. New York: Vintage, 1989.

Kahneman, Daniel. *Thinking, Fast and Slow*. New York: Farrar, Straus & Giroux, 2011.

Keating, Thomas. "Afterword." In *The Common Heart: An Experience of Interreligious Dialogue*, edited by Netanel Miles-Yepez, 125–26. New York: Lantern, 2006.

———. "Introduction." In *The Common Heart: An Experience of Interreligious Dialogue*, edited by Netanel Miles-Yepez, xvii–xix. New York: Lantern, 2006.

Keener, Craig S. *The Gospel of Matthew: A Socio-Rhetorical Commentary*. Rev. ed. Grand Rapids: Eerdmans, 2009.

Kern, Philip H. "'The Word of the Cross': The Language of the Cross in 1 Corinthians." In *The Wisdom of the Cross: Exploring 1 Corinthians*, edited by Brian S. Rosner, 78–99. Nottingham, UK: Apollos, 2011.

Kidd, Thomas S. *American Christians and Islam: Evangelical Culture and Muslims from the Colonial Period to the Age of Terrorism*. Princeton, NJ: Princeton University Press, 2013.

Kinlaw, Dennis F. *Let's Start with Jesus: A New Way of Doing Theology*. Grand Rapids: Zondervan, 2005.

Kiuchi, Nobuyoshi. *Leviticus*. Apollos Old Testament Commentary. Nottingham, UK: Apollos, 2007.

Klimecki, Olga, and Tania Singer. "Empathic Distress Fatigue Rather Than Compassion Fatigue? Integrating Findings from Empathy Research in Psychology and Social Neuroscience." In *Pathological Altruism*, edited by Barbara A. Oakley et al., 368–83. New York: Oxford University Press, 2012.

Knight, Henry H., III. "Wesley's 'Orthopathy.'" *Catalyst: Contemporary Evangelical Perspectives for United Methodist Seminarians*, April 1, 2003. Online. http://www.catalystresources.org/consider-wesley-21.

Knitter, Paul F. *No Other Name? A Critical Survey of Christian Attitudes Toward the World Religions*. American Society of Missiology 7. Maryknoll, NY: Orbis, 1985.

Kok, Jacobus, et al., eds. *Sensitivity towards Outsiders: Exploring the Dynamic Relationship between Mission and Ethics in the New Testament and Early Christianity*. Wissenschaftliche Untersuchungen zum Neuen Testament 2.364. Tübingen: Mohr/Siebeck, 2014.

Koleva, Spassena P., et al. "Tracing the Threads: How Five Moral Concerns (Especially Purity) Help Explain Culture War Attitudes." *Journal of Research in Personality* 46.2 (2012) 184–94.

Koltko-Rivera, Mark E. "The Psychology of Worldviews." *Review of General Psychology* 8.1 (2004) 3–58.

Koskie, Steven J. "Seeking Comment: The Commentary and the Bible as Christian Scripture." *Journal of Theological Interpretation* 1 (2007) 237–49.

Kossowska, Małgorzata, et al. "The Impact of Submissive Versus Dominant Authoritarianism and Negative Emotions on Prejudice." *Personality and Individual Differences* 45.8 (2008) 744–49.

———. "Many Faces of Dogmatism: Prejudice as a Way of Protecting Certainty Against Value Violators Among Dogmatic Believers and Atheists." *British Journal of Psychology* 108 (2017) 127–47.

Kreisel, Howard. "*Imitatio Dei* in Maimonides's *Guide of the Perplexed*." *AJS Review* 19.2 (1994) 169–211.

Kress, Michael. "Jewish-Christian Relations Today." *My Jewish Learning*. Online. https://www.myjewishlearning.com/article/jewish-christian-relations.

Krull, Douglas S. "Religiosity and Moral Foundations: Differing Views about the Basis of Right and Wrong." *Journal of Psychology and Christianity* 35.1 (2016) 41–51.

Kteily, Nour, et al. "The Ascent of Man: Theoretical and Empirical Evidence for Blatant Dehumanization." *Journal of Personality and Social Psychology* 109.5 (2015) 901–31.

Kuss, Katarina, et al. "A Reward Prediction Error for Charitable Donations Reveals Outcome Orientation of Donators." *Social Cognitive and Affective Neuroscience* 8.2 (2013) 216–23.

Lakoff, George, and Mark Johnson. *Metaphors We Live By*. With a new afterword. Chicago: University of Chicago Press, 2003.

Land, Steven J. *Pentecostal Spirituality: A Passion for the Kingdom*. Sheffield, UK: Sheffield Academic, 1993.

Laplane, Lucie, et al. "Opinion: Why Science Needs Philosophy." *Proceedings of the National Academy of Sciences* 116.10 (2019) 3948–52.

Larsen, Randy J., and Timothy Ketelaar. "Personality and Susceptibility to Positive and Negative Emotional States." *Journal of Personality and Social Psychology* 61.1 (1991) 132–40.

Lewis, C. S. *The Abolition of Man*. 1944. Reprint, San Francisco: HarperSanFrancisco, 2001.

———. *The Four Loves*. 1960. Reprint, New York: Harcourt Brace, 1988.

Lewis, John David. *Solon the Thinker: Political Thought in Archaic Athens*. London: Duckworth, 2006.

Lewis, Paul. "'The Springs of Motion': Jonathan Edwards on Emotion, Character, and Agency." *Journal of Religious Ethics* 22.2 (1994) 275–97.
Løgstrup, Knud Ejler. *Beyond the Ethical Demand*. English Language ed. Notre Dame, IN: University of Notre Dame Press, 2007.
———. *The Ethical Demand*. Philadelphia: Fortress, 1971.
Lombardo, Nicholas E. *The Logic of Desire: Aquinas on Emotion*. Washington, DC: Catholic University of America Press, 2011.
Longenecker, Richard N. *Galatians*. Word Biblical Commentary 41. Dallas: Word, 1990.
Loose, Jonathan J., et al., eds. *The Blackwell Companion to Substance Dualism*. Blackwell Companions to Philosophy. Hoboken, NJ: Wiley Blackwell, 2018.
Luther, Martin. "The Freedom of a Christian." Translated by W. A. Lambert. In *Career of the Reformer I*, edited by Harold J. Grimm, 327–78. Vol. 31 of *Luther's Works*. Minneapolis: Fortress, 1957.
———. *Lectures on Galatians, 1535, Chapters 1–4*. Translated and edited by Jaroslav Pelikan. Vol. 26 of *Luther's Works*. St. Louis: Concordia, 1963.
———. *Lectures on Romans, Glosses and Scholia*. Edited by Hilton C. Oswald. Vol. 25 of *Luther's Works*. St. Louis: Concordia, 1972.
———. "On the Bondage of the Will." In *Luther and Erasmus: Free Will and Salvation*, edited by E. Gordon Rupp and Philip S. Watson, 99–334. Library of Christian Classics. Ichthus ed. Philadelphia: Westminster, 1969.
MacIntyre, Alasdair. *After Virtue: A Study in Moral Theory*. 3rd ed. Notre Dame, IN: University of Notre Dame Press, 2007.
———. *Dependent Rational Animals: Why Human Beings Need the Virtues*. Paul Carus Lecture Series 20. Chicago: Open Court, 1999.
———. *Three Rival Versions of Moral Enquiry: Encyclopaedia, Genealogy, and Tradition*. Notre Dame, IL: University of Notre Dame Press, 1990.
Mackie, Diane M., and Eliot R. Smith. "Intergroup Emotions Theory: Production, Regulation, and Modification of Group-Based Emotions." In vol. 58 of *Advances in Experimental Social Psychology*, edited by James M. Olson, 1–69. Cambridge, MA: Academic, 2018.
Madhani, Aamer. "Study: 27 Percent of Americans Say ISIL Represents True Islam." *USA Today*, February 11, 2015. Online. http://www.usatoday.com/story/news/2015/02/11/27-americans-isil-true-islam-lifeway-research/23231713.
Marsden, George M. *Fundamentalism and American Culture: The Shaping of Twentieth-Century Evangelicalism, 1870–1925*. Oxford: Oxford University Press, 1980.
———. "Introduction: The Evangelical Denomination." In *Evangelicalism and Modern America*, edited by George M. Marsden, xii–xix. Grand Rapids: Eerdmans, 1984.
Martin, Walter. *The Kingdom of the Cults*. Rev. ed. Minneapolis: Bethany, 1977.
Matthews, Miriam, and Shana Levin. "Testing a Dual Process Model of Prejudice: Assessment of Group Threat Perceptions and Emotions." *Motivation and Emotion* 36.4 (2012) 564–74.
Mauss, Marcel. *The Gift: The Form and Reason for Exchange in Archaic Societies*. Translated by W. D. Halls. 1990. Reprint, New York: Norton, 2000.
McClymond, Michael J., and Gerald R. McDermott. *The Theology of Jonathan Edwards*. New York: Oxford University Press, 2012.
McDermott, Gerald R. *God's Rivals: Why Has God Allowed Different Religions? Insights from the Bible and the Early Church*. Downers Grove, IL: IVP Academic, 2007.

McDermott, Gerald R., and Harold A. Netland. *A Trinitarian Theology of Religions: An Evangelical Proposal*. Oxford: Oxford University Press, 2014.

McGregor, Holly A., et al. "Terror Management and Aggression: Evidence That Mortality Salience Motivates Aggression Against Worldview-Threatening Others." *Journal of Personality and Social Psychology* 74.3 (1998) 590–605.

McInerny, Ralph. *Aquinas on Human Action: A Theory of Practice*. Washington, DC: Catholic University of America Press, 2012.

McQuilkin, Robertson, and Paul Copan. *An Introduction to Biblical Ethics: Walking in the Way of Wisdom*. 3rd ed. Downers Grove, IL: InterVarsity, 2014.

Melanchthon, Philip. *Loci communes theologici*. Translated by Lowell J. Satre with revisions by Wilhelm Pauck. In *Melanchthon and Bucer*, edited by Wilhelm Pauck, 18–152. Library of Christian Classics. Ichthus ed. Philadelphia: Westminster, 1969.

Melina, Livio. *Sharing in Christ's Virtues: For a Renewal of Moral Theology in Light of* Veritatis Splendor. Translated by William E. May. Washington, DC: Catholic University of America Press, 2001.

Metzger, Paul Louis. "Christian Interaction with Other Religions." In *Handbook of Religion: A Christian Engagement with Traditions, Teachings, and Practices*, edited by Terry C. Muck et al., 27–40. Grand Rapids: Baker Academic, 2014.

———. "How Multi-Faith Engagement Matters: An Interview with John W. Morehead, Part II." *Patheos* (blog), July 6, 2018. Online. https://www.patheos.com/blogs/uncommongodcommongood/2018/07/how-multi-faith-engagement-matters-an-interview-with-john-w-morehead-part-ii.

Milgrom, Jacob. *Leviticus: A Book of Ritual and Ethics*. Continental Commentaries. Minneapolis: Augsburg Fortress, 2004.

Miner, Robert. *Thomas Aquinas on the Passions: A Study of Summa Theologiae Ia2ae 22–48*. Cambridge: Cambridge University Press, 2009.

Mitchell, Donald W., and James A. Wiseman, eds. *The Gethsemani Encounter: A Dialogue on the Spiritual Life by Buddhist and Christian Monastics*. New York: Continuum, 1999.

Moltmann, Jürgen. *Theology of Hope: On the Ground and the Implications of a Christian Eschatology*. Translated by James W. Leitch. London: SCM, 1967.

Montague, P. Read, et al. "Imaging Valuation Models in Human Choice." *Annual Review of Neuroscience* 29.1 (2006) 417–48.

Moo, Douglas J. *The Epistle to the Romans*. New International Commentary on the New Testament. Grand Rapids: Eerdmans, 1996.

———. *Galatians*. Baker Exegetical Commentary on the New Testament. Grand Rapids: Baker Academic, 2013.

Moreau, A. Scott. "Syncretism." In *Evangelical Dictionary of World Missions*, edited by A. Scott Moreau, 924–25. Baker Reference Library. Grand Rapids: Baker Academic, 2000.

Morehead, John W. "Author: John W. Morehead." *Evangelical Chapter of the Foundation for Religious Diplomacy* (blog), March–July 2019. Online. https://www.evangelicalfrd.org/blog/author/John-W.-Morehead.

Morehead, John W., et al. "Multi-Faith Matters: Evangelical Multi-Faith Engagement, Purity Concerns, and Persuasive Storytelling." *Louisville Institute*. Online. https://louisville-institute.org/our-impact/awards/collaborative-inquiry-team/13611.

———. "Who We Are." *Multi-Faith Matters*. Online. https://multifaithmatters.org.

Mouw, Richard J. *Adventures in Evangelical Civility: A Lifelong Quest for Common Ground.* Grand Rapids: Brazos, 2016.

———. *Talking with Mormons: An Invitation to Evangelicals.* Grand Rapids: Eerdmans, 2012.

———. *Uncommon Decency: Christian Civility in an Uncivil World.* 2nd ed. Downers Grove, IL: InterVarsity, 2010.

Mouw, Richard J., and Robert L. Millet, eds. *Talking Doctrine: Mormons and Evangelicals in Conversation.* Downers Grove, IL: InterVarsity, 2015.

Moyaert, Marianne. *Fragile Identities: Towards a Theology of Interreligious Hospitality.* Currents of Encounter 39. Amsterdam: Rodopi, 2011.

———. *In Response to the Religious Other: Ricoeur and the Fragility of Interreligious Encounters.* Lanham, MD: Lexington, 2014.

Muck, Terry C. "Interreligious Dialogue: Conversations that Enable Christian Witness." *International Bulletin of Missionary Research* 35.4 (2011) 187–92.

———. "Interreligious Dialogue and Evangelism." *Buddhist-Christian Studies* 17 (1997) 139–51.

———. "The New Testament Case for Interreligious Dialogue." *Insights* 110 (1995) 7–21.

———. *Why Study Religion? Understanding Humanity's Pursuit of the Divine.* Grand Rapids: Baker Academic, 2016.

Muck, Terry C., and Frances S. Adeney. *Christianity Encountering World Religions: The Practice of Mission in the Twenty-First Century.* Grand Rapids: Baker Academic, 2009.

Murphy, Nancey, and Warren S. Brown. *Did My Neurons Make Me Do It? Philosophical and Neurobiological Perspectives on Moral Responsibility and Free Will.* Oxford: Oxford University Press, 2007.

Myers, David G., and Jean M. Twenge. *Social Psychology.* 12th ed. New York: McGraw-Hill, 2016.

Nair, Remya, et al. "A Self for Others: Joint Self-Other Representation of Value During Morally Relevant Action." Paper presented at the EuroAsianPacific Joint Conference on Cognitive Science, Turin, Italy, September 25–27, 2015. Online. http://ceur-ws.org/Vol-1419/paper0051.pdf.

Nathan, Marco J., and Guillermo Del Pinal. "Mapping the Mind: Bridge Laws and the Psycho-Neural Interface." *Synthese* 193.2 (2016) 637–57.

Neely, Brent. "Jesus at the Well (John 4:4–42): Our Approach to the 'Other.'" *Theology* 121 (2018) 332–40.

Netland, Harold. *Christianity and Religious Diversity: Clarifying Christian Commitments in a Globalizing Age.* Grand Rapids: Baker Academic, 2015.

———. "Toward Contextualized Apologetics." *Missiology* 16.3 (1988) 289–303.

Neuberg, Steven L., and Catherine A. Cottrell. "Intergroup Emotions: A Biocultural Approach." In *From Prejudice to Intergroup Emotions: Differentiated Reactions to Social Groups,* edited by Diane M. Mackie and Eliot R. Smith, 265–84. New York: Psychology, 2002.

Neuberg, Steven L., and Mark Schaller. "An Evolutionary Threat-Management Approach to Prejudices." *Current Opinion in Psychology* 7 (2016) 1–5.

Newberg, Andrew, et al. "The Measurement of Regional Cerebral Blood Flow During the Complex Cognitive Task of Meditation: A Preliminary SPECT Study." *Psychiatry Research* 106.2 (2001) 113–22.

Neyrey, Jerome H. "What's Wrong with This Picture? John 4, Cultural Stereotypes of Women, and Public and Private Space." *Biblical Theology Bulletin* 24.2 (1994) 77–91.
Nietzsche, Friedrich. *Human, All Too Human*. Translated by R. J. Hollingdale. Cambridge Texts in the History of Philosophy. Cambridge: Cambridge University Press, 1996.
Numbers, Ronald L., ed. *Galileo Goes to Jail and Other Myths about Science and Religion*. Cambridge, MA: Harvard University Press, 2009.
Oaks, Dallin H. "Teaching and Learning by the Spirit." *Ensign* 27.3 (1997). Online. https://www.churchofjesuschrist.org/study/ensign/1997/03/teaching-and-learning-by-the-spirit?lang=eng.
Obama, Barack. *The Audacity of Hope: Thoughts on Reclaiming the American Dream*. New York: Three Rivers, 2006.
O'Day, Gail R. "Surprised by Faith: Jesus and the Canaanite Woman." In *A Feminist Companion to Matthew*, edited by Amy-Jill Levine with Marianne Blickenstaff, 114–25. Feminist Companion to the New Testament and Early Christian Writings 1. Cleveland: Pilgrim, 2001.
Olivera, Bernardo. *How Far to Follow? The Martyrs of Atlas*. Cistercian Studies 197. Kalamazoo, MI: Cistercian, 1997.
Olson, Roger E. "Postconservative Evangelicalism." In *Four Views on the Spectrum of Evangelicalism*, edited by Andrew David Naselli and Collin Hansen, 161–87. Counterpoints Series. Grand Rapids: Zondervan, 2011.
Pannenberg, Wolfhart. *Basic Questions in Theology: Collected Essays*. Translated by George H. Kelm. Vol 2. Minneapolis: Fortress, 1971.
Panofsky, Dora, and Erwin Panofsky. *Pandora's Box: The Changing Aspects of a Mythical Symbol*. Bollingen Series 52. New York: Pantheon, 1956.
Pape, Robert A. *Dying to Win: The Strategic Logic of Suicide Terrorism*. New York: Random, 2005.
Pascal, Blaise. *Pensées*. Translated by A. J. Krailsheimer. New York: Penguin, 1995.
Pell, Patty. *Hospitality: God's Call to Compassion*. Downers Grove, IL: IVP Connect, 2008.
Pelser, Adam C. "Emotion, Evaluative Perception, and Epistemic Justification." In *Emotion and Value*, edited by Sabine Roeser and Cain Todd, 106–22. Oxford: Oxford University Press, 2014.
———. "Reasons of the Heart: Emotions in Apologetics." *Christian Research Journal* 38.1 (2015) 32–39.
Pennartz, Cyriel M. A. "Consciousness, Representation, Action: The Importance of Being Goal-Directed." *Trends in Cognitive Sciences* 22.2 (2018) 137–53.
Pessoa, Luiz. "Cognitive-Motivational Interactions: Beyond Boxes-and-Arrows Models of the Mind-Brain." *Motivation Science* 3.3 (2017) 287–303.
Petersen, Alan, and Iain Wilkinson. "Editorial Introduction: The Sociology of Hope in Contexts of Health, Medicine, and Healthcare." *Health* 19.2 (2015) 113–18.
Peterson, Gregory R. "Can One Love the Distant Other? Empathy, Affiliation, and Cosmopolitanism." *Philosophy, Theology, and the Sciences* 2.1 (2015) 4–24.
———. *Minding God: Theology and the Cognitive Sciences*. Theology and the Sciences. Minneapolis: Fortress, 2003.

Peterson, Gregory R., et al. "The Rationality of Ultimate Concern: Moral Exemplars, Theological Ethics, and the Science of Moral Cognition." *Theology and Science* 8.2 (2010) 139–61.

Pettigrew, Thomas F., and Linda R. Tropp. "A Meta-Analytic Test of Intergroup Contact Theory." *Journal of Personality and Social Psychology* 90.5 (2006) 751–83.

Pew Research Center. "Americans Express Increasingly Warm Feelings Toward Religious Groups." *Numbers, Facts, and Trends Shaping the World*, February 15, 2017. Online. http://assets.pewresearch.org/wp-content/uploads/sites/11/2017/02/15093007/Feeling-thermometer-report-FOR-WEB.pdf.

———. "Global Survey of Evangelical Protestant Leaders." *The Pew Forum on Religion & Public Life*, June 22, 2011. Online. http://www.pewresearch.org/wp-content/uploads/sites/7/2011/06/Global-Survey-of-Evan.-Prot.-Leaders.pdf.

———. "How Americans Feel About Religious Groups." *Numbers, Facts, and Trends Shaping the World*, July 16, 2014. Online. http://www.pewresearch.org/wp-content/uploads/sites/7/2014/07/Views-of-Religious-Groups-07-27-full-PDF-for-web.pdf.

———. "Middle Easterners See Religious and Ethnic Hatred as Top Global Threat." *Numbers, Facts, and Trends Shaping the World*, October 16, 2014. Online. http://www.pewresearch.org/wp-content/uploads/sites/2/2014/10/Pew-Research-Center-Dangers-Report-FINAL-October-16-2014.pdf.

Pfänder, Alexander. *Phänomenologie des Wollens: Eine psychologische Analyse*. Leipzig: Verlag von Johann Ambrosius Barth, 1900.

———. *Phenomenology of Willing and Motivation*. Translated by Herbert Spiegelberg. Northwestern University Studies in Phenomenology and Existential Philosophy. Evanston, IL: Northwestern University Press, 1967.

Phelps, Elizabeth A., et al. "Emotion and Decision Making: Multiple Modulatory Neural Circuits." *Annual Review of Neuroscience* 37 (2014) 263–87.

Pilgrim, Walter E. *Good News to the Poor: Wealth and Poverty in Luke-Acts*. 1981. Reprint, Eugene, OR: Wipf & Stock, 2011.

Pinnock, Clark H. *A Wideness in God's Mercy: The Finality of Jesus Christ in a World of Religions*. Grand Rapids: Zondervan, 1992.

Pope, Alexander. *Essay on Man and Other Poems*. Dover Thrift ed. Mineola, NY: Dover, 1994.

Pope, Stephen J. "Agape and Human Nature: Contributions from Neo-Darwinism." In *An Evolving Dialogue: Theological and Scientific Perspectives on Evolution*, edited by James B. Miller, 421–40. Harrisburg, PA: Trinity, 2001.

———. *Human Evolution and Christian Ethics*. New Studies in Christian Ethics. New York: Cambridge University Press, 2007.

Powell, Samuel M. *The Impassioned Life: Reason and Emotion in the Christian Tradition*. Minneapolis: Fortress, 2016.

Pratto, Felicia, et al. "Social Dominance Orientation: A Personality Variable Predicting Social and Political Attitudes." *Journal of Personality and Social Psychology* 67.4 (1994) 741–63.

Premack, David, and Guy Woodruff. "Does the Chimpanzee Have a Theory of Mind?" *Behavioral and Brain Sciences* 1.4 (1978) 515–26.

Preston, Stephanie D., and Frans B. M. de Waal. "Empathy: Its Ultimate and Proximate Bases." *Behavioral and Brain Sciences* 25.1 (2002) 1–19.

Prince, Matthew. *Winning through Caring: The Handbook on Friendship Evangelism*. Grand Rapids: Baker, 1981.

Prinz, Jesse. "Against Empathy." *Boston Review*, August 26, 2014. Online. http://bostonreview.net/forum/against-empathy/jesse-prinz-response-against-empathy-prinz.

Pyszczynski, Tom, et al. "Thirty Years of Terror Management Theory: From Genesis to Revelation." In vol. 52 of *Advances in Experimental Social Psychology*, edited by James M. Olson and Mark P. Zanna, 1–70. Waltham, MA: Academic, 2015.

Rae, Murray. "The Ethics of Jesus." *Cultural Encounters* 3.2 (2007) 47–64.

Rah, Soong-Chan, and Gary VanderPol. *Return to Justice: Six Movements that Reignited Our Contemporary Evangelical Conscience*. Grand Rapids: Brazos, 2016.

Rahner, Karl. *Writings of 1965–67, 2*. Vol. 10 of *Theological Investigations*. Translated by David Bourke. New York: Seabury, 1973.

Rawls, John. *Justice as Fairness: A Restatement*. Edited by Erin Kelly. Cambridge, MA: Belknap, 2001.

———. *Political Liberalism*. Exp. ed. Columbia Classics in Philosophy. New York: Columbia University Press, 2005.

Reeves, Jayme R. *Safeguarding the Stranger: An Abrahamic Theology and Ethic of Protective Hospitality*. Cambridge: Lutterworth, 2017.

Reimer, Kevin S. *Living L'Arche: Stories of Compassion, Love, and Disability*. Collegeville, MN: Liturgical, 2009.

Reimer, Kevin S., et al. "Maturity Is Explicit: Self-Importance of Traits in Humanitarian Moral Identity." *Journal of Positive Psychology* 7.1 (2012) 36–44.

Reiterer, Friedrich, et al., eds. *Hospitality: A Paradigm of Interreligious and Intercultural Encounter*. Amsterdam: Rodopi, 2012.

Richards, E. Randolph, and Brandon J. O'Brien. *Misreading Scripture with Western Eyes: Removing Cultural Blinders to Better Understand the Bible*. Downers Grove, IL: InterVarsity, 2012. Kindle.

Richardson, Don. *Eternity in Their Hearts*. Ventura, CA: Regal, 1981.

Ricoeur, Paul. "'Associate' and Neighbour." In *Love of Our Neighbour*, edited by Albert Plé, 149–60. Translated by Donald Attwater and R. F. Trevett. London: Blackfriars, 1955.

Ritter, Ryan S., et al. "Imagine No Religion: Heretical Disgust, Anger, and the Symbolic Purity of Mind." *Cognition and Emotion* 30.4 (2016) 778–96.

Ritter, Ryan S., and Jesse Lee Preston. "Gross Gods and Icky Atheism: Disgust Responses to Rejected Religious Beliefs." *Journal of Experimental Social Psychology* 47.6 (2011) 1225–30.

Roberts, Michelle Voss. *Tastes of the Divine: Hindu and Christian Theologies of Emotion*. Comparative Theology: Thinking across Traditions. New York: Fordham University Press, 2014.

Roberts, Robert C. *Emotions: An Essay in Aid of Moral Psychology*. Cambridge: Cambridge University Press, 2003.

———. "Emotions Among the Virtues of the Christian Life." *Journal of Religious Ethics* 20.1 (1992) 37–68.

———. *Emotions in the Moral Life*. Cambridge: Cambridge University Press, 2013.

———. *Spiritual Emotions: A Psychology of Christian Virtues*. Grand Rapid: Eerdmans, 2007.

———. "Unconditional Love and Spiritual Virtues." In *The Wisdom of the Christian Faith*, edited by Paul K. Moser and Michael T. McFall, 156–72. Cambridge: Cambridge University Press, 2012.

Robinson, Bob. "Christian-Hindu Dialogue—Are There Persuasive Biblical and Theological Reasons for It? A Critical Assessment." *Dharma Deepika* 10.2 (2006) 7–22.

———. *Christians Meeting Hindus: An Analysis and Theological Critique of the Hindu-Christian Encounter in India*. Regnum Studies in Mission. Carlisle, UK: Paternoster, 2004.

———. *Jesus and the Religions: Retrieving a Neglected Example for a Multicultural World*. Eugene, OR: Cascade, 2012.

Rooker, Mark F. *Leviticus*. New American Commentary 3A. Nashville: B & H, 2000.

Rorty, Richard. *Philosophy and Social Hope*. New York: Penguin, 1999.

Ross, Allen P. *Holiness to the Lord: A Guide to the Exposition of the Book of Leviticus*. Grand Rapids: Baker Academic, 2002.

Rothschild, Zachary K., et al. "Does Peace Have a Prayer? The Effect of Mortality Salience, Compassionate Values, and Religious Fundamentalism on Hostility toward Out-Groups." *Journal of Experimental Social Psychology* 45.4 (2009) 816–27.

Rowatt, Wade C., et al. "Religion, Prejudice, and Intergroup Relations." In *Religion, Personality, and Social Behavior*, edited by Vassilis Saroglou, 170–92. New York: Psychology, 2013.

Różycka-Tran, Joanna. "Love Thy Neighbor? The Effects of Religious In/Out-Group Identity on Social Behavior." *Personality and Individual Differences* 115 (2017) 7–12.

Runyon, Theodore H. "A New Look at 'Experience.'" *Drew Gateway* 57.3 (1987) 44–55.

———. "Orthopathy and Criteria for Religious Experience." In *Exploring the Range of Theology*, by Theodore H. Runyon, 141–55. Eugene, OR: Wipf & Stock, 2012.

Saliba, John A. *Understanding New Religious Movements*. 2nd ed. Walnut Creek, CA: AltaMira, 2003.

Sanders, E. P. *Jesus and Judaism*. Philadelphia: Fortress, 1985.

Sanders, Julia. *Stockholm Syndrome: Bonding with Captors; True Stories of a Psychological Phenomenon*. Self-published, 2017.

Sataline, Suzanne. "Befriending Witches Is Still a Problem in Salem, Mass." *Wall Street Journal*, October 31, 2006. Online. https://www.wsj.com/articles/SB116225928137808417.

Saunders, Ernest W. *Searching the Scriptures: A History of the Society of Biblical Literature*. Biblical Scholarship in North America 8. Chico, CA: Scholars, 1982.

Saxe, Rebecca, and Sean Dae Houlihan. "Formalizing Emotion Concepts within a Bayesian Model of Theory of Mind." *Current Opinion in Psychology* 17 (2017) 15–21.

Schein, Chelsea, et al. "Harm Mediates the Disgust-Immorality Link." *Emotion* 16.6 (2016) 862–76.

Schein, Chelsea, and Kurt Gray. "The Theory of Dyadic Morality: Reinventing Moral Judgment by Redefining Harm." *Personality and Social Psychology Review* 22.1 (2018) 32–70.

———. "The Unifying Moral Dyad: Liberals and Conservatives Share the Same Harm-Based Moral Template." *Personality and Social Psychology Bulletin* 41.8 (2015) 1147–63.

Schjoedt, Uffe, et al. "Highly Religious Participants Recruit Areas of Social Cognition in Personal Prayer." *Social Cognitive and Affective Neuroscience* 4.2 (2009) 199–207.

Schleim, Stephan. "How Empathy Became a Brain Function: A Neurophilosophical Case Study." *Philosophy, Theology and the Sciences* 2.1 (2015) 41–62.

Schnabel, Eckhard J. *Acts*. Zondervan Exegetical Commentary on the New Testament. Grand Rapids: Zondervan, 2012.

Schneider, Dana, et al. "Current Evidence for Automatic Theory of Mind Processing in Adults." *Cognition* 162 (2017) 27–31.

Schröder, Tobias, et al. "Intention, Emotion, and Action: A Neural Theory Based on Semantic Pointers." *Cognitive Science* 38.5 (2014) 851–80.

Scott, David. "Priests, Prophets, and Pastors: The Historical Role of the Prison Chaplain." *Justice Reflections* 32 (2013). Online. https://www.academia.edu/11405930/Priests_prophets_and_pastors_the_historical_role_of_the_prison_chaplain.

Seidman, Steven. "The End of Sociological Theory: The Postmodern Hope." *Sociological Theory* 9.2 (1991) 131–46.

Seth, Anil K., and Karl J. Friston. "Active Interoceptive Inference and the Emotional Brain." *Philosophical Transactions of the Royal Society B* 371.1708 (2016). Online. doi.org/10.1098/rstb.2016.0007.

Shaw, Karen L. H. "Divine Heartbeats and Human Echoes: A Theology of Affectivity and Implications for Mission." *Evangelical Review of Theology* 37.3 (2013) 196–209.

———. "Four Encounters with One Religious Other." Sermon delivered at the Middle East Consultation of the Arab Baptist Theological Seminary, Mansourieh, Lebanon, June 20, 2018.

———. "A Pauline Anthropology of the Religious Other." Lecture delivered at the Middle East Consultation of the Arab Baptist Theological Seminary, Mansourieh, Lebanon, June 19, 2018.

Sherif, Muzafer, et al. *Intergroup Conflict and Cooperation: The Robbers Cave Experiment*. Norman, OK: Institute of Group Relations, University of Oklahoma, 1961.

Sherwin, Michael S. *By Knowledge and by Love: Charity and Knowledge in the Moral Theology of St. Thomas Aquinas*. Washington, DC: Catholic University of America Press, 2005.

Shortt, Rupert. *Christianophobia: A Faith under Attack*. Grand Rapids: Eerdmans, 2013.

Sibley, Chris G., and John Duckitt. "Personality and Prejudice: A Meta-Analysis and Theoretical Review." *Personality and Social Psychology Review* 12.3 (2008) 248–79.

Siddiqui, Mona. *Hospitality and Islam: Welcoming in God's Name*. New Haven, CT: Yale University Press, 2015.

Simon, Herbert A. "A Behavioral Model of Rational Choice." *Quarterly Journal of Economics* 69.1 (1955) 99–118.

Singer, Michael. *The Legacy of Positivism*. New York: Palgrave Macmillan, 2005.

Singer, Peter. "Against Empathy." *Boston Review*, August 26, 2014. Online. http://bostonreview.net/forum/against-empathy/peter-singer-response-against-empathy-peter-singer.

Singer, Tania, and Olga M. Klimecki. "Empathy and Compassion." *Current Biology* 24.18 (2014). Online. doi.org/10.1016/j.cub.2014.06.054.

Sjogren, Steve, et al. *Irresistible Evangelism: Natural Ways to Open Others to Jesus*. Loveland, CO: Group, 2004.

Smith, Eliot R., and Diane M. Mackie. "Intergroup Emotions." In *Handbook of Emotions*, edited by Lisa Feldman Barrett et al., 412–23. 4th ed. New York: Guilford, 2016.

Smith, J. Warren. *Passion and Paradise: Human and Divine Emotion in the Thought of Gregory of Nyssa*. New York: Crossroad, 2004.

Snyder, Charles R., et al. "Hope Theory: A Member of the Positive Psychology Family." In *Handbook of Positive Psychology*, edited by Charles R. Snyder and Shane J. Lopez, 257–76. Oxford: Oxford University Press, 2002.

Solivan, Samuel. *The Spirit, Pathos and Liberation: Toward an Hispanic Pentecostal Theology*. Journal of Pentecostal Theology Supplement 14. Sheffield, UK: Sheffield Academic, 1998.

Sorabji, Richard. *Emotion and Peace of Mind: From Stoic Agitation to Christian Temptation*. Oxford: Oxford University Press, 2000.

Spezio, Michael L. "Brains, Minds, Persons: Interaction within—and among—Individuals." In *Interactive World, Interactive God: The Basic Reality of Creative Interaction*, edited by Carol Rausch Albright et al., 113–43. Eugene, OR: Cascade, 2017.

———. "The Cognitive Sciences: A Brief Introduction for Science and Religion." In *The Routledge Companion to Religion and Science*, edited by James W. Haag et al., 285–95. New York: Routledge, 2011.

———. "Embodied Cognition and Loving Character: Empathy and Character in Moral Formation." *Philosophy, Theology and the Sciences* 2.1 (2015) 25–40.

———. "Forming Identities in Grace: *Imitatio* and Habitus as Contemporary Categories for the Sciences of Mindfulness and Virtue." *Ex Auditu* 32 (2016) 125–41.

———. "The Moral Life and the Structures of Rational Selves." In *Theology as Interdisciplinary Inquiry: Learning with and from the Natural and Human Sciences*, edited by Robin W. Lovin and Joshua Mauldin, 23–49. Grand Rapids: Eerdmans, 2017.

Spezio, Michael L., et al. "Humility as Openness to Others: Interactive Humility in the Context of l'Arche." *Journal of Moral Education* 48.1 (2019) 27–46.

Spicq, Ceslaus. *Agape in the New Testament*. 3 vols. New York: Herder, 1963–66.

Spiegelberg, Herbert. *Phenomenology in Psychology and Psychiatry*. Northwestern University Studies in Phenomenology and Existential Philosophy. Evanston, IL: Northwestern University Press, 1972.

Stackhouse, John G., Jr. "Generic Evangelicalism." In *Four Views on the Spectrum of Evangelicalism*, edited by Andrew David Naselli and Collin Hansen, 116–42. Counterpoints Series. Grand Rapids: Zondervan, 2011.

Stålsett, Sturla J. "From Dia-logos to Dia-pathos? Politics, Emotions, and Interreligious Dialogue." *Studies in Interreligious Dialogue* 26.1 (2016) 20–36.

Stark, Rodney, and Katie E. Corcoran. *Religious Hostility: A Global Assessment of Hatred and Terror*. Waco, TX: ISR, 2014.

Stein, Robert H. *Luke*. New American Commentary 24. Nashville: B & H, 1993.

Stenschke, Christoph. "Interreligious Encounters in the Book of Acts." In *Interreligious Relations: Biblical Perspectives*, edited by Hallvard Hagelia and Markus Zehnder, 135–79. T & T Clark Biblical Studies. London: Bloomsbury T & T Clark, 2017.

Stephan, Walter G., et al. "Intergroup Threat Theory." In *Handbook of Prejudice, Stereotyping, and Discrimination*, edited by Todd D. Nelson, 43–59. New York: Psychology, 2009.

Stephan, Walter G., and Cookie White Stephan. "Predicting Prejudice." *International Journal of Intercultural Relations* 20.3 (1996) 409–26.

Stetzer, Ed. "Rick Warren Interview on Muslims, Evangelism, and Missions (Responding to Recent News Reports)." *Christianity Today*, March 2, 2012. Online. https://www.christianitytoday.com/edstetzer/2012/march/rick-warren-interview-on-muslims-evangelism-missions.html.

Strange, Daniel. "Ministry in a Multi-faith Society Means Confrontation: Learning from Paul at the Areopagus, the Epicenter of Evangelism." *Christianity Today*, October 31, 2016. Online. https://www.christianitytoday.com/ct/2016/october-web-only/ministry-in-multi-faith-society-means-confrontation.html.

Sudworth, Richard J. "Missional Discipleship: Following Christ the Lord in a Multi-faith Society." *Anvil* 25.2 (2008) 85–94. Online. https://biblicalstudies.org.uk/pdf/anvil/25-2_085.pdf.
Swidler, Leonard J. *Dialogue for Interreligious Study: Strategies for the Transformation of Culture-Shaping Institutions*. New York: Palgrave Macmillan, 2014.
Tajfel, Henri, and John C. Turner. "An Integrative Theory of Intergroup Conflict." In *The Social Psychology of Intergroup Relations*, edited by William G. Austin and Stephen Worchel, 33–47. Monterey, CA: Brooks-Cole, 1979.
Talbot, Mark R. "Godly Emotions (Religious Affections)." In *A God-Entranced Vision of All Things: The Legacy of Jonathan Edwards*, edited by John Piper and Justin Taylor, 221–56. Wheaton, IL: Crossway, 2004.
Tallon, Andrew. "Christianity." In *The Oxford Handbook of Religion and Emotion*, edited by John Corrigan, 111–24. Oxford: Oxford University Press, 2008.
Tang, Yi-Yuan, and Michael I. Posner. "Tools of the Trade: Theory and Method in Mindfulness Neuroscience." *Social Cognitive and Affective Neuroscience* 8.1 (2013) 118–20.
Taylor, Florence. "Islam Is 'Dangerous,' Say Over Half of US Protestant Pastors." *Christianity Today*, October 23, 2015. Online. http://www.christiantoday.com/article/islam.is.dangerous.say.over.half.of.us.protestant.pastors/68518.htm.
Thagard, Paul. *Mind: Introduction to Cognitive Science*. 2nd ed. Cambridge, MA: MIT Press, 2005.
———. "Why Cognitive Science Needs Philosophy and Vice Versa." *Topics in Cognitive Science* 1.2 (2009) 237–54.
Thagard, Paul, et al. *Hot Thought: Mechanisms and Applications of Emotional Cognition*. Cambridge, MA: MIT Press, 2008.
Thagard, Paul, and Terrence C. Stewart. "The AHA! Experience: Creativity Through Emergent Binding in Neural Networks." *Cognitive Science* 35.1 (2011) 1–33.
Titchener, Edward Bradford. *Lectures on the Experimental Psychology of the Thought-Processes*. New York: Macmillan, 1909.
Tolbert, Keith Edward. *ARC Cult Literature Index, 1987, Module 4*. Trenton, MI: Apologetics Research Coalition, 1988.
Tripathi, Rama C., and Rashmi Srivastava. "Relative Deprivation and Intergroup Attitudes." *European Journal of Social Psychology* 11.3 (1981) 313–18.
Trueman, Carl. *The Real Scandal of the Evangelical Mind*. Chicago: Moody, 2011.
Turner, David L. *Israel's Last Prophet: Jesus and the Jewish Leaders in Matthew 23*. Minneapolis: Fortress, 2015.
Turner, John C., and Penelope J. Oakes. "Self-Categorization Theory and Social Influence." In *Psychology of Group Influence*, edited by Paul B. Paulus, 233–75. Hillsdale, NJ: Erlbaum, 1989.
Tversky, Amos, and Daniel Kahneman. "The Framing of Decisions and the Psychology of Choice." *Science* 211.4481 (1981) 453–58.
Uenal, Fatih. "Disentangling Islamophobia: The Differential Effects of Symbolic, Realistic, and Terroristic Threat Perceptions as Mediators Between Social Dominance Orientation and Islamophobia." *Journal of Social and Political Psychology* 4.1 (2016) 66–90.
Vacek, Edward Collins. "Orthodoxy Requires Orthopathy: Emotions in Theology." *Horizons* 40.2 (2013) 218–41.
Van Camp, Debbie, et al. "People Notice and Use an Applicant's Religion in Job Suitability Evaluations." *Social Science Journal* 53.4 (2016) 459–66.

Van den Bos, Kees, et al. "On the Psychology of Religion: The Role of Personal Uncertainty in Religious Worldview Defense." *Basic and Applied Social Psychology* 28.4 (2006) 333–41.

Verwilghen, Albert. "Jesus Christ: Source of Christian Humility." In *Augustine and the Bible*, edited and translated by Pamela Bright, 301–12. Vol. 2 of *The Bible through the Ages*. Notre Dame, IN: University of Notre Dame Press, 1999.

Vithayathil, Varkey. "St Paul, Model for Mission in India and Asia." *AsiaNews*, June 30, 2008. Online. http://asianews.it/news-en/Card.-Vithayathil:-St-Paul,-model-for-mission-in-India-and-Asia-12636.html.

Voorwinde, Stephen. *Jesus' Emotions in the Gospels*. London: T & T Clark International, 2011.

Walker, William O., Jr. "The Timothy-Titus Problem Reconsidered." *Expository Times* 92.8 (1981) 231–35.

Weithman, Paul J. "Rawlsian Liberalism and the Privatization of Religion: Three Theological Objections Considered." *Journal of Religious Ethics* 22.1 (1994) 3–28.

———. *Religion and the Obligations of Citizenship*. New York: Cambridge University Press, 2002.

Wellman, Jack. "What Is the Biblical or Christian Definition of Hope?" *Patheos*, May 26, 2014. Online. http://www.patheos.com/blogs/christiancrier/2014/05/26/what-is-the-biblical-or-christian-definition-of-hope.

West, M. L. "Introduction." In *"Theogony" and "Works and Days,"* by Hesiod, vii–xxii. Translated by M. L. West. Oxford World's Classics. Oxford: Oxford University Press, 1988.

West, Ryan, and Adam C. Pelser. "Perceiving God through Natural Beauty." *Faith and Philosophy* 32.3 (2015) 293–312.

Wiles, Rose, et al. "Hope, Expectations, and Recovery from Illness: A Narrative Synthesis of Qualitative Research." *Journal of Advanced Nursing* 64.6 (2008) 564–73.

Willard, Dallas. "Apologetics Glossary." *DWillard.org*. Online. http://www.dwillard.org/articles/individual/apologetics-glossary1.

Williford, Kenneth, et al. "The Projective Consciousness Model and Phenomenal Selfhood." *Frontiers in Psychology* 9.2571 (2018). Online. doi.org/10.3389/fpsyg.2018.02571.

Wilson, Erika. *Emotions and Spirituality in Religions and Spiritual Movements*. Lanham, MD: University Press of America, 2012.

Wirtz, Coen, et al. "Negative Attitudes toward Muslims in The Netherlands: The Role of Symbolic Threat, Stereotypes, and Moral Emotions." *Peace and Conflict* 22.1 (2016) 75–83.

Witherington, Ben, III. *The Christology of Jesus*. Minneapolis: Augsburg Fortress, 1990.

Wolter, Allan B. "Introduction." In *Duns Scotus on the Will and Morality*, edited by William A. Frank, 1–123. Translated by Allan B. Wolter. Rev. ed. Washington, DC: Catholic University of America Press, 1997.

World Council of Churches (WCC). *The Church: Towards a Common Vision*. Geneva: World Council of Churches, 2013.

World Council of Churches (WCC) et al. "Christian Witness in a Multi-Religious World: Recommendations for Conduct." *World Council of Churches*, June 28, 2011. Online. https://www.oikoumene.org/en/resources/documents/wcc-programmes/interreligious-dialogue-and-cooperation/christian-identity-in-pluralistic-societies/christian-witness-in-a-multi-religious-world/@@download/file/ChristianWitness_recommendations.pdf.

---. "Religious Plurality and Christian Self-Understanding." *Current Dialogue* 45 (2005) 4–12. Online. https://www.oikoumene.org/en/resources/documents/assembly/2006-porto-alegre/3-preparatory-and-background-documents/religious-plurality-and-christian-self-understanding.

Worthen, Molly. *Apostles of Reason: The Crisis of Authority in American Evangelicalism.* Oxford: Oxford University Press, 2016.

Wright, N. T. *Jesus and the Victory of God.* Christian Origins and the Question of God 2. Philadelphia: Fortress, 1996.

Yancey, Philip. *What's So Amazing about Grace?* Grand Rapids: Zondervan, 1997.

Yoder, Christine Roy. "The Shape and Shaping of Emotion." *At This Point* 6.1 (2011). Online. http://www.atthispoint.net/professional-responses/the-shape-and-shaping-of-emotion/220.

Yong, Amos. *Beyond the Impasse: Toward a Pneumatological Theology of Religions.* Grand Rapids: Baker Academic, 2003.

---. *The Bible, Disability, and the Church: A New Vision of the People of God.* Grand Rapids: Eerdmans, 2011.

---. "Christological Constants in Shifting Contexts: Jesus Christ, Prophetic Dialogue, and the *Missio Spiritus* in a Pluralistic World." In *Mission on the Road to Emmaus: Constants, Contexts, and Prophetic Dialogue*, edited by Stephen B. Bevans and Cathy Ross, 19–33. Maryknoll, NY: Orbis, 2015.

---. *The Dialogical Spirit: Christian Reason and Theological Method in the Third Millennium.* Eugene, OR: Cascade, 2014.

---. *Discerning the Spirit(s): A Pentecostal-Charismatic Contribution to Christian Theology of Religions.* Journal of Pentecostal Theology Supplement 20. Sheffield, UK: Sheffield Academic, 2000.

---. "Francis X. Clooney's 'Dual Religious Belonging' and the Comparative Theological Enterprise: Engaging Hindu Traditions." *Dharma Deepika: A South Asian Journal of Missiological Research* 16.1 (2012) 6–26.

---. "Guests, Hosts, and the Holy Ghost: Pneumatological Theology and Christian Practices in a World of Many Faiths." In *Lord and Giver of Life: Perspectives on Constructive Pneumatology*, edited by David H. Jensen, 71–86. Louisville: Westminster John Knox, 2008.

---. *Hospitality and the Other: Pentecost, Christian Practices, and the Neighbor.* Maryknoll, NY: Orbis, 2008.

---. "The Spirit of Hospitality: Pentecostal Perspectives toward a Performative Theology of the Interreligious Encounter." *Missiology* 35.1 (2007) 55–73.

---. *Spirit of Love: A Trinitarian Theology of Grace.* Waco, TX: Baylor University Press, 2012.

---. "Toward a Trinitarian Theology of Religions: A Pentecostal-Evangelical and Missiological Elaboration." *International Bulletin of Mission Research* 40.4 (2016) 294–306.

Zagzebski, Linda Trinkaus. *Divine Motivation Theory.* Cambridge: Cambridge University Press, 2004.

Scripture Index

Old Testament

Genesis

4:9	139

Exodus

33	128
33:18	128
33:19	128
34	128
34:6	129

Leviticus

17–19	140n19
17–26	140n19
19	139
19:1	140
19:11–16	140
19:13	140
19:15	143, 143n31
19:15–18	140
19:17	139–40
19:17–18	7n27
19:18	135, 138–39
19:33	140
19:34	7n27

Numbers

6:24–26	154

Deuteronomy

6:5	138

2 Kings

5:20–27	157

2 Chronicles

16:9	197

Psalms

19:1	174
51:10–13	197

Proverbs

1:7	9n31
2:14	9n31
4:6	9n31
4:13	197

Proverbs (continued)

5:18–19	9n31
8:17	9n31
8:21	9n31
12:1	9n31
14:17	9n31
15:27	9n31
24:17	7n27
28:16	9n31

Ecclesiastes

9:4	105

Isaiah

61	26

Jeremiah

31:29–30	139

Ezekiel

18	139
37	109
37:11–14	110

Hosea

6:6	142

Joel

2:28	193

New Testament

Matthew

5–7	14
5:43–44	140
5:43–48	135, 140, 209
5:44	26
5:46–47	141
6:25–34	177
7:6	160
8:5–13	17
8:10	19
8:11–12	24
8:23–27	177
9	76–77, 206
14:26–31	177
15:21	28
15:21–28	17
18:15–17	139
18:15–35	141
22:36–40	77
22:37–40	4
23	136n7
23:3	136
23:4	136
23:13–36	136, 209
25:31–46	195
25:41	195
28:20	201

Mark

2:13–17	137
7:24–30	17
11:15–19	136
12:28–34	142
12:29–31	138
12:31–33	135
12:33	142

Luke

4	18, 25–26, 28
4:16–30	17
4:21	25
7:1–10	17
9:50	26
9:51–56	26
10:25–37	4, 17, 23, 77, 128, 135, 200, 209
10:30–37	142
10:35	128

SCRIPTURE INDEX 241

10:37	23
14:26	139
17:12–19	18
19:1–10	137
19:8	137
24:22–24	170
24:25–27	170
24:30–32	170

John

1:1–5	16
1:9	16
1:14	16
3:16	169
4	20, 27, 29, 203
4:4	20, 28
4:4–42	17
4:40	28
8:48	29
9:16	29
9:24	29
10:10	169
13:34–35	179
14:6	17, 169
16:33	94
17:3	177

Acts

2:2–4	194
2:11	184
2:17	193
4	15
9:1–2	163
10:2	15
10:35	15
13:47	160n19
14:11–12	161
14:14	153
14:15–17	161
14:17	158–59
15:1	137
15:2	153
15:36	153
16:1–5	138

17	15, 181
17:16	161, 181
17:22–23	15
17:23	181
17:26–28	159
17:27	161
17:27–28	15
17:32	182
17:34	182
19	15
20:31	153
23:3	153
26:14	155
28:25–28	160n19

Romans

1	159
1:5	155
1:7	154, 161
1:9	164
1:11	153
1:14	155
1:16	166
1:18–32	157
1:24	159
1:25	153
2	157
2:4	157, 160
2:5	157
2:14–15	158
2:14–16	175
2:23–34	157
3:9	158
3:10–18	162
3:22–24	158
3:27	158
5:1	162, 169
5:3	153
5:9	160
5:15–21	154
6:1–2	157
6:15	157
6:17	164
8:6	161
8:23	153, 194
8:24–25	83

Romans (continued)

8:26	194
9:5	153
9:22	159
10:1	162, 165
10:2	163
10:3	163
10:14–17	163
11:13	155–56
11:13–14	160n19
11:36	153
12:1	153
12:2	77
12:18	162
12:19–20	160
13:1–7	162
13:8	142
13:8–10	135, 142
13:9	142
13:9–10	142
13:10	142–43
14:17–19	161
15:13	166
15:14	161
15:15–16	155
15:20	163
15:24	153
16:20	154
16:25–27	153

1 Corinthians

1:3	154, 161
1:3–5	164
1:23	138
1:26–29	167
1:29	158
2:1–5	166
2:3	153, 165–66
3	164
3:6–7	93n16
3:10	155
3:16	194
3:21	158
4:6	158
4:8–13	165
4:9	153
5:1	164
5:6	158
5:11	161n19
6:1	164
6:19	194
7:15	161
7:25	155
9:3–18	156
9:11–23	156
9:15–18	159
9:19–22	162
9:19–23	138, 164
9:24–27	165
11:1	21
12:7	166
13:4–6	180
15:10	155, 165
15:58	164
16:22	153
16:23	153–54

2 Corinthians

1:2	154, 161
1:3–11	165
1:8	153, 166
1:12	166
1:24	156
2:2	153
2:4	165
2:7–8	161n19
3:1–3	176
4:1	155, 166
4:7–12	165
4:10	167
4:16	166
4:16–18	102, 208
5:2	153
5:8	166
5:11	162, 211
5:14	162–63
5:20	162, 211
6:3–10	165–66
7:3	155
7:4	159
7:5	166

7:14	159
8:1–2	156
8:9	155
8:17	163
8:22	163
9:2	156
9:8	155
9:14–15	155
10:15	77
11:3	153
11:20–21	166
11:28	153, 165
11:29	153
11:30	159
11:33	153
12:10	153, 155, 159
13:4	166
13:11	161
13:14	154
14:23	164

Galatians

1:3	154, 161
1:4–5	153
1:6–10	136, 209
1:8–9	137, 145, 146n42, 153
1:10	164
1:13–14	163
1:15	155
2:3	137
2:6	164
2:9	155
2:11	137
2:11–16	156
2:12	137
2:14	137
3:1	153
3:10	137
3:28	158
4:8–10	157
4:11	153
5:12	153
5:14	135, 138, 143
5:14–15	143
5:15	143

5:22–23	4, 176
5:25	4
6:14	159
6:16	161
6:18	154

Ephesians

1:2	154, 161
1:4–6	155
1:9–10	16
1:10	161
1:15–20	165
1:18	171–72
1:18–19	166
1:19–21	166
2:8–9	158
2:9	158
2:14	161
2:17	162
3:2	155
3:2–8	155
3:4–6	163
3:7–8	155
3:8	155
3:14–21	165
3:16—4:16	162
3:20–21	153
4:2–4	162
4:7–11	155
4:14	177
4:15	134
4:26–27	160
6:10–11	163, 166
6:12	198
6:15	162
6:18–20	163
6:19–20	163
6:23	161
6:24	154

Philippians

1:1	155
1:2	154, 161
1:8	153

Philippians (continued)

1:14	165
1:20	153
1:23	153
1:27–28	164
1:29–30	155
2:3	157
2:4	162
2:5	30
2:12–15	157
2:14–16	167
2:17	156
3:1–3	136, 209
3:18	153
3:18–19	136, 209
4:1	153
4:4	7n27
4:7	161
4:11–12	153
4:11–13	166
4:20	153
4:23	154

Colossians

1:1–15	16
1:2	154
1:11	166
1:17–20	161
1:24	153
1:27	166
1:28–29	166
2:16	164
2:20–23	157
3:8	160
3:12	158
4:5–6	164
4:6	156
4:18	154

1 Thessalonians

1:1	155, 161
1:10	159
2:2	164
2:5	166
2:16	159
2:19–20	159
4:11–12	162
4:13	178
5:15	160, 165
5:28	155

2 Thessalonians

1:2	155, 161
1:4	159
1:6–9	159
2:16–17	166
3:16	161
3:18	155

1 Timothy

1:2	155, 161
1:12	166
1:13–16	155
1:17	153
1:20	161n19
2:1	166
2:1–4	162
2:3–4	161
2:3–7	158
2:4	92
2:8	160
4:16	77
6:1	164
6:14–16	153
6:21	155

2 Timothy

1:2	155, 161
1:4	153
1:6–8	164, 166
1:12	153, 166
2:9–10	164
2:10	163
3:2	158
3:5	161n19
4:16–17	166

4:18	153
4:22	155

Titus

1:4	155, 161
2:12	157
2:14	165
3:1–2	162
3:3–8	158
3:15	155

Philemon

3	155, 161
7	153
25	155

Hebrews

2:14	193
2:17	193
4:15	193
11	102
11:1	102n21

James

1:2–4	177
1:20	160
2:8	135, 138, 143, 160

1 Peter

1:3	103
3:15	178, 198, 200

1 John

2:6	30
4:4	198
4:18	180, 198
4:20	180

www.ingramcontent.com/pod-product-compliance
Lightning Source LLC
Chambersburg PA
CBHW050348230426
43663CB00010B/2034